AKIMITSU TAKAGI was born in Japan in 1920 and went on to work as an aeronautical engineer until the end of the Second World War. He later decided to become a mystery writer on the recommendation of a fortune teller. He went on to become one of the country's most popular crime authors, winning the prestigious Mystery Writers Club Award. *The Tattoo Murder* was Takagi's debut and is considered one of the great classic Japanese whodunits. It was first published in 1948 but has never been published in the UK until now.

THE TATTOO MURDER

AKIMITSU TAKAGI

Translated and adapted by Deborah Boehm

PUSHKIN VERTIGO

Pushkin Press
65–69 Shelton Street
London WC2H 9HE

English translation rights arranged with The Heirs of Akimitsu Takagi through The Sakai
Agency

The Tattoo Murder was originally published in Japanese as Shisei Satsujin Jiken in 1948

First published in English in the USA by Soho Press in 1998
First published by Pushkin Press in 2022

1 3 5 7 9 8 6 4 2

ISBN 13: 978-1-78227-828-3

Designed and typeset by Tetragon, London
Printed and bound by Clays Ltd, Elcograf S.p.A.

www.pushkinpress.com

In the shadowy depths of Mount Togakushi in Nagano Prefecture, there lived three powerful, wicked sorcerers who were masters of the black arts of magic and enchantment. These mysterious magicians were known as Tsunedahime, Jiraiya, and Orochimaru, and their legendary exploits have been the subjects of folk tales, Kabuki plays, woodblock prints, and some of the most spectacular Japanese art tattoos ever created.

This is the tragic story of three of those tattoos.

1

It was the summer of 1947, and the citizens of Tokyo, already crushed with grief and shock over the loss of the war, were further debilitated by the languid heat. The city was ravaged. Seedy-looking shacks had sprung up on the messy sites of bombed-out buildings. Makeshift shops overflowed with colorful black-market merchandise, but most people were still living from hand to mouth.

Even in formerly posh neighborhoods around the Ginza, the same pathetic scenario was being played out. During the day, ragged crowds of people with empty eyes would meander aimlessly about the crossroads, mingling with the American soldiers who strutted along triumphantly in their dashing uniforms. When evening rolled around, the rubble-strewn streets teemed with prostitutes, petty criminals, and vagabonds seeking a cheap night's lodging. The uneasy silence of the night was frequently shattered by the report of a pistol.

"Tokyo has really changed. The Ginza's changed, too," muttered Dr. Heishiro Hayakawa, as he stood beside a shuttered building on a side street in the West Ginza district. He was nattily dressed in an off-white linen suit with a precisely knotted necktie of ecru satin, and he carried a rattan walking stick.

Dr. Hayakawa struck several matches, without success. When one finally flared, he held it up to the nameplate on the building. The bright flame illuminated the professor's aquiline profile, with its dramatic, deeply carved features. There was something vaguely Mephistophelean about his magnified shadow, which loomed on the wall like that of a gigantic Balinese puppet.

"Six-Chome, Number fifty-eight. This must be the place," Dr. Hayakawa murmured as he rang the bell below the nameplate.

There was a small sound as a peephole slid open. From inside, two eyes peered into the darkness. "Who's there, please?" a woman asked in a low voice.

"My name is Heishiro Hayakawa, but the newspapers call me Dr. Tattoo. In any case, Miss Nomura should know who I am. Just tell her Professor Hayakawa is here."

"And may I ask who sent you?"

"Takezo Mogami is my nephew."

The woman's next question sounded like a riddle, or a nursery rhyme: "The snake, the frog, and the slug?" she said cryptically.

"The snake eats the frog, the frog eats the slug, the slug dissolves the snake," the professor replied without hesitation.

The Arabian Nights door opened to reveal a steep, narrow staircase, lit dimly by a naked bulb. The sphinx behind the door turned out to be an innocent-looking young girl with a vaguely foreign appearance, dressed in a Chinese sheath-dress of white silk embroidered with blue and yellow dragons. Following this lovely apparition, the professor climbed the stairs.

At the end of the hall, on the right side, was a closed door bearing a discreet sign that read simply serupan. Professor Hayakawa, being something of a linguist, recognized the word right away as the Japanized French for "serpent," and he shivered with pleasure at the prospect of being admitted into the snake-woman's inner sanctum.

The girl in white knocked on the door, then vanished down the hall. The professor's heart was pounding with excitement. Kinue Nomura and he were practically related, by common-law marriage, if not by blood. Surely that would count for something.

8

After a moment the door was opened by a striking-looking young woman with a long face, narrow eyes, and the delicate classical features of one of Utamaro's woodblock-print beauties. She looked at Professor Hayakawa with undisguised suspicion.

"Welcome," she said automatically, but her voice didn't sound very welcoming. The woman was tall and slender, and she was dressed Japanese-style, in a kimono patterned with white polka dots on a black ground and sashed with a red-and-black striped obi.

"Kinue—Miss Nomura—it's me! Don't you remember?"

"Professor Hayakawa?" Kinue Nomura's pale oval face flushed cherry-blossom pink with recognition, but instead of looking relieved she seemed even more suspicious. "So, the famous skin-peeler survived the war. How long has it been since we've seen each other, Sensei?" she asked in a distant tone, using the term of respectful address for teachers and masters of any art. In her mouth, though, it sounded facetious, almost insulting.

He said, "It must have been six or seven years, at least. You've really changed, haven't you?" The remark was obviously meant as a compliment, for over that time Kinue had blossomed from an attractive teenager into a breathtakingly beautiful woman.

"Now that you mention it, so have you."

Behind the terse words was the clear implication that the professor had changed for the worse. It was true. The hardships of war had turned his hair half-white and deepened his wrinkles, making him look considerably older than his forty-six years. His skin had a slightly jaundiced cast, and even his jaunty costume looked weary and worn in the light.

Kinue Nomura eyed the professor warily. "Well, Doctor Tattoo, I assume you've come here to offer me your famous obscene proposition?" Her tone was acerbic.

"You know me, I'm a slave to my obsession. But let's not rush things. Won't you let me come into your bar and have a drink? I am an old friend of your family's, after all. And now that you're, uh, seeing my nephew Takezo, I'm practically your uncle."

Kinue pursed her shapely lips, which were painted a deep cherry red to match her obi. "Well, Uncle, I'm afraid the Serpent Bar is full up at the moment," she said coldly. "Besides, it's for members only."

Through the crack the professor could see several empty tables, and he knew that even with the tenuous family connection, an uphill battle lay ahead. Start with innocuous small talk, he told himself, and the door will swing open soon enough. "So tell me," he said casually, "what's your talented older brother Tsunetaro doing these days?"

"He was sent down south to the Philippines in 1943, and I haven't seen him since. Nobody came to deliver his ashes, and he's officially listed as missing, so I think he must have been killed in the war. I've given up hope by now."

In the background the professor could hear a drunken male voice shouting, "Hey, madam! Come back and show us your sexy tattoo!" Kinue Nomura paid no attention. Somewhere in the noisy room behind her a defective gramophone kept playing the same melancholy postwar ballad over and over, but she didn't seem to notice that either.

"And what about your sister?" the professor asked, prolonging the conversation.

"Poor Tamae, I guess she was born under an unlucky star. She was in Hiroshima when the bomb fell, and no one's seen her since. Even if she had survived by some miracle, she probably would have died soon after from her injuries." Kinue's tone was oddly clinical and offhanded, as if she were discussing the fate of a stranger.

"You two were never close, were you, even as children?" the professor asked.

"That's putting it mildly." Kinue's exquisite face was suddenly distorted into a mask of unpleasantness.

"I thought sisters so close in age were supposed to be inseparable," ventured Professor Hayakawa.

Kinue Nomura shrugged her elegant shoulders. "To tell you the truth, I never felt close to her at all," she said. "I always thought Tamae was an evil changeling, left on the doorstep, who just happened to look like me."

The professor was taken aback. He had forgotten about Kinue's habit of saying outrageous things, true or not, just to shock people. Returning to his own agenda, he said, "I can't remember the last time I saw your sister. I think it was when you two were still in middle school, long before your father gave you that magnificent snake tattoo. What about Tamae, did she ever get any tattoos?"

"You really do have a one-track mind, don't you?" Kinue sounded angry, but it could have been an act. "What ever happened to, 'My condolences on the loss of your entire family'? But to answer your prying question, Tamae was very competitive, not to mention insanely envious of everything I did, so she couldn't very well have stood by watching me get tattooed without wanting one too."

"What did your sister's tattoo look like?" The professor leaned forward eagerly, his eyes gleaming behind wire-rimmed spectacles.

"I'd rather not discuss that. It's too creepy, like counting the birthdays of a child who died a long time ago."

"If it's true that both your brother and sister are gone, then the Orochimaru tattoo on your back has become a national treasure. Please take care of yourself, and live a long, healthy life."

11

"What a lousy liar you are!" Kinue erupted. "What you really mean is, 'Be careful not to injure the skin on your back, and please die as soon as possible.'"

Professor Hayakawa was so stunned that he couldn't think of anything to say. Kinue Nomura stood there glaring at him, her crimson lips curved in a mirthless laugh.

After a moment she said, "By the way, the answer is still no." And with that, she slammed the door in his face.

2

Let's celebrate the Japanese art tattoo! read the crudely mimeo-graphed flyer, under a blurry photograph of a glowering, muscular man covered from shaven head to foot with tattoos of exotic sea creatures in a matrix of stylized Hokusai-style waves. The fine print gave the date and time for the first postwar meeting of the Edo Tattoo Society, and solicited entrants for a tattoo contest. Kenzo Matsushita had seen the posters around town, and had thought nothing of them at first. Eventually, though, it occurred to him that a passing knowledge of the tattoo culture might be useful to a future doctor of forensic medicine, if only because tattooed people (whose ranks included a great many gun-toting gangsters) had a tendency to become involved or implicated in crimes. Not without some trepidation, Kenzo showed up at the tattoo competition around twilight on a warm August evening. His long hair was uncombed as usual, and he was casually dressed in a short-sleeved open-necked white shirt, khaki slacks, and a pair of American-made combat boots. In this costume he joined the predominantly male crowd filing through the gate: dapper young men with squared-off haircuts and flashy outfits, hoodlums in sunglasses and sharkskin suits, khaki-uniformed American GIs—black, Caucasian, and a few Asian-Americans—with their sleeves rolled up and newly purchased Japanese cameras around their necks.

Kenzo Matsushita was twenty-nine years old, and like every-one else in Japan he was still reeling from the effects of the Great War. By necessity, Kenzo lived in a small, rent-free room at his married brother's home. His primary leisure-time activities were reading foreign mystery novels and playing board games, and he would have been hard pressed to remember the last time he had gotten dressed up or slicked back his thick black hair for a night on the town. As for female companionship, there had been very little of that in Kenzo's life so far, aside from a few sordid, unsatisfactory wartime encounters.

Kenzo was intelligent and well-educated, but he had never developed the delicate instincts that would have enabled him to understand the flamboyant Edo Style, an aesthetic that found its most spectacular expression in the full-body tattoos to which the Tattoo Society was dedicated. Indeed, aside from what he had learned during one brief visit to the famous Specimen Room at Tokyo University, Kenzo had no particular interest in or affinity for tattoos.

Kenzo Matsushita had grown up in the farm country of Nagano Prefecture, where tattoos were few and far between. Since graduating from Ikko Preparatory Academy and subsequently from Tokyo University Medical School—two of the most elite schools in the country—Kenzo had become a military medic. He had survived the war with limbs and faculties intact, although even after he was repatriated from the Philippines a sort of tropical torpor seemed to linger in his mind.

Kenzo's older brother, Detective Chief Inspector Daiyu Matsushita, was a prominent police detective who had taken advantage of the postwar chaos to skip the usual hierarchical steps and vault to the position of chief of the main criminal investigation division of the Metropolitan Police Department. With his brother's help, Kenzo was planning eventually to join the police medical staff. Since there were no vacancies at the moment, he had returned to the university, where he was refreshing his skills by studying forensic medicine and working desultorily on a PhD dissertation about an arcane aspect of the limbic system.

As the surging throng swept him into the garden, Kenzo felt one of his sudden mood-swings coming on. He had first experienced this disturbing phenomenon while stranded in the depths of the mountains of the Philippines, resigned to imminent death. It had been diagnosed as a post-traumatic nervous disorder, and in certain situations it would flare up suddenly, without warning.

In the manic phase, Kenzo would feel on top of the world, as if he were already a full-fledged medical doctor, a PhD, and a member of the faculty of a prestigious medical school. When he was depressed, though, he became convinced that his talents were mediocre, his existence worthless, and his dissertation a total waste of time. The wisest thing, he would think at those emotional low tides, would be to throw himself under a train, because there was nothing for him to contribute, and no place in the world where he could ever feel at home.

On this summer evening, Kenzo felt uncomfortable from the moment he walked through the gate. Crowds made him nervous, and he felt like a leaf being tossed about on a stormy ocean. Rather than following the other spectators into the large hall where the meeting was to take place, Kenzo fled toward the far corner of the garden in search of solitude.

Just as there were exclusive clubs in Tokyo for the descendants of samurai lords and the winners of literary prizes, there was an association called the Edo Tattoo Society whose membership was limited to men and women with substantial art tattoos. (Edo was the archaic name for Tokyo, and many tattooed Edoites referred to themselves as *edokko*—literally, "children of Edo.") There were only a hundred members in

1947, but this was by no means the total number of people in Tokyo who had tattoos. For example, there were gentlemen and ladies of high social standing who might have gotten a tiny tattoo on some spur-of-the-moment whim during their salad days, but who had grown ashamed of those badges of reckless youth and did their utmost to conceal them. There were vast armies of gangsters, whose dubious profession made club-joining impractical. Many laborers and firemen boasted full-body tattoos, but were too busy trying to make a living to go to a meeting and stand around with their clothes off.

The Edo Tattoo Society's activities tended to be annual rather than monthly. Every year a number of tattooed men were called upon to carry the miniature *mikoshi* shrines in various Shinto festivals. They might also be asked to appear at the christening of monuments and the formal celebration of marriage announcements, or to act as pallbearers at funerals. Aside from such occasions, the annual general meeting was the only opportunity for members to get together and mingle en masse. Those meetings had to be suspended during the wartime era, but after the war ended, the tattoo society sprang back to life with a flourish.

There was a suggestion that the first postwar meeting should be a memorial service for the members who had died, but that idea was rejected, because the country was still in turmoil and many people remained unaccounted for. Also, it seemed more upbeat to have a friendly get-together to see old faces (and familiar tattoos) and to celebrate the miracle of survival.

As an afterthought it was decided to include a tattoo competition, to liven things up. The usual meeting place, Nanushi Waterfall in Oji, had been badly damaged in the war, so the organizers arranged to rent a garden restaurant that was housed in a former nobleman's estate near Kichijoji. The date was set, and advertising flyers were printed in the basement of a society member who owned a rusty old mimeograph machine.

As August 20 approached, excitement about the contest mounted, particularly when it was announced that there would be a first prize of ten thousand yen for the best tattoos, male and female. Even with spiraling inflation, ten thousand yen was a sizable sum. The members of the society, being true children of Edo, tended to be relatively unconcerned about cash, but times were hard and they couldn't very well eat their tattoos. Besides, everyone secretly believed that his or her tattoo was the most magnificent in Japan.

With the lures of artistic pride, prize money, and sociability, the meeting managed to attract most of the surviving members of the society and some outside participants. There were more than a hundred men and women entered in the competition. The eye-catching flyers, posted all over town, attracted a good deal of attention, and a large number of newspaper reporters and spectators showed up, including Kenzo Matsushita.

Kenzo had found his haven in the depths of the garden when someone placed a hand on his arm. He turned and found himself looking into the face of a bespectacled stranger, a short, slight, middle-aged man with wispy yellowish-white hair crowned by an unseasonal beret of thick black wool. The man wore a summer kimono of dark green cotton, and he was holding an old-fashioned *kiseru* pipe, shaped like a long cigarette holder with a brass bowl at the end. Kenzo's suspicion that his accoster would turn out to be a fatuous academic type was confirmed when the man opened his mouth. "There's nothing quite so lonely as a crowd, is there?" he said.

Kenzo nodded, and before he could reply the man said, "Have you seen the ridiculous Americans strutting about, showing off their pathetic 'sushi' tattoos?" He pointed toward a small clump of GIs who were chatting with two young Japanese women in identical short red dresses. "Unlike the Japanese tattoo, which flows over the contours of the body like a river over stones, the Americans cover their arms with a hodgepodge of unsightly, obvious designs—hearts, anchors, flags, and the like. I suppose an upstart country like the United States doesn't have any folklore or tradition to draw upon, but still, there's no excuse for the total lack of artistry. No imagination. And the shading techniques are appallingly primitive, like something from the Stone Age! The subtle shadowing that sets the Japanese tattoo apart is achieved by the use of natural pigments which are applied with immeasurable skill by a true artist manipulating a variety of needles, with each bundle of needles encased in a wooden handle. But the Americans! They use a single needle, which is why their designs are as thin as a bowl of milk that's been left out in the rain."

As a physician, Kenzo had taken the required courses in psychology, and he recognized the pipe-smoker's tirade as the most transparent sort of jingoistic overcompensation. Kenzo had no grudge against the American victors, and he thought of saying, "Their appalling tattoos didn't keep them from winning the war." But he knew that would prolong the conversation, and turn it into an argument. So he just said, "Thank you very much for the edifying lecture, but I really must go meet someone now." As he walked away Kenzo wished he had thought to ask what the man had meant by "sushi tattoos," but it didn't seem worth the trouble to turn back.

The aroma of the talkative stranger's pipe tobacco had made Kenzo crave a lungful of nicotine, and as soon as he reached the safety of the far garden wall he took a hand-rolled cig-arette from his stainless-steel cigarette case. After a moment's blissful, smoky silence, another strange voice spoke into his ear, causing him to levitate in surprise.

3

"Excuse me, kind sir, could you please lend me a match?"

Kenzo turned in alarm and saw that the question had come from a young woman standing behind him. She was tall and slender, yet voluptuous, and she wore a high-collared, white, Western-style dress with flowing sleeves. The woman had a long oval face, and her hair was piled on top of her head to show off her swanlike neck and delicate features. Her enchanting profile reminded Kenzo of an aristocratic cat, or an Egyptian goddess.

"Oh, a match? Here you are." Kenzo spoke playfully, in the overblown style of an advertising poster: "Thanks to the progress of twentieth-century science, these matches are guaranteed to strike a light the very first time." He handed over the box.

The woman lit an Asahi cigarette and blew a cloud of lavender smoke. "Thank you," she said with a coquettish laugh. "That's delicious."

That laugh, combined with the woman's elegant yet slightly dissolute appearance, had a bewitching effect on an unsophisticated country boy like Kenzo. When the woman lifted her arm to light her cigarette, the sleeve of her dress slid back and Kenzo caught a glimpse of pattern and color, of darkness and light. He thought it was odd that she was wearing a dress of such thick material on such a hot evening. Unable to control his curiosity, he ventured a casual-sounding inquiry.

"There certainly are a lot of people here tonight," he said. "Of course I suppose the majority came as I did, just to observe, but I'm still amazed by the turnout."

"Yes," the woman replied through a cloud of smoke, "there are a lot of people in this world who like strange things."

"I read somewhere that there were a hundred entrants in the men's division and about twenty in the women's," Kenzo said. "I wonder if there really are that many tattooed women here tonight."

"Oh, absolutely. I know at least ten personally."

"And are you going to participate as well?"

Kenzo immediately regretted the boldness of his question, for the woman seemed annoyed by his lack of subtlety. Furrowing her pale brow with its crescent-shaped eyebrows, she shrugged her shoulders and spread her hands in an exaggerated manner, like an actress in a foreign movie.

"Hey, mister," she said feistily, "do I really look like a tattooed hussy?"

Totally taken aback, Kenzo stammered an incoherent reply. "No, really, I'm sorry, that was terribly rude of me. I didn't mean to pry or anything, it's just that you look so stylish, and after all this is a tattoo society meeting, and I just sort of thought you might have a couple of tattoos; it was just a weird feeling I had. What I said was totally inappropriate, and I'm very sorry if I offended you."

The woman gave a heedless laugh. "That's really funny," she said, still chuckling. "There's no need to take everything so seriously. Besides, I'm sure you could tell just by looking at me that I'm in the business of entertaining men."

"So I was right! What do your tattoos look like?"

"On my arms I have a few men's names, and some calligraphed poems—you know, the one by Akiko Yosano, where she says that her naked body looks like a white lily submerged in the bathtub."

"I see." Kenzo assumed the woman was telling the truth, and he was filled with admiration for her candor. She stared at his credulous face in astonishment, then began to laugh again.

"What's so funny?" Kenzo asked.

"You're really gullible, aren't you? You're just like a child. Do you really think I could hold my own at this competition with a couple of measly tattoos like that?"

Kenzo blushed. "In that case, you must have some really serious tattoos," he said.

"I know it's not very becoming for a woman, but the truth is I'm tattooed all over, down to my knees and my elbows, and everywhere in between."

Kenzo stood stunned and speechless, as if he had been hit on the head with a cudgel. With a seductive sidelong glance, the woman added, "You would have found out in any case when the meeting started. The unveiling will take place any minute, so there's no point in trying to hide it. If you'll excuse me…"

She turned and headed toward what had been the main house of the estate. Kenzo peered intently at the back of her white dress, wishing he had X-ray vision. No trace of color or pattern was visible through the thick fibers, and Kenzo thought that the woman must have been joking about being tattooed all over.

4

Feeling disoriented and overstimulated, Kenzo headed for the meeting hall in a daze. As he passed a thicket of trees, a young man in a dark blue shirt brushed past him. The man glanced at Kenzo's face and stopped in his tracks, staring in disbelief.

"If I'm mistaken, please forgive my rudeness," he said, "but are you by any chance Kenzo Matsushita?"

"Yes." Kenzo stared into the startlingly handsome face, trying in vain to recall where he might have seen it before. There was something slightly contemptuous about the way the man's mouth turned up at the corners, and his sculpted, sensual lips were so naturally rosy that Kenzo wondered for a moment whether he might be an actor who had neglected to remove his stage makeup. The man had a long, well-shaped nose and a deep vertical furrow between his thick, straight brows. His brooding black eyes sparkled with intelligence, and his hair was combed straight back from his face. He had broad shoulders and an athletic build, and he carried himself with a self-assured, almost cocky air, as if he knew very well that he was a type that men find intimidating and women find irresistible.

Flustered, Kenzo searched his memory, but he still had no idea who this charismatic person might be. "I'm sorry, you are… ?" he ventured.

"Have you forgotten? I'm Hisashi Mogami." The man's tone was incredulous, as if he were not accustomed to being unremembered.

"Oh, that's right, of course." Suddenly a memory from long ago swam into the front of Kenzo's mind. "Forgive me, I had a pretty rough time in the Philippines and I'm afraid I'm still not thinking too clearly."

Hisashi Mogami had been a friend in middle school, but they hadn't seen each other in over ten years, so it was no wonder Kenzo hadn't recognized him. Although Hisashi was three years older than Kenzo, he had taken two years off, from school due to heart trouble and they had ended up in the same class, sitting at adjacent desks.

It might have been sexual precocity or a naturally wild nature, but at that time Hisashi Mogami had already begun to acquire a reputation as the black sheep of the school. On one occasion he copied a love letter word for word from a famous foreign novel, audaciously substituted his own name for that of the dead writer, and sent copies to ten different female students.

Hisashi Mogami studied judo, and by the third year of middle school he was already a black belt. While he was out of school, recuperating from his illness, he had become very good at playing *shogi*, Japanese chess, and he used to brag that he would have no trouble earning a first-grade certification, which was reserved for the most accomplished players. Hisashi did have a remarkable aptitude for mathematics so it was possible that he really had mastered the complex and sophisticated board game.

The two boys graduated. Kenzo managed by a once-in-a-lifetime fluke to get into Ikko Academy, the premier feeder-school for prestigious Tokyo University. Hisashi went to a less illustrious high school and from there to the engineering department of a small private college, where he majored in applied chemistry. The two men drifted apart.

Kenzo had heard rumors that Hisashi was living an unconventional, rootless life as a freelance experimental chemist and womanizer, with financial support from his prosperous older brother.

"Well, well," Hisashi was saying. "Fancy meeting you here! I never dreamed you were interested in tattoos."

"No, it's not that I'm interested," Kenzo stammered. "I'm just here to do some scientific research."

"That's fine—whatever the nature of your interest. You never even used to look at girls. I guess you've grown up. Come on, you don't need to hide it. I know you came to ogle the tattooed women!"

"You always did try to make sex the underlying motive for everything, didn't you? You really are a Freudian at heart." Kenzo didn't appreciate being reminded of his lifelong lack of success with women. Besides, it wasn't so much that he didn't look at them. They usually didn't look back.

"So I'm a Freudian. Is that a problem?" Hisashi's tone was mock-belligerent. "As far as human behavior goes, if you strip away the thin veneer of appearances, there's nothing left but the desire for food, sex, material goods, and power. Why do you suppose all these spectators have flocked to this meeting? For most of them the motivation is purely sexual. Putting aside the artistic merit of the tattoos, there's nothing particularly unusual about seeing men who are tattooed all over. There's no way all these spectators would take the time and trouble, and spend money on train fare, just to see a bunch of tattooed dolts milling around in their skivvies. But if you have the chance to see twenty tattooed *women* in the same place, that would be well worth taking a day off from work."

"Do you really think there are that many tattooed women in Japan nowadays?"

"Oh, they're out there, for sure. If you look at the women who hang out with members of the underworld, you'd be hard pressed to find a single one with undecorated skin. Getting tattooed is almost a prerequisite to being accepted in that world, but no one forces them into that idiotic life. They choose it by themselves. It's a distorted underground society, where going to prison is like a badge of honor. By getting tattooed all over and cutting themselves off from normal society, the women show their commitment to a particular man and to the renegade-outlaw life in general."

"That makes sense," Kenzo said slowly. "Yes, I can see your point. There certainly could be ten or twenty such women out of the millions living in Tokyo. But I'm still amazed that so many have shown up here."

"These days, ten thousand yen has an undeniable appeal," Hisashi said, making the Japanese hand-symbol for money: thumb and forefinger joined to form a circle. "So the women are here out of greed, and we're here out of lust. Any way you look at it, it all comes down to primal instincts." His sophistry was as glib and flawless as ever.

"So then you, too… ?" Kenzo raised his eyebrows interrogatively.

"No, I personally don't have the slightest interest in such barbaric customs. I did some research into the tattoo subculture a while ago, but I just ended up feeling contempt for that whole way of life. The truth is I was forced to come here on my older brother's orders, to keep an eye on his tattooed moll. He really is absurdly jealous."

"Your brother?" Kenzo started to add, *Oh, the one who pays your bills?* but decided that might be less than tactful.

"Yes," Hisashi said, "he runs a civil engineering and construction firm called the Mogami Group. If you ask me, though, he's a kind of war criminal. During the war, he collaborated with the army and made pots of money. After the war ended, he turned to funneling hoarded goods into the black market in collusion with the Army of Occupation. I must admit it, though, he's really got a good thing going, the slimy bastard." Hisashi apparently felt a pang of conscience after this scathing attack on his brother's character because he added, "Not that it's my place to criticize anyone else; I'm not exactly Albert Schweitzer myself. Let's just say that my brother has a good business sense, and leave it at that. On the personal front, he has been greatly influenced by our uncle, Professor Hayakawa. So when he got tired of dating normal women, he went out and found the most beautiful tattooed woman in Japan, and made her his mistress."

To illustrate this point, Hisashi Mogami held up the little finger on his left hand, a gesture that denotes an intimate male-female relationship. "She isn't my type at all, but I have to admit she's a real looker, and she's got quite a figure." Hisashi leered and sketched an exaggerated hourglass shape in the air. "Her name is Kinue Nomura. She's the daughter of a tattoo artist named Horiyasu, and she has a bizarre design, called Orochimaru, tattooed on her back. But the thing is, she isn't educated or cultured at all, and her interests are very superficial. I swear, if you talked to her for an hour you'd be bored to tears. Like I always say, give me a woman with large breasts and a big brain, and I'll be happy as a clam."

It suddenly occurred to Kenzo that Hisashi was talking about the intriguing woman in the garden. "Is she still young, this Kinue Nomura?" he asked.

"Of course she's young. She's in her early to mid-twenties, just the age when women start to fill out, and since she got her tattoos when she was eighteen, they're only five or six years old. You're a physician. You know that when you put pigment into human skin, the color will eventually be absorbed, the images will start to migrate, and the tattoo will fade and become discolored. But right now this woman is in her prime, and her tattoo is at its best. I must say, I'm really amazed that my brother would allow her to strut around practically naked in front of strangers like this. We may have the same blood in our veins, but I don't understand him at all."

"Do you suppose she's an exhibitionist, that woman?"

"It's very possible. After all, she's the daughter of a tattoo artist. Given the circumstances of her birth and her upbringing, it's no wonder she's a bit abnormal. When you see her all dressed up in kimono, you can somehow tell she works at a bar, but you would never guess that she's hiding such extreme tattoos under her clothes. When I saw her bare tattooed arms for the first time, I was so shocked that I couldn't say a word. I mean, if you think of a tattoo as a substitute for clothing, then I suppose you could be naked and not feel naked, but still…"

5

As Kenzo and Hisashi were reminiscing about their antic schooldays, they were approached by a man in a cream-colored seersucker suit. He was stout but not obese, with heavy brows, deep-set eyes, and an imposing physical presence. The expression on his face, though, seemed to reveal a subtle darkness of the soul. It was the restless, tormented expression of one who had been sneered at for being nouveau riche and had taken those jibes to heart.

The man wore several heavy gold rings, and the gold chain of a pocket watch hung from his waistcoat, but he didn't seem to feel completely at home with those expensive adornments. He had the look of someone who enjoys sensual pleasures, and behind that complicated forty-year-old face, with all its timidities and desires, there seemed to lurk a certain slyness. The man's eyes darted nervously, alighting on some passing face, then quickly glancing away.

"Oh, here you are, Hisashi," he said. "I wondered where you'd gotten to."

"I was wondering where you were, too." Just a few moments earlier Hisashi had been deriding his brother. Now his tone was deferential, almost sycophantic.

"Have you seen Kinue?" asked the man in the seersucker suit.

"No, not really," Hisashi replied. "I lost track of her a while ago. Sorry about that." His apology sounded singularly insincere.

"The contest is about to begin, and I've looked everywhere for her but she doesn't seem to be around." The man's eyes roamed the crowd as he spoke.

"Maybe she's feeling embarrassed," said Hisashi.

"Don't be ridiculous. She was the one who wanted to enter the contest in the first place, remember?" While his brother was looking around with a displeased expression on his face, Hisashi leaned over and whispered two or three words in his ear. At that, the older man's demeanor suddenly changed.

Turning to Kenzo, he bowed and said, in an extremely polite manner, "Well, well, I had no idea. Please forgive my rudeness. I'm Takezo Mogami. Thank you very much for all you've done for my brother in the past."

"No, on the contrary, he's the one who's helped me." Kenzo responded with the appropriate formulaic phrase.

"By the way, I hear that you're the brother of Detective Chief Inspector Matsushita of the Metropolitan Police. I've known of your brother by reputation for some time, and I've been thinking recently that I would like to meet him face to face, just once. This is really fortuitous, meeting you like this. I'd like to buy you a glass of sake and a nice big American-style steak sometime, but unfortunately tonight I have an appointment with some foreigners. What day might you be free to honor me with your company?"

If you want to shoot the general, first you kill his horse, Kenzo thought bitterly. Clearly the man had some dark ulterior motive—probably financial—for wanting to use Kenzo to make a connection with his brother Daiyu, or with the police department in general.

"Thank you ever so much for your kind offer," Kenzo said, using the same excessively polite language. "Unfortunately, I'm not much of a drinker." The truth was, he was able to hold his own perfectly well and had even been accused on occasion of having a hollow leg, but this sly, overfed mogul was not his idea of a convivial drinking companion.

"Now, now, don't say that," said Takezo Mogami in a hearty

voice. "I can see by looking at you that you like to have a good time. After all, isn't that what brought you here tonight?"

"Actually, I'm here as a scientific observer," Kenzo replied coolly. "I'm working on my dissertation at the Tokyo University research laboratory. That may sound rather grand," he added self-deprecatingly, "but the truth is I'm just a humble intern who doesn't even know how to take anyone's pulse." *More polite lies*, he thought. In fact, he could take a pulse or do a tracheotomy with one highly skilled hand tied behind his back.

"I've always enjoyed this sort of event, myself," Takezo Mogami declared, gesturing expansively at the ebullient crowd around them. "And of course I've been influenced by my uncle, Professor Heishiro Hayakawa, whom you may know better by his nickname, Dr. Tattoo. At any rate, my woman insisted on entering this contest as a foolish prank, against my wishes, and I just hope she doesn't embarrass me."

Kenzo felt a twinge of jealousy at the thought of the tattooed beauty in bed with this corpulent crook. "I just heard about that from Hisashi," he said. "It sounds to me as if she's the odds-on favorite to win tonight."

"*Hahaha*. Seriously, though, this is the sort of race where there are so many dark horses that the favorite might go home hungry. Well, I'll see you around. In the meantime, here's someone else who wants a word with you." Takezo Mogami jerked his chin in the direction of his hitherto silent companion, who then stepped forward, bowed very low, and handed Kenzo his business card.

"I'm Gifu Inazawa, manager of the Mogami Group," he said effusively. "I can't begin to tell you how delighted I am to meet you." Gifu Inazawa was a small thin man, flashily dressed in a blue plaid suit of prewar vintage. He had a sharp-chinned, ferret-like face, and his thinning hair was artfully combed over a nascent bald spot. He wore what appeared to be a permanent synthetic smile, and he reeked of hair oil, lavender water, and tobacco.

"Likewise I'm sure," said Kenzo drily, for he had taken an instantaneous dislike to the man.

"Do you reside with your honorable brother?" Gifu Inazawa's super-polite language failed to disguise the cheekiness of the question.

"Yes, I'm just a poor graduate student, so I can't get anyone to marry me."

"No, don't be silly. You're probably just setting your sights too high."

What a dreadful creep, Kenzo thought. He couldn't put his finger on what it was he disliked about Gifu Inazawa, he only knew that his first impression of the manager of the Mogami Group was entirely negative.

"We'll look forward to seeing you next time." Takezo Mogami and his obsequious employee took their leave, bowing from the waist and trailing elliptical pleasantries in their wake.

When Kenzo saw Takezo Mogami from behind, he couldn't help being startled, for the man's rear view was radically different from the front. Melodramatic as it might sound, he appeared to be walking in the shadow of death. Kenzo shuddered. When he was working as a military medic in China and the Philippines, he had often seen that same shadow hovering around Japanese soldiers as they walked away from his hospital tent on their way to battle. There was no logical explanation for the phenomenon. It was just an instinctive feeling, an irrefutable premonition of death. No matter how healthy and full of life the soldiers might have appeared to be at the moment, Kenzo always knew with absolute certainty that the only thing the future held for those high-spirited young men was a fatal bullet from an enemy gun.

6

The large meeting room of the restaurant was a hundred tatami mats in area. Even so, it was crammed to capacity. Half the occupants were spectators with unembellished skin, aside from the occasional arrow-pierced heart or Stars-and-Stripes tattoo on an American GI's forearm. The other half were the tattooed contestants who stood around in scanty undergarments, looking like colorful statues. The room was hot and stuffy and the male contestants, without exception, were dressed according to contest regulations in cool white cotton *fundoshi* loincloths that covered their private parts but left their tattooed buttocks exposed.

It was, undeniably, a grand spectacle. Each person was an individual work of art. But seeing such a multitude assembled in one place, with such a profusion of magnificent skin-pictures on their backs, the philosophical observer was tempted to view them as an independent race, separated by their immortal tattoos from the transience of life on earth. With the force of a tidal wave, the sculpturesque group made a profound impression on the spectators. In the hallucinatory excitement, some people even forgot that they were living in the postwar depression of 1947, and were transported back to the carefree days of the Edo Period.

The female contestants, too, had congregated in a corner of the room, but only about half of them had stripped down to their underpants. Some lounged around wearing nothing but white loincloths and fanning themselves, just like men. Takezo Mogami's "woman," Kinue Nomura, was standing at the center of one wall, between the seating areas for spectators and contestants, leaning against a pillar and smoking a cigarette. Kinue was still wearing her white dress, and the eyes of many of the spectators kept straying in her direction. Standing there with sleeves flapping and arms akimbo, she looked like some exotic creature of myth, a giant white bat with an angel's face.

"Are you tattooed, too?" A woman who was sitting next to Kinue suddenly spoke to her, out of boredom or curiosity. The woman had a picture of Kintaro (Golden Boy), the legendary wunderkind of Japanese folklore, tattooed on her back.

"Just a little bit," Kinue replied cagily.

"Well then, you'd better take off your clothes. Everyone else is already undressed, so there's no need to hold back. That dress must be unbearably hot."

"When I look at all these splendid tattoos, my own scribbles seem like a bad joke, and I feel embarrassed. I think I'll stay like this until my number is called." When Kinue said this the woman with the Kintaro tattoo, obviously miffed, stuck her nose in the air and looked the other way.

The meeting room had a slightly raised area that was used as a stage. On this makeshift platform the expert judges—five middle-aged and elderly men, including Professor Heishiro Hayakawa—were seated at a long table. One by one the society members paraded up and down in front of the row of judges, in the order in which they had registered. The numbers were assigned in the same manner, so that while Kinue was one of twenty or so female entrants, her number was forty-seven.

The greatest applause for a male competitor was for number twenty-one, a young man with a shaved head and gothic eyebrows who was tattooed everywhere except his face, his neck, the soles of his feet, and the palms of his hands. Rather than the usual designs, he was imprinted from hairless head to hammer-toed foot with mystical Sanskrit scriptures rendered in scarlet, black, and blue. The applause escalated when he raised his arms to show the arabesque runes in his armpits, for everyone knew that the tender underarm flesh was the second most painful place to receive a tattoo.

When the man paused in his jaunty promenade and let his white loincloth drop to the stage, there was a universal gasp as the audience saw that the man's penis was tattooed from top to bottom as well. No one in the crowd was unaware that this was by far the most sensitive spot on the male body, and most of them had heard stories of how such tattoos were done. While the tattoo master plied his bundles of sharp-tipped needles as gently as possible, an assistant would stretch the skin taut, and four strong men would immobilize the arms and legs of the shrieking, writhing subject.

"Ouch! That must have hurt like hell!" shouted a wag in the first row as the tattooed man showed off his illustrated sex organ, and everyone laughed uproariously.

The women's competition began when a woman whom Kinue had met many times took off her white *yukata* summer kimono and walked in front of the judges. The woman was the proprietor of a restaurant in Yokohama and had formerly been the wife of an influential organized-crime boss from Kanagawa. As was the custom, she was known by her own name in conjunction with that of her tattoo: O-Kichi of the Fiery Chariot. O-Kichi was well filled out, even a bit overweight, and on the plump flesh of her back two blue demons were shown pulling a flaming chariot while above them a naked beauty writhed in torment in the raging fire.

The breathtaking exhibition continued, and the atmosphere in the hot, stifling room became electric with anticipation. "Number forty-seven, Miss Kinue Nomura." Kinue was the final entrant in the women's division, and when her name was called at last she didn't reply. She just stood by her pillar, with the impermeable dignity of a sumo grand champion toeing the mark before a match.

"Orochimaru: Miss Kinue Nomura," Professor Hayakawa called again, and this time Kinue stepped forward. Flicking away her half-smoked cigarette, she threaded her way through the contestants' seating area with long strides, while the spectators watched her as if with a single eye. Still fully dressed, she stopped in front of the judges' table.

"We have to see you naked, Miss, so please take off your clothes." The professor's voice was as crisp and businesslike as if he were addressing a stranger.

"All right, I will," Kinue replied saucily. "As long as I've come this far, I may as well put myself on the chopping block, like a dead carp." She stepped out of her white one-piece dress and stood in front of the judges in a thin-strapped chemise of translucent white silk that revealed the colorful tattooing on her upper arms. It was a strikingly beautiful sight: her bare skin was flushed a pale pink, and against a blue-black background the tattooed cherry blossoms appeared to be in fragrant bloom, with vermilion maple leaves floating through the air around them.

As Kinue had known, the beauty of her tattooed body was tantalizingly visible through the thin silk of her chemise. She was well aware that the flimsy fabric would act as a conductor of light, and that the indescribably gorgeous colors of the tattoos—the vermilion, the pink, the purple, the indigo, the luminous yellow-green—would shine through with subtle glory. She also knew that if she appeared to be shyly concealing her superb tattoos it would have a bewitching effect on the audience, and would make the ultimate unveiling that much more dramatic. After twirling around once or twice to

36

heighten the suspense, Kinue casually stepped out of her silk chemise and stood in front of the crowd, dressed only in a pair of skimpy tailor-made underpants cut high on the hips, like the two-piece bathing suits worn by foreign women.

Kinue couldn't see her own back, but she could feel a blush of excitement spreading over her full breasts, and she could feel them undulating gently as she walked. As the flush engulfed her body it appeared to the spectators as if the wild-eyed sorcerer on her back was blushing in shame, and the giant snake seemed to be wriggling like a living thing. The meeting hall, which had been dead silent, suddenly erupted in cheers, shouts, and whistles.

When she heard that thunderous roar Kinue knew without a doubt that she would be crowned the queen of the tattoo contest. Raising her crescent-moon eyebrows in triumph, she looked first at the five male judges and then turned to face the rowdy, cheering audience. The young man who had given her a match in the garden was standing near the front, shoulder to shoulder with Hisashi Mogami, staring hungrily up at her. Kinue caught his eye and gave him a small, secret smile.

"What's your headline going to be?" a photographer in a filthy tan trench-coat asked a cigar-chewing newspaper reporter, as they left the hall after the contest.

"Hmm," said the reporter, scratching his head with a tooth-marked yellow pencil. "How about 'A Beautiful Snake-Woman Sheds Her Skin'?"

"Perfect," said the photographer. He jammed a new roll of film in his camera, then ran off in pursuit of the woman in question.

The tattoo competition was over, and everyone agreed that it had been a huge success. As expected, Kinue Nomura was awarded the grand prize. After the judging ended and the musical entertainment began, a number of contestants wandered out into the garden without bothering to put their clothes back on. Some refreshed themselves under a small manmade waterfall, while others relaxed in the cool shadows of the trees.

Kenzo Matsushita and Hisashi Mogami strolled amid the flowering shrubs. "How about it?" Hisashi asked. "Would you like to meet the snake-woman face to face?"

Kenzo still hadn't recovered from the excitement of being in such a decadent, sensual atmosphere, and he answered deliriously, "Yes, by all means, let me bask in the glory of the radiant queen."

"I don't mind introducing you, but I have to warn you that she has a tendency to take over people's lives. Also, she sometimes comes out with bizarre and even paranoid remarks, and the best thing is just to say 'Yes, yes' and act sympathetic. I think she's probably a little strange in the head because of the sort of upbringing she had, if you know what I mean." Hisashi spoke in a serious tone, and Kenzo nodded.

Kinue Nomura was standing in the garden under a large cryptomeria tree, dressed in her demure white dress and surrounded by admirers. A large crowd of newspaper reporters was laying siege to the newly crowned queen, waving notebooks and cameras and yelling the usual questions.

"No, no!" Kinue shouted back, flapping her hands at a couple of photographers who had gotten too close. "Show's over, boys. No more photographs. If you want to see my tattoos, you'll have to come again next year."

Kinue was still trying to shoo the journalists away when Kenzo and Hisashi approached. As they elbowed their way through the surging crowd, Hisashi called out, "How's it going, Kinue? You seem to be having a hard time."

"Oh, Hisashi, your timing is perfect. Please make these annoying creatures go away."

"You don't need me. If you just bare one shoulder like a gambler and shout a few insults at them, they'll creep away in terror with their tails between their legs."

"Bare one shoulder? That's not exactly a brilliant suggestion. I mean, that's what they're hoping for, to see some skin."

"Well, we're living in a democracy now, remember. Why not give them a break and let them take a few pictures?"

"Absolutely not. You're no help at all!" Kinue's tone of voice was playful.

"Excuse me, Miss Nomura, but I was wondering what motivated you to get that tattoo?" A young reporter seized on the chance to ask a question.

"I got tattooed because I was deceived by a disgusting, manipulative, lecherous man, just like you!" Kinue shouted. Everyone started to laugh, and the young reporter turned bright red and rushed off toward the meeting hall. The rest of the journalists seemed to realize then that their siege was in vain, and they, too, began to drift away.

"Kinue," Hisashi said, "I'd like to introduce one of your admirers. Actually, he's an old school friend of mine. His name is Kenzo Matsushita, and he's a doctoral candidate at the Tokyo University Medical School."

Kinue stared at Kenzo in amazement. "So it was you?" she said softly.

"Oh, do you two know each other?" Hisashi said. "Just as I thought, there's more here than meets the eye."

"Don't be ridiculous," Kinue scoffed. "He just lent me a match a while ago."

"Hmm, is that so? Sounds pretty fishy to me," Hisashi said, winking at Kenzo.

"What on earth are you talking about?" Kinue demanded, but she said it with a smile. "Actually," she said, turning to Kenzo, "my husband Takezo was just asking me about you, too. Don't tell me you're another skin-peeler!" She pronounced the last phrase with the bitterest sarcasm, and Kenzo knew right away that she was talking about Professor Hayakawa, who was notorious for his obsession with harvesting and collecting tattooed human skins.

"No, no," Kenzo said quickly. "I have no interest in that sort of thing at all."

"Forgive me," said Kinue. "It's just that when I hear that someone is a doctor, I immediately think they want to peel me like a grape and steal my skin. Listen, why don't we go over there and have a nice leisurely chat?" She led the way into the garden without looking back.

"Say, Matsushita, do you feel like stopping off somewhere for a drink on the way home?" Hisashi asked as they walked along behind the willowy, glamorous woman in white. Kenzo mumbled something about making it another time, and Hisashi went off on his own. The reporters had all dispersed by this time, and no one pursued Kinue and Kenzo into the dark.

In the shadows of a quiet grove of trees, there was a wooden bench. As they sat down, Kinue looked at Kenzo from under her eyelashes and said, "So, tell me the truth. Were you shocked to see the sort of woman I am?"

"Not in the least," Kenzo said. "When Hisashi first told me that there was a stunning young woman with an Orochimaru tattoo who was certain to win first place in the contest, I had a feeling it would turn out to be you."

"But an educated person like you must think I'm a foolish woman. I'm sure you must feel contempt for me for having defaced my body like this."

"Not in the least," Kenzo repeated. "The truth is, I took some classes in med school from Dr. Tattoo—that is, from Professor Hayakawa—and I had often heard him talk about the tattoo as an underrated art form, but I didn't realize how right he was until today. When I saw your tattoo up there on the stage, it was almost like a Zen satori. You know, the flash of enlightenment when everything becomes clear? At that moment, I suddenly understood the beauty of tattooed skin with every cell of my being. There's absolutely no need for you to be so defensive about it. Better that you should be proud of your tattoo and let the reporters take pictures, instead of running yourself down."

"The problem is, I really hate reporters. They treat me like a freak, like a two-headed zebra or a sideshow snake-lady, not a human being."

"There's probably some truth in that. I've always thought that heartlessness must be a prerequisite for a career in tabloid journalism."

"That's so true. You're a very perceptive man, do you know that? You're not too bad to look at, either." Kinue Nomura was staring into Kenzo's eyes with an intensity he had never encountered before.

Kenzo blushed and looked down at his army boots. "I must say, you really handled the reporters."

"That's because I'm a woman," Kinue said. "That's the one thing I know how to do, handle men." Seemingly lost in thought, she let out a sigh. Then she said dreamily, "I guess I was born with a taste for tattoos. When I was a child, no matter how hard I might be crying, my tears would stop the minute I saw my parents' tattoos. It finally got to the point where I couldn't stand not to have my own tattoos, and I virtually forced my father to tattoo me. It was really unbelievably painful. Even though you're a doctor, I'm not sure if you could understand that sort of pain unless you had endured it yourself. The process took three years, and it was finished just a couple of months before my father died. When I looked in the mirror and saw that I was finally tattooed all over, I felt like a full-fledged woman for the first time. I was totally happy."

Just then, Gifu Inazawa came up to where they were sitting, smiling his phony smile. "Doctor Tattoo wants to talk to you about something," he told Kinue, after treating Kenzo to several deferential hand-puppet bows.

"Don't you dare go away, Mr. Kenzo Matsushita," Kinue said with a dazzling smile, and she followed Inazawa to a nearby gazebo, where the professor was waiting.

Shamelessly eavesdropping from twenty feet away, Kenzo could catch only a word here and a phrase there. First Gifu Inazawa took his unctuous leave, then Professor Hayakawa said something in a low voice and Kinue snapped, "Over my dead body!"

More maddeningly inaudible murmurs, then Professor Hayakawa said in a normal tone, "Can't you see that you're being unreasonable? I'm only asking for a photograph, not your skin."

"Yes, but we all know it's my skin you want, to hang in your creepy parlor."

"Kinue, my dear, I'm deeply hurt." The professor's tone was mocking, as usual. "As an old friend of your family, I wish you only the best. And besides, you'll surely outlive me by a good many years. I just want to make sure that your glorious tattoo is preserved for posterity, that's all."

"Well, for your information, I've made arrangements to be cremated when I die, and there's nothing you can do to stop me." Kinue's tone was defiant.

The two voices lapsed once more into animated whispers for a moment and then Kinue suddenly shouted, "Just stay away from me, you perverted skin-peeler!" There was the sound of a slap, then silence.

A moment later Kenzo heard Kinue's light footsteps coming back to their bench, and he pretended to be engrossed in winding his watch. He looked up expectantly into her beautiful, stormy face, but it was clear from the stubborn set of her jaw that she didn't want to discuss what had just happened. She sat down beside Kenzo, and he could almost hear her blood boiling.

"The nerve of some people," she muttered after a moment. Giving her head a vigorous shake as if to clear her troubled mind, she turned to Kenzo and said, "Look, it's really impossible to carry on a relaxed conversation in a public place like this with all the annoying interruptions, and I'm afraid that I have to run along now, anyway." There seemed to be an unspoken invitation hovering in the air, and Kenzo decided to give the bold approach another try.

"I'd like very much to have a long talk with you sometime if your, er, husband wouldn't mind." Kenzo was wildly infatuated with the queen of the tattoo contest by this time, and his voice trembled as he spoke.

"Oh, don't worry about that," said Kinue blithely. "After all, my husband was saying he'd like to get together with you, too. How about Monday, the day after tomorrow. Are you by any chance free to meet us at my bar in the evening, around nine?"

"Absolutely," Kenzo said. "I'll look forward to seeing both of you then."

In his secret, guilty, smitten heart, though, he was praying that the tattoo queen's porcine "husband" would get hit by a bus, or choke to death on a big chunk of black-market steak.

7

"This must be the place," Kenzo said as he rang the bell. The front of the building was shuttered for the night, but if you had happened to pass by in the daytime, you would have seen SOUVENIRS written on the glass door in dubious gold letters. Inside, a jumble of cheap goods—pottery, parasols, yellowing woodblock prints—was arrayed in the hopes of catching the eyes of foreign shoppers. In the evening, the upper floors sprang to life when a gambling club and a members-only drinking place called Serpent opened for business. On this Monday, though, all was dark upstairs as well.

The peephole in the wooden door on the side of the building slid open. "Who's there, please?" a woman asked in a low voice.

"It's Kenzo Matsushita. I'm here to see Miss Nomura and, um, Mr. Mogami." *Please,* Kenzo prayed, *let that fat capitalist pig be out of town.* The door opened, revealing a narrow, dimly lit staircase. Kinue Nomura was standing behind the door, looking like one of the floating-world beauties in a woodblock print by Utamaro. She greeted Kenzo with a graceful bow and warm words of welcome, then led him upstairs. As he watched her lithe hips moving under the shimmering saffron-colored kimono she wore with a butterfly-patterned obi sash, Kenzo found it difficult to catch his breath. *It's the stairs,* he told himself. *I'm out of shape.*

Kenzo followed Kinue into a deserted room with three tables and a counter along one wall. Above the counter was a tier of mirrored shelves stacked with "keep bottles" of brandy and whiskey, each with a customer's name written on the label in black ink.

"What is this place?" Kenzo asked, looking around.

"This is the private bar I run, Serpent," Kinue said. "The police have been giving me a hard time so I can't put out a sign. In any case, we're closed until further notice. Don't worry, it's perfectly safe. The bell won't ring and the door is locked from the inside. No one will disturb us. Please relax and make yourself at home. Would you like something to drink?" She glanced at Kenzo, who was still looking around nervously, and held up a bottle of expensive imported whiskey.

"Where's your husband?" Kenzo asked. "Isn't he supposed to be here too?"

"Oh, he had some sudden business in Nagoya, and he left on the morning express. He asked me to give you his best regards," Kinue said breezily.

This was the answer to Kenzo's most fervent prayers, but he was suddenly filled with trepidation about what might happen if he stayed. After all, what could a beautiful, sophisticated woman like this, a woman with a rich and powerful lover, possibly see in an ordinary man like him? What if he made an unwelcome overture and she slapped him, or told her jealous husband?

"I think I'd better be going now," he said, his voice cracking like a teenager's. "It doesn't seem proper to be here alone, just the two of us."

"I think you're being very silly, but if you want to go home, go right ahead. No one's stopping you." Kinue folded her arms and stared stonily off into space, but there were tears running down her long, perfectly oval face.

Kenzo had been thinking of Kinue Nomura as a very tough type of woman, like the female gamblers in samurai movies who would bare one tattooed shoulder and hurl insults at men. He was totally nonplussed by her tears. "What's the matter?" he asked gently, placing one hand on her silk-covered forearm.

"Idiot! Idiot! Idiot!" Kinue suddenly began pounding his chest with her fists, sobbing convulsively all the while. "Are you going to force me to say the words out loud? Are you so determined to humiliate me?"

At that moment, Kenzo finally realized what was going on. All the blood in his body seemed to rush to his head, and he was breathing heavily as he tried to subdue his feverishly pounding heart. "What about the room next door?" he whispered.

"It's used for gambling. You know, mah-jongg, poker, roulette, that sort of thing. There's no one using it now, so we can relax in there." Kinue had been perched on a bar stool, delicately blotting her tears with a cocktail napkin. Now she stood up and opened the adjoining door.

The gambling club was a medium-size Western-style room with a white linoleum floor. In the middle of the room stood a black-and-red roulette table, and under the window was a large sofa covered in textured gold velvet. When they entered the room, Kinue closed the door behind her.

"No one will come in here, so please don't worry," she said. Kenzo suspected that she had spoken those same words many times before, to many other men, but he didn't care. He was utterly spellbound, like a frog hypnotized by a voracious, gimlet-eyed snake.

"You may be a doctor," Kinue was saying, "but I'll bet you've never touched the skin of a tattooed woman." With a mysterious smile on her lips, she went on talking in a way guaranteed to inflame the passion of any man. "My skin is cold, you know," she murmured. "It's like the skin of a carp, or some cold-blooded reptile. Even in the heat of summer, it will chill you to the bone. Come, don't you want to touch it?"

More than anything in the world, Kenzo thought as he stretched out a trembling hand.

Several hours later, Kinue lay on the sofa like an exquisite odalisque, wearing nothing but her magnificent tattoos. Her long almond-shaped eyes were partly closed, and she made no attempt to wipe away the tears that coursed down her lovely cheeks.

"Are you crying because of what we just did?" Kenzo asked as he lay beside her, stroking her long silky hair. He was perfectly happy, and he wouldn't have minded a bit if her husband had burst in right then and shot them both.

"No," Kinue replied in a soft voice. "I'm not worried about my old man, if that's what you mean. It's just that it's a very sad thing to be a woman. I always mean to keep my foolish heart in check, but then I end up doing something reckless and unladylike like this, just because I'm a woman of strong desires."

"Well, tonight was really wonderful for me," Kenzo murmured. He felt shy about expressing his true feelings, which were running along the lines of rapture, bliss, and eternal adoration. Instead he said, "For one thing, I had my first glimpse into the mystical ecology of a tattoo. I realized that when a tattoo master designs a tattoo, he has to think about what effect the subtle movements of the human body will have on the picture he paints on the subject's back. It truly is a living work of art."

"Of course that's true. Otherwise we couldn't bear the discomfort of running a fever every day while we were being tattooed. I got tattooed because I wanted to. The first day the ink was injected into my skin I felt a strange jumble of emotions, and I have to admit I shed a few tears. But I just kept telling myself, 'In the end, all this pain will be forgotten and you'll be left with something beautiful that can never be erased.' I didn't want to be one of those shameful cowards who gets part of a tattoo, then quits because she can't stand the pain. Getting tattooed is sort of like a love affair. You have to see it through to the end, no matter how much it hurts."

"I suppose that's true," Kenzo said. He couldn't help wondering whether she considered their liaison a budding love affair, or just a one-night fling.

She said, "You understand, don't you, darling Kenzo? I really feel as if you understand me now. Until you make love to a tattooed person, you can never understand the true beauty of the tattoo. But I'm afraid it might be upsetting for someone like you, with your high-class education, getting involved with a woman from the seamier side of life."

Kenzo felt a frisson of hope, for the word "involved" seemed to imply the possibility of other nights like this one. "It isn't upsetting at all. On the contrary, it's the best thing that's happened to me in years," he said, planting a light kiss on the top of Kinue's silky head. "There's no need for you to speak of yourself in such negative terms. Your tattoo is a splendid and beautiful thing, but there are prejudices in society that make some people perceive even the most artistic tattoo as loathsome and repellent. I really admire someone who would ignore those biases and make such a commitment, who would sacrifice her future possibilities and endure so much pain and suffering just to create a thing of beauty."

"Thank you, darling. You're the only person I know who would say something like that to me. I'm so glad there's one man in the world who treats me like a human being." Kinue stretched like a cat, then snuggled against Kenzo's naked, sweaty body.

"Tell me how you came to have these tattoos," he said, tracing the sinuous lines of the snake with his index finger.

"Are you sure you want to hear my boring story?"

"Of course," Kenzo said. "I want to know everything about you."

Kinue sighed. "All right, my darling, if you insist. How would it be if I made it like a fairy tale?"

"Anything you want," Kenzo murmured, wrapping his arms around her from behind, like a boa constrictor.

8

"Once upon a time [Kinue began], there was a famous tattoo master named Horiyasu. In addition to a son, he had two daughters. 'Please let my daughters' skin be as smooth as silk, and as beautiful as a precious jewel,' Horiyasu prayed every night as he gazed at their sleeping faces. His prayer was echoed in the first part of the names of his two girls: Kinu ('silk') and Tama ('jewel'). Sure enough, both his daughters grew up to have pale ivory skin that everyone said was as beautiful as drawing-silk.

"Kinue, the older daughter, had had a secret desire to be tattooed for as long as she could remember. This was hardly surprising, for she grew up surrounded by tattoos. Both her parents were beautifully tattooed, and among the many visitors who came to the house, there wasn't a single person—male or female—who sported the unembellished white skin he or she had been born with. Naturally, Kinue began to feel ashamed of her undecorated skin as she got older.

"Kinue's first love affair, at seventeen, was with a good-look-ing yakuza, a failed photographer who had been tattooed by Horiyasu. 'Do you really think I would marry a woman with plain white skin?' this uncouth man used to say, over and over, and Kinue ended up feeling even more certain that her untattooed skin was an obstacle to happiness.

"Kinue's older brother Tsunetaro had been taught the techniques of tattooing from earliest childhood, and he had spent countless hours watching his father wield his needles and brushes. Horiyasu had his heart set on making his son his successor, and he systematically taught him all the tricks and secrets of his art. Just before Tsunetaro took his physical exam for conscription into the army, Horiyasu began tattooing his son's back as an expression of fatherly devotion, in lieu of the traditional coming-of-age ceremony at a Shinto shrine.

"Until that time Kinue had been struggling to conceal her increasingly desperate desire to be tattooed, but when she saw her brother stretched out on the table she couldn't bear it any longer. 'Please tattoo me too, Papa,' she pleaded. 'I want a great big beautiful one, just like the one you're giving to Tsunetaro.'

"Horiyasu scolded Kinue soundly for even suggesting such a thing, and he explained to her that it would be impossible for him to deface the skin of his own daughter at such a young age. In truth, it had wrenched his heart to refuse his favorite daughter's request, and he asked himself afterward why he hadn't spent a few minutes giving her a tiny hidden tattoo of some sort. If he had just begun the process, it would have been easy to complete it later, once she was married to an understanding husband. But as a parent, he couldn't very well change his mind after taking such a firm stand.

"On the evening of the second day, Horiyasu returned from making a house call, and Kinue greeted him with a meaning-ful smile. 'Papa, I have something to show you. Do you still refuse to tattoo me after this?' She pulled the right sleeve of her kimono up to the shoulder. One portion of the white skin of her upper arm was pink where the blood had gathered, and it appeared to be somewhat swollen. On that spot, three small cherry blossoms had been finely drawn with indigo ink.

"Horiyasu immediately recognized the flowers as the work of his son, Tsunetaro. His eyes were filled with indescribably deep emotion as he stared at his daughter's face. 'See, Papa,' she said, 'since you wouldn't tattoo me, I'm going to get Tsunetaro to tattoo my entire body, so there.'

"*All right,* Horiyasu thought, *you win.* His emotions were a mix of pride and sorrow and relief. 'Go upstairs and take off all your clothes,' he murmured with shining eyes, as he unpacked his drawing pens and his bundles of needles. Over a period of three excruciating years Horiyasu tattooed the handsome, evil mountain sorcerer and his menacing snake-familiar on his daughter's supple skin, and thus was born Kinue of the Orochimaru.

"On the night that her brilliantly colored tattoos were completed, Kinue lay in the rococo arms of her yakuza lover and wept with joy. 'When the two of us are embracing like this, you can't see a single bit of white skin,' she said. 'This is good. This is perfect. As long as these pictures remain on my skin, my feelings for you will never change.'

"The tattoos didn't disappear, but the love Kinue thought would last forever soon vanished in a cloud of acrimony and recriminations. After that stormy breakup, Kinue embarked on an aimless odyssey around Japan. She traveled first with one attractive, disreputable man, then another. Eventually she ended up in Yokohama, where she worked as a geisha and indulged her acquired passion for gambling.

"Before long the Great War began. Almost overnight, life in the Land of the Rising Sun became a flaming nightmare of death and destruction, like a medieval image of hell. By some miracle Kinue managed to survive, although her brother and sister were not so lucky. When the smoke finally cleared, Kinue was running a bar called Serpent in the Yurakucho area, and living with a fat, rich, insanely possessive man whom she didn't love a bit. Such are the compromises of life, she told herself. But her heart and soul were dead.

"Then one day Kinue entered a tattoo contest, and won. As a bonus, on that same day she met a young man who was intelligent, kind, handsome, and loving. Kinue felt her soul returning to life and she thought that maybe, just maybe, the young man might care about her, too. For the first time in a very long time, she began to think that fairy tales might come true, even for a woman who had defaced her body with a snake tattoo."

9

Toward the end of Kinue's story, Kenzo had been unconsciously holding his breath. He was afraid to believe his ears. Could she really be saying that she cared for him, and that he might have a role in her tattooed–Cinderella fairy tale?

They were still lying cozily in spoon formation, back to belly. Kinue looked over her decorated shoulder at Kenzo with an expectant expression, and he let out his breath with an almost snakelike hiss. "That was a fascinating story, very well told," he said. "Can I ask you one terribly personal question?"

"Anything," Kinue said, kissing his fingertips.

"Do you ever regret having gotten tattooed?"

"No, though I do wish I hadn't gotten tattooed with such an unlucky design. Maybe an angel, or a princess, or the medieval dancer Shizuka Gozen. Even now I often regret that I didn't request one of those designs—something gentle, and feminine. And ladylike."

"When you say unlucky, do you mean because it's associated with sorcery?"

"No, not exactly that. You must have heard of the Three Curses? You know. 'The snake eats the frog, the frog eats the slug, the slug dissolves the snake.'"

Kenzo shook his head. "It sounds kind of like 'Paper, Scissors, Rock,' only with slimy creatures," he joked. "But what does that have to do with your tattoo?"

"I'm surprised you don't know, didn't you say you were from the Nagano area? Anyway, Orochimaru has a big snake as his sorcerer's familiar, right?" She pointed at the snake's head on her shoulder. "If you read the story, you'll see that Jiraiya's familiar was a giant toad, and Tsunedahime was always seen riding on an enormous slug. Those three characters lived in the depths of Mount Togakushi in Nagano Prefecture, and they were constantly competing to see who could create the wickedest, most powerful spells. My father saw an old woodblock-print version of the story, and he fell in love with the images. So he tattooed the three curses on his three children—Jiraiya on my older brother, Tsunedahime on my sister Tamae, and Orochimaru on me."

"And… ?"

"And both my brother and sister were killed in the war, while I've somehow managed to survive until now. But I have a feeling that I don't have much longer to live myself. Jiraiya and Tsunedahime both met untimely deaths, and there's no reason to believe that only Orochimaru would be allowed to live a long, healthy life."

"That's just silly superstition." Kenzo spoke lightly, but he shivered in spite of himself.

"Silly superstition? Before you dismiss it so easily, you should try living inside the skin of someone with one of those doomed tattoos. In any case, it's not as if I have any great desire to live to a ripe old age, so it doesn't matter. If I can just live a short life, and live it fully, that's enough for me. Cry a little, laugh a little, and then it's over."

"I don't know. That strikes me as rather bleak and pessimistic."

"Oh, please, spare me the sermon. If I were to die right now, at least Professor Hayakawa would be ecstatic. That man is so obsessed with his collection, I wouldn't put it past him to commit a crime in order to get what he wanted. I really feel sometimes that he might kill me just to get his hands on my tattoo. Remember when he called me away after the contest? He was pestering me to give him some photographs of my tattoo, and he tried yet again to persuade me to let him harvest my skin after I die. I mean, how creepy is that? Then there's the famous story about the time a yakuza boss from Ueno was brought into the university hospital with one arm chopped off at the shoulder. That boss was a patient of Professor Hayakawa's, and the professor had already paid the man up front for the right to remove his tattooed skin when he died. The professor was eating lunch with some colleagues in the university cafeteria when he heard the news. Apparently he dropped his chopsticks, jumped to his feet, and cried, 'But what happened to the tattoos? Are the tattoos all right?' Isn't that awful? I mean, he didn't even ask about the condition of his patient; all he cared about was getting his grubby hands on the man's tattoos. Doctor Tattoo isn't the only weirdo who's approached me, either. The world is full of men with strange obsessions who will stop at nothing to get what they want." Kinue seemed terribly upset, and after she finished speaking she buried her face in the sofa and dissolved in tears.

It was an illusion, of course, but Kenzo thought he could hear the rustling of the scales on the great serpent that reared its head on Kinue's right shoulder. There was no question in his mind but that the same chilly blood was flowing in the veins of Kinue Nomura and her snake tattoo. Was she a woman, or a snake?

After all that had happened on that entrancing evening, the distinction had become blurred in Kenzo's mind. He was certain of one thing, though. All the old folk tales he had read about the passionate lubriciousness of snake-women were true, to judge from the intoxicating feast he had experienced that night.

"Please don't cry," Kenzo whispered. "I want to make love to you again." He got down on his knees and gently placed his lips on Kinue's back, right on the tattooed lips of the fearsome sorcerer Orochimaru.

"Oh," Kinue sighed, with a catch in her breath. "My dear darling Kenzo, my wonderful, beautiful lover."

10

Near the entrance to the famous Specimen Room at Tokyo University, there was a lavishly gilded casket that housed an ancient Egyptian mummy, said by some to have been the favorite concubine of King Tut himself. Elsewhere in the room, the disembodied brains of such celebrated novelists as Natsume Soseki and Kanzo Uchimura were on display, floating dreamily in formaldehyde. Then there was the distinguished married couple, both professors of medicine, who had willed their bodies to science in the 1920s. Now their perfect ivory skeletons stood at attention by the entrance, like a pair of sentries. Interesting though these objects were, the most riveting thing in the room was the collection of vividly colored, intricately-tattooed skins hanging on the walls and suspended from the ceiling. They looked to Kenzo like an eerie parade of souls in limbo, and he gazed at them in awe and fascination.

The amber-patinaed human hides, preserved with fixative and stretched over special frames, had the visual appeal and textural richness of a Flemish tapestry. Horned demons, folk heroes, Chinese lions, dragons, peonies, cherry blossoms, sea creatures, characters from Kabuki plays, the designs were elaborate, and diverse. Kenzo could almost see the people writhing in agony under the needle while the tattoo master, breathing heavily from the sheer physical exertion, poured his soul into the creation of a picture that would outlive its mortal host.

Taken one by one, you could certainly say that these leathery specimens were valid works of art. Unlike a gallery of paintings, though, the assembly of human skins created a surrealistic, unsettling atmosphere. Kenzo was staring at the otherworldly torsos in a trance, trying to imagine those desiccated, decorative skins wrapped around living human flesh. When someone tapped him on the shoulder, he almost jumped out of his shoes.

Standing behind him was Professor Hayakawa, dressed in his trademark ice-cream suit, with the familiar ironical smile tugging at the corners of his mouth. He wore a starched white shirt and a precisely knotted necktie of sea-blue silk, and he carried a walking stick of lacquered rattan. Something about the professor's natty getup suggested that he had managed to maintain a certain sartorial style, even in those desperate times. The dapper attire was like a suit of armor, worn as a shield against a world in chaos.

"Ah, Sensei," Kenzo stammered. He was so surprised that he forgot to bow.

"Don't 'Ah, Sensei' me," said the professor tartly. "What's wrong with you, anyway, wandering around looking as if you'd been bewitched by foxes? You'd better watch out. I've heard there are a lot of supernatural creatures at large in Tokyo these days."

Kenzo felt awkward and embarrassed, for he was certain that the professor must be able to tell just by looking at him that he had spent the previous night immersed in illicit passion with Kinue Nomura. Earlier that morning Kenzo had awakened in his own bed with only three desires—to eat breakfast, to make love to Kinue again, and to learn more about tattoos. Since the second was not an immediate option, Kenzo downed a hasty meal of miso soup and seaweed-wrapped rice balls, then set off to revisit the tattoo exhibit at Tokyo University, where he was a postgraduate research fellow.

"Come along," said Professor Hayakawa. "As long as you're here, I'll give you the tour." Leading the way, the professor expounded on his favorite topic. "So you see, even after people die their skin outlives them!" he said in an agitated voice, gesturing around the room. The expression on his face was a curious mixture of excitement and rapture.

"Tattooing is definitely an art form," Kenzo said. "I do agree with you about that, and I've recently learned to appreciate the beauty of the art tattoo. But tell me, speaking not as a collector but strictly as a physician and a rational man, don't you think it's stupid to undergo so much pain and expend so much energy on self-mutilation? I mean, surely no one with an iota of common sense would ever do such a thing."

"If you say it's idiotic, maybe it is," the professor retorted. "And if you say it shows a complete lack of common sense, that's probably true as well. But on the other hand, tattooing has something of the same seductive, addictive appeal as opium. Once you become enslaved by its charm, that's the end. You're hooked for life, and there's no way to resist. Here's a perfect example." He gestured in the direction of one of the specimen room's more striking exhibits—a complete human skin, tattooed from head to foot, and everywhere in between.

"This is a former president of the Edo Tattoo Society named Yasokichi Murakami. Murakami was an usher at the Shintomi Theater in Asakusa, and he wasn't merely tattooed on his back, chest, thighs, and upper arms, as is customary. As you can see, his tattoos also covered his face and head, his fingers and toes, his eyelids, the insides of his ears, and even his private parts. The only place where his skin remained as blank as the day he was born were the palms of his hands. When strangers saw the man's face from a distance, they often mistook him for a foreigner. And when they got close enough to see that his face was a solid mask of tattoos, many people couldn't help shrieking in surprise."

The professor paused to light a cigarette, in open defiance of the NO SMOKING signs posted above every door. He took three or four wolfish drags, then stubbed the cigarette out on the bottom of his beige leather shoe and kicked the butt under a glass table. On top of that table was a display of disarticulated hand bones with missing finger joints. YAKUZA EXTREMITIES, the label read, referring to the custom among Japanese gangsters of chopping off bits of their fingers to atone for errors in judgment or social gaffes in that highly ritualistic world.

"Anyway," the professor went on, "when I try to imagine the state of mind that made Murakami want to penetrate every pore with the most permanent of ink, I always get a chilly feeling in my heart. He may have been a living work of art, but I think what he did to himself goes beyond mere enthusiasm, into the dark realm of obsession. Not that I wouldn't give my left arm to have his skin hanging in my living room, you understand." The professor paused for a moment with a distracted look on his face, then continued. "As you know, if you walk around the men's side of a public bathhouse you'll often see a number of decorated bodies. One man might have a woman's name or two tattooed amateurishly on his arms, while another might sport a half-finished portrait of some folklore hero on his back. But the fully realized fine-art tattoos, like the exhibits here, are another matter altogether. You could count on two hands the number of tattoo artists who could legitimately be called masters, and still have some fingers left over…"

Kenzo couldn't stop himself from making the obvious joke. "Maybe not, if you were a yakuza," he quipped, holding up a hand with the pinkie folded back.

Dr. Hayakawa glared at him. "As I was saying before I was so rudely interrupted, after the Meiji Period, which lasted from 1869 to 1912, these persecuted artists led lives of bare subsistence in slums and narrow alleys. Struggling to elude the vigilant eyes of the government, which had outlawed tattooing, they kept their skills alive by creating works of art that could never be shown in public. The names that spring to mind are Horiuno I and II, followed by Horikane, Horikin, Horigoro, Horiyasu, and a couple of others.

"Of course, no list of post-Meiji tattoo artists would be complete without the renowned Honcho the First. As you may know, he created a nationwide scandal in Japan in 1900 by committing 'love suicide' with a woman who was not his wife. Horicho had already left his mark on posterity, not just in Japan but overseas as well, by tattooing highly publicized dragons on the forearms of the English Duke of York, who became King George V, and the czarevitch of Russia, later Czar Nicholas II. At the time, Horicho's was the only legal tattoo parlor left open in Yokohama. It was there—attracted, no doubt, by a sign that read 'For Foreigners Only'—that both George and Nicholas got their dragons.

"Aside from these serious tattoo artists, the only people who were doing tattoos in those days were rank amateurs who didn't even have the skill to work with red pigments. Hence, the murky blue-black coloration of their clumsy designs. Even for the most accomplished masters, though, expressing their artistic sensibilities wasn't as simple as running an ink-dipped brush over a clean sheet of paper. With a living canvas such as human skin, whether or not a tattoo artist could produce a work of art that satisfied him depended in great measure upon the subject. The ideal, of course, was pale, velvety, fine-grained skin without a single birthmark, scar, or blemish.

"Assuming that the tattoo artist could find someone who possessed such flawless skin, there remained the question of whether that person would want to be tattooed. Most people on the higher rungs of society would never even consider such a thing. There was a strong societal prejudice at work, exacerbated by the natural human fear of pain and permanent commitment. Once you cross the line into being tattooed you can never go back. However beautiful the design may be, a tattoo is a brand that cannot easily be removed from the skin."

Kenzo nodded dreamily, thinking of Kinue's exotically decorated flesh, which he had memorized inch by lovely inch. "You've got that bewitched-by-foxes look again," Professor Hayakawa said sharply, and Kenzo thought, *If you only knew.*

11

Professor Hayakawa took a silver flask from his leather brief-case, unscrewed the cap, and offered Kenzo the first sip. "No, thank you," Kenzo said. He was a bit shocked that his companion would be tippling so early in the day.

"It's only green tea, you know," the professor said, but Kenzo still demurred.

The professor drained the flask, wiped his lips with a large plaid handkerchief, and then resumed his monologue precisely where he had left off.

"When a person gets a major tattoo, there are also some permanent physiological side effects, including a perceptible change in metabolism. As a fellow physician, I'm sure you're aware that having tattoos over a large area of the body radic-ally lowers the body temperature. Even on the most torrid summer day, tattooed skin is cool to the touch. I once knew a woman, the wife of a prominent tattoo artist, who said that when she embraced her husband it was like making love to a refrigerated fish. She had a pathological fear of needles, but she finally got tattooed all over in self-defense, so that her naked skin would be as chilly as his."

The professor paused to light another forbidden cigarette, and Kenzo had a sudden vision of Kinue saying, "My skin is cold, you know. Don't you want to touch it?" He shivered involuntarily at the memory of that first electrifying touch, and what had followed. Professor Hayakawa began speaking again, and Kenzo snapped to attention.

"Even if a person has a sincere desire to have his body covered with a splendid tattoo," the professor said, blowing twin plumes of smoke through his narrow nostrils, "that goal cannot be accomplished without an extraordinary amount of effort. Over the span of many months, there will be constant sharp pain as thousands of needles are plunged into the skin, and the inks, dyes, and pigments are poured into the resulting openings. There are unpleasant side effects, too, including the fever that is the body's defense against this invasion, the physical exhaustion brought on by the accompanying decrease in white blood cells, and the drain on one's finances. Good tattoos aren't cheap, you know." Kenzo nodded mutely, for he knew a reply was neither desired nor expected.

"At any rate, with all these drawbacks, it's hardly surprising that so many people who set out to get tattooed end up dropping out at some point in the process. Thus it can be said without exaggeration that the person who ends up with a completed full-body art tattoo is truly one in a million. Locating these rare examples of the tattooer's art is no easy matter. Aside from occasional public appearances at festivals and the like, spectacularly tattooed people tend to be rather private, preferring to stay within their own tightly knit social groups.

"My old friend, the late Professor F., who single-handedly assembled most of the specimens in the Tokyo University Pathology Department, was constantly on the lookout for beautiful tattoos to add to the university's collection. Year after year, without missing a day, he would make the rounds of all the public bathhouses, searching for completed tattoos. He would mine every possible connection in order to make contact with the sort of people who were likely to be tattooed all over. He deliberately sought out gangsters, construction workers, firemen, and so on. In this shadowy realm of society, Professor F. met many men who had left their tattoos unfinished due to financial pressures. He wasn't a wealthy man, but he would pay out of his own pocket for the work to be completed.

"Even after a work-of-art tattoo was located, the problems were just beginning. The next obstacle in the collector's path was obtaining a contract for posthumous conveyance of the tattoo. The potential difficulty of this cannot be overemphasized, for people tend to be passionately attached to their own skins, even after death. No matter how hard up he might be, a person would have to be mad to blithely sell the tattooed skin off his back just to raise a bit of cash. Professor F. would pay visit after visit to the subject's house, explaining the reasons why a great tattoo artist's work should be left to posterity. Eventually, with patience, luck, and persuasion, he might manage to overcome the subject's initial superstitious reluctance. The contract for posthumous dissection and conveyance of the tattoo would be drawn up and signed, and the fee paid in advance.

"When the negotiations were concluded and the papers signed, the next step was to wait for the owner of the tattoo to die. There was no way of knowing whether this would happen in ten years, or twenty, or thirty. However, it is a medical fact that all-over tattooing decreases life span because heavily tattooed skin doesn't breathe properly. No matter how frustrated and impatient the collector might become during this long wait, he couldn't very well slip the tattooed person a dose of poison to hasten the process. All he could do during those long years was to pray that the tattoo would remain safe, for there are so many potential disasters that can befall a wonderfully decorated body. Natural calamities, war damage, domestic accidents, automobile wrecks, violent crime, to name a few. Then there's the possibility that the tattooed person will decide to disappear, absconding with his own skin to avoid the imagined horror of being flayed after death.

"All that suffering—the pain of the tattooing process, the struggle of the collector—is enshrined in every one of the hundred or so skins in this room. As a result of his lifetime's work in building this remarkable collection, Professor F. came to be called Dr. Tattoo, and I'm honored to have inherited that nickname. Many of the tattoos on these walls belonged to gangsters, and to show their gratitude,. crime bosses from all over the Tokyo area chipped in and bought a magnificent stone lantern for the garden.

"It is common knowledge that if it hadn't been for the noble efforts of Professor F., Tokyo University would not have this world-class collection to illustrate the unique art of the Japanese tattoo. However, it cannot honestly be said that these posthumous relics are an accurate representation of the opulent beauty of the tattoo. The background ink that appears as a deep, rich indigo on living skin grows darker after death, while the brilliant clear reds are transmuted into a reddish brown, like scorched brick. Putting aside for a moment the problem of changes in color and hue, there is also the matter of distortion of the design. When you take a tattooed human skin with all its subtle curves and contours and stretch it out flat, it will not meet the standards of a one-dimensional work of art."

Kenzo's eyes glazed over momentarily as he visualized the subtle curves and lush contours of Kinue's body, but he quickly resumed his attentive-pupil stance before the professor could accuse him again of being under a fox-spell.

Oblivious to Kenzo's reveries, the professor lectured on. "If you visit a Japanese tattoo artist at his studio and see his design-sketches, what Western tattoo artists call 'flash,' you will understand this very clearly. Like a picture on a paper kite, when the tattoo designs are drawn in a notebook, every part of the human body will appear to be out of balance. The head will look immense, while the arms and legs appear diminished. At first glance there seems to be something artless, almost childlike, about the awkward asymmetry of the figures in these drawings. But when the designs are removed from paper and transposed onto the complex canvas of a living human skin, what animation and luster are revealed! I have been surprised on many occasions by the startling disparities between the flat drawing and the living tattoo. As one famous tattoo artist so aptly said, a tattoo should not be viewed as a flat painting, but rather as a three-dimensional sculpture.

"Of course, an eminent authority like Professor F. was well aware of the problems in displaying posthumously-preserved tattoos. The torsos that are hanging in the middle of this room illustrate his ultimate solution to that problem. The skins have been restored to the curved shape of a human body, thus giving the impression of three-dimensionality. This method also avoids the unnatural feeling that results when a tattoo is stretched tightly across a frame, like needlepoint. Many of the bodies have neither heads nor arms nor legs, just a disembodied trunk, and the uncanny shapes with their splendid coloration seem to float in empty space. As you can see, the illusion of ghostliness is intensified by the way the dim golden light shines through the torsos, illuminating the elaborate, mythopoeic designs." Kenzo gazed around at the spectral hanging tattoos with renewed appreciation, while the professor went on talking.

"At first glance it is impossible to tell whether the departed souls whose skins live on in this room were men or women. It is safe to assume that most of them were not pillars of polite society, and we can only guess at the lives of turmoil and transformation they must have led. For example, one of these tattooed skins is said to have belonged to a famously wicked adventuress named O-Den Takahashi, whose beautiful severed head stood on a pike in the center of Tokyo for a week after she was hanged for her crimes. However, no one has been able to corroborate that story. The same is true of a skin that was willed to the Osaka College of Medicine. It is popularly believed to have once adorned the body of the notorious female bandit known as O-Shin Kaminari, but..."

As the professor rambled on in his articulate, erudite fashion, it seemed to Kenzo that the older man was talking for his own pleasure rather than trying to impress or educate his audience of one. Finally the lecture ended and, after agreeing that it was time for both of them to go to work, the two men walked past the skeletal sentries to the door.

"That woman still hasn't given me a picture of her tattoo," the professor complained with an enormous, windy sigh, as he and Kenzo stepped out of the sarcophagal dimness of the specimen room into a bright August day.

"When you say 'that woman,' who do you mean?" Kenzo asked disingenuously.

"Haven't you been listening to a word I've been saying? I'm talking about Kinue Nomura, the beauty who has the magnificent Orochimaru tattoo on her back."

"Oh, *that* woman." Kenzo tried to keep his voice casual. "I thought you would have long since gotten a photograph of her tattoo, since I gather it was finished six or seven years ago."

"No, I haven't been around. During most of that time I was going from Manchuria to China on official military business. By the time I returned to Tokyo, her father Horiyasu had moved out of his old house, and I couldn't track him down.

When I saw Kinue recently, it was the first time in several years. But since we aren't exactly unrelated—her patron is my nephew, in case you didn't know—I don't see why she couldn't give me a measly photograph, at least."

"Maybe it's because you're always hounding her, asking her to leave you her skin when she dies. I overheard your conversation by accident, in the garden after the contest."

"Humph." Professor Hayakawa snorted derisively. "That's not the case at all. If you look at it from a psychoanalytic point of view, a tattoo is a form of perpetual suicide. It's as if the person has some subconscious awareness of having sinned, and their way of atoning for a guilty conscience is to inflict pain on their own body. Not just criminals, but martyrs and celibates too; what they all have in common is deep feelings of guilt. So the collector's request to remove their skin after death and preserve it for posterity is actually the fulfillment of their deepest desires."

"I wonder if that's really so. What you say may make sense in theoretical terms, but I think Miss Nomura is truly frightened. If you want to dismiss it as superstition that's fine, but the fact is that the bearers of the other two cursed tattoos, Jiraiya and Tsunedahime, are already dead, and she's afraid her turn will be next."

"Tsunedahime?" Professor Hayakawa's face was suddenly transfigured by an expression of sheer terror. "Who had a tattoo of Tsunedahime? Who was it?"

"I heard it was that woman's sister, Tamae. Surely you must have known about that, Sensei?"

Professor Hayakawa shook his head emphatically. "That's the most ridiculous thing I've ever heard. It's impossible I refuse to believe it."

"Why is that?"

"Because it's simply shocking, and inconceivable. If Horiyasu really did give Tamae the Tsunedahime tattoo, he must have been out of his mind."

"I don't understand what you're talking about," Kenzo said, shifting from one weary foot to the other. The two men had been walking or standing for more than an hour, first in the Specimen Room and now on the sun-splashed steps of the building.

"Listen carefully, all right? I'm only going to explain this once." The professor's tone was impatient, and emotional. "Among tattoo artists, there are certain taboos which it is absolutely forbidden to break. For example, they believe that if you tattoo a snake wrapped around a person's torso you have to make a little cut under the armpit or somewhere else where it won't show. Otherwise the throttling power of the snake's embrace will make it difficult to sleep, and within three years the person who has the snake tattoo will be dead. There are lots of persistent beliefs like that, call them superstitions if you like. Anyway, one of the most taboo of all tattoos is the Three Curses."

"The Three Curses?" Kenzo asked, feigning ignorance.

"Surely you've heard that saying: 'The snake eats the frog, the frog eats the slug, the slug dissolves the snake.' At any rate, those creatures are the familiars of the three rival sorcerers. The sorcerer Jiraiya always appears riding on a giant toad, Orochimaru on a snake, and Tsunedahime on a slug. If anyone ever tattooed a snake, a frog, and a slug on one person's body, the three creatures would fight to the death. That's why such a tattoo is forbidden. Even if a client begged for that tattoo and offered to pay a fortune for it, the artist would be morally obliged to refuse."

"What if the three tattoos were divided among three separate people?"

71

"That's a valid point, but it doesn't apply in this case. If the three separate people were totally unrelated that would be a different matter, but when it's three siblings with the same blood flowing in their veins, and on top of that, his own children! I really don't understand what could have possessed Horiyasu to do such a reckless thing. As a man, as a father, as a tattoo artist..." Professor Hayakawa's usually precise speech lapsed into incoherence. He lit a cigarette and inhaled deeply, like a drowning man gasping for air. After a moment he spoke again, more calmly.

"If what you say is true, then it's as if Horiyasu put a curse on his own children. Maybe he carved the anger he felt at their mother into the skin of his children."

"What did their mother do to make Horiyasu so angry?" Kenzo asked, but Professor Hayakawa chose to ignore that question. The professor heaved a great sigh, then whispered some terrifying words. "If the other two are already dead, then Kinue probably doesn't have long to live. I may get my wish sooner than I expected. But it's just as well for her that the other two are already dead. If all three of them were living, they would probably end up destroying each other."

Those were not the sort of words Kenzo expected to hear from a rational, scientific sort of person. The realization that a scholar like Professor Hayakawa believed in the superstition of the Three Curses was very disturbing, indeed. After taking his leave of the older man, Kenzo walked to his office feeling almost dizzy with concern for the safety of his newfound love.

12

Kenzo's professional mail was usually singularly unexciting, but on this morning he arrived at the university research laboratory to find a large square envelope waiting for him. His address was written on the front in feminine, rather hesitant calligraphy. When he turned the envelope over, the sender's name seemed to leap out at him: KINUE NOMURA.

Hastily Kenzo stuffed the envelope into his briefcase. He went into an empty classroom, and after looking around to make sure he hadn't been followed, he opened it. Several photographs fell out onto the table. He sat down. They showed a man and two women; there were eight shots in all, and all three of the people in the photos were heavily, beautifully tattooed.

"Jiraiya, Tsunedahime, Orochimaru," Kenzo whispered softly. He shook the envelope again and a letter fell out.

Dearest Kenzo, it began. Kenzo felt deeply ashamed of himself as he looked at the letter, which was sloppily written and full of childish mistakes. When he read the words, his shame changed to alarm.

I feel that I am going to be killed very soon, she wrote. *A terrible death is stalking me, and I am terrified of what may lie in wait... I fear my days are numbered, and the happiness I've found with you will be cruelly snatched away... You're the only one who can rescue me, my love.*

At the bottom of the page was a postscript: *The other night you said that you would like to have a photograph of me. Since I don't have a new photo, I'm enclosing some old ones. I am including some pictures of my sister and brother, too, and I'd appreciate it if you would keep them safe for me.*

"Just my luck," Kenzo muttered, looking at the photographs. "The woman I love belongs to another man, and she's seriously paranoid to boot." Not that he cared very much about either of those drawbacks. He had spent every waking moment since leaving the Serpent Bar reliving his wondrously erotic night with Kinue and fantasizing about a sequel, consequences be damned.

The pictures appeared to be several years old and were somewhat discolored. There were bits of glue sticking to the backs, as if they had been peeled out of an album. Two of the photographs were group poses showing the front and back views of a man standing between two women who looked remarkably similar apart from their very different tattoos. All three were dressed only in loincloths to show off the magnificent designs on their torsos. The remaining photos were individual front and rear portraits of the trio.

The man's tattoo was of Jiraiya, the wild-haired mountain sorcerer who rides on the back of a giant toad. On the back of the photograph someone had written *Tsunetaro Nomura* with a fountain pen. The two women in the pictures resembled one another so closely that if they had both been dressed in kimonos, Kenzo would have had a hard time telling them apart.

He examined the photographs carefully, staring for a long time at the image of Kinue Nomura with her snake-and-sorcerer tattoo. When he looked at the pictures of the other woman—obviously her sister, Tamae—he was more than a little surprised. *This woman must have really liked tattoos,* he thought. *She took the process much farther than Kinue did.*

Men are another matter entirely, but women, however much they may love their tattoos, are usually reluctant to show them off to strangers. For that reason, to keep people from peeking up their sleeves in summer, most women, and many men, choose designs that stop just above the elbow. For similar reasons, the majority of tattoos end above the knee.

The woman in the photograph, though, had tattoos below her elbows. From the shoulder all the way to the wrist, her arms were gorgeously tattooed with a traditional design of reddish-golden carp climbing a waterfall. She had designs on her calves as well, of crabs and cherry blossoms against a background of stylized clouds. On her back was a splendid tattoo of the sorcerer known as Tsunedahime riding on a giant slug, which was in no way inferior to the other two tattoos, Jiraiya and Orochimaru. There was a strange quality to the photograph, a lack of shadow that gave the woman's entire body a garish cast, which Kenzo thought must have been a result of shooting with available light.

Kenzo put the photographs back in his briefcase and went to the research room. Miss Ogi, the attractive young department secretary, was standing in the door looking oddly upset. "Sensei, you have a phone call," she said. Miss Ogi was usually wreathed in smiles, but now her round face was downcast, and her tone of voice sounded almost reproachful.

"From whom?" Kenzo asked wonderingly, for no one ever called him at work.

"From a young woman." Biting her lip, Miss Ogi turned and ran into the restroom.

"Hello," Kenzo said, picking up the telephone. A woman's voice flowed through the receiver and seemed to twine around his heart.

"Kenzo, darling, it's me, Kinue."

"Miss Nomura?" Losing his composure for the second time that morning, Kenzo glanced around to make sure no one was listening.

"Did you get the photos and the letter I sent you?" Kinue whispered.

"Yes, I did receive them. Thank you very much for your kindness."

"Why are you being so cold, darling? That's not—Oh, I get it. Is someone listening? Please take good care of the photos for me," she said softly. "If I should be killed—"

"Don't talk like that, it's bad luck. Nothing's going to happen to you, I promise. I won't let it."

Kinue was silent for a moment. "I really can't tell you the details on the phone," she whispered, "so I was wondering if you could come to my house tomorrow morning. There's a reason... There's a reason why it isn't silly for me to be afraid. I'd like to see you tomorrow and tell you about it, and borrow some of your strength. Tomorrow morning at nine. You'll be there, won't you?"

"Yes, but..." Kenzo had been hoping to meet at a more romantic time, after dark.

"Don't worry about a thing. My husband won't come by, and the maid won't be there. It'll just be you and me, with all the time in the world to be together, just like the other night. And since it'll be daylight, you won't have to be concerned about what people will think. Are you ready for the directions? Go out the north exit of Kitazawa Station, and walk through the market that runs along the tracks. You'll come to a business district. Go straight, and when you get to a dead end, turn right. You'll see a public bathhouse called Asahi-Yu on the corner. Turn right there and my house is just a few steps farther along."

"Are you sure it's all right?"

"Don't be silly, of course it's all right. I'm counting on you to save me. I'm so very frightened, and I need you so much." Kinue hung up abruptly, but her cry for help—and, he thought wishfully, for affection—echoed in Kenzo's ears for the rest of the day.

13

In the evening, shortly before eight o'clock, there was a bit of a ruckus at Asahi-Yu, the public bathhouse in Kitazawa. Due to the postwar fuel shortage, the bathhouse's hours of operation had been shortened, and it was getting toward closing time. The women's bath was so crowded that when a statuesque stranger walked in wearing a leaf-patterned summer kimono, no one took any special notice at first. The moment the woman shed her clothing, though, thirty or forty pairs of eyes were immediately riveted upon her colorful naked body.

It would have been different if the bathhouse had been in downtown Tokyo, where tattoos were a common sight. In the quiet residential district, it was extremely unusual to see a tattooed female in the public bath. The woman herself seemed unaware of the stir she was causing. She wasn't even blushing as she made her way through the crowd with a long, graceful stride. When she got to the large bathtub, the woman dipped steaming water from it with a wooden bucket and poured it over her body with a self-confident air that bordered on arrogance.

"Who is that?" whispered a local kimono maker.

"Does someone like that really live in this neighborhood?" said a fish seller.

"No way she's anybody's wife. She has to be a mistress, or a bar girl," chimed in a florist's apprentice.

"She looks like a bandit to me. I'll bet she has a criminal record," said the seamstress, squinting into the mirror as she carefully shaved off all her facial hair, including the eyebrows.

"Maybe she's a professional gambler," said a caterer.

"I've never seen such a big tattoo, even on a man," said a mother of five. Huddled in bunches, the neighborhood women stared at the glamorous interloper and gossiped in scandalized whispers.

Whether she was under the taps or in the middle of the big communal tub, the subject of all this speculation conducted herself with quiet, regal dignity. Her tattoos, though, were another matter. The giant snake that wriggled on her back appeared to be sticking out its long red tongue at the people in the bathhouse, while the sorcerer Orochimaru seemed to be watching the nervous behavior of the local women and sneering in disdain.

"Mommy, why is that lady going in the bathtub with her snake kimono on?" Nobody laughed at the child's innocent question. They just went on staring at the tattoo, not head on but rather sideways, with eyes filled with fear and curiosity.

After about twenty minutes, Kinue Nomura got out of the bath. She stood in front of the mirror for a moment, admiring her spectacular reflection, and then slowly put on her clothes.

Kenzo was at home playing a rather sloppy game of *shogi* chess with his brother, Detective Chief Inspector Daiyu Matsushita. Daiyu—who was also known as "Matsu the Demon" and "the Locomotive"—was a tall, bulky, crewcut man. He had a square-jawed face with a wide mouth, deep-set eyes, and a low, broad nose that had been flattened still further during his career as a collegiate judo champion at Nihon University. Daiyu had wanted to be a police detective since boyhood, and he spent almost every waking moment either doing his job or thinking about it. His taste in entertainment ran to drinking beer and reading an occasional pulp novel about a sword-wielding medieval magistrate, while his only hobby, if you could call it that, was blowing smoke rings. Daiyu and his pianist wife, Mariko, had met at the university and married for love. Their standing joke was that someday when they were old and gray they would spend a leisurely day together, and maybe even go out to dinner.

Next to the chessboard stood a nearly empty bottle of medium-grade whiskey. It was obvious from Kenzo's flushed face, and from the crooked way the pieces were lined up on the chessboard, that both he and his brother were more than a little tipsy. Daiyu had been scowling at the chessboard, trying to figure out his next move. Now he raised his eyes and said, "Kenzo, how are things going at the university?"

"Same as usual, I guess. Sometimes I get the feeling I've been in school forever."

"Of course, that's only natural. But since you've been studying forensic medicine, you seem to have become more of a realist."

"A realist, huh? Yes, I suppose I have…"

"Aha, I see you're trying to get me to jump your rook. Well, if you insist, I'll just help myself. So tell me, have you finally graduated from reading detective novels?"

"Wait a minute… Check!"

"That move doesn't scare me at all. No, what I mean is, I've been handling murder cases for ten years, but so far there hasn't been a single one that bears any resemblance to the exaggerated cases in your detective novels. Hey, how's this for a defensive maneuver?"

As Daiyu moved a chess piece, he knocked over a celadon vase containing three stalks of purple clematis. Nonchalantly, he jammed the flowers back into the vase and mopped up the puddle of water with one sleeve of his lounging kimono.

"I don't know why you haven't had any interesting cases, and since I'm not God I can't very well predict the future," Kenzo said airily, taking a big gulp of whiskey.

"There won't be any interesting cases in the future, either. That's my form of realism. Hey, I seem to have accidentally captured your bishop. Oops... checkmate!"

Kenzo stared at the chessboard and then began to laugh.

"What is it? What's so funny?" his brother asked.

"It's just that you aren't as much of a realist as you'd like to think, at least not when it comes to chess. You can't promote your bishop that way, and in any case my king is still guarded by two pawns."

"Who? Which? Where?" Daiyu looked at the chessboard for a moment, then joined in the laughter. "Oh, now I see," he said. "Where the hell did those blasted pawns come from?"

Kenzo laughed even more loudly. "Even if you were sober, if you can't at least remember the previous moves, I don't think you should be permitted to play chess without a sizable handicap."

"Hahaha, that's a good one. In that case, shall we call it a draw?" Still chuckling, Daiyu began tossing the chess pieces back in the box. "It's really muggy tonight," he said. "It's going to be hard to sleep."

"Yes," said Kenzo, "it's an awful night. I have a weird feeling, too, as if something terrible is about to happen."

"Don't even say that. On a night like this I wouldn't mind having a nice long rest, so please don't upset me with talk of terrible things. When bad things happen in this city, it usually means a phone call in the middle of the night for me."

"What? Don't tell me that Matsu the Demon actually craves rest and relaxation once in a while?"

"Hey, in this new age of democracy, even the demons in

hell can go on strike!" Daiyu quipped. He said good-night and started up the stairs, still smiling at his own joke.

It was, indeed, an unusually muggy late-summer night. Kenzo found it impossible to sleep. There was no breeze at all, and the wind bells that hung in the garden were completely silent. As the hours ticked by on his alarm clock, he hugged his pillow and fantasized about having Kinue in bed beside him, with her ripe body, silken skin, and fragrant hair.

Kenzo tossed and turned in his sweat-soaked bed until the clock downstairs chimed three A.M., and the air finally began to cool off. He had just drifted into a shallow dream-state when the sudden sound of a faraway train pierced the stillness. Startled, Kenzo sat bolt upright in bed with his heart racing a mile a minute, for the train whistle sounded uncannily like a scream.

14

On the morning of the twenty-eighth of August, there wasn't a cloud in sight. Kenzo Matsushita got off the train at Kitazawa Station in the throes of a serious hangover and squinted resentfully up at the bright blue sky with bleary eyes. In front of him was a line of the sort of cheap market stalls that had sprung up around every station after the war.

The people milling about the open market all seemed to reek of garlic, and Kenzo felt certain they were staring at him with suspicion and contempt. He immediately blushed, for he had a guilty conscience about going to call on Kinue Nomura with such patently dishonorable intentions. The hangover didn't help his equilibrium, and every time he thought about holding his tattooed queen in his arms again, he felt so dizzy that he could hardly stand up.

Kinue had said, "Go straight," but the route she had suggested turned out to be strangely circuitous. The narrow, crooked street wound absurdly around and around. Just when Kenzo was sure he must have left the train tracks far behind, they would suddenly appear on the other side of the road, gleaming in the sun. *It's like some weird hallucination, I must be even more hung over than I realized,* he thought. A few blocks later he stopped in the shadow of a rice storehouse and lit a hand-rolled cigarette.

Calm down, calm down, Kenzo ordered his pounding heart, to no avail, for he was filled with carnal desire and nervous anticipation.

On that hot summer morning there wasn't a single person out on the streets of the plush residential district. The Kitazawa area had survived the fire-bombing that reduced so much of Tokyo to rubble, but all the life had gone out of the town, giving it the vaguely haunted look of an abandoned movie set. As Kenzo was thinking these rather bleak thoughts, a lone man, walking with an unsteady gait and looking distractedly about, approached from the opposite direction. The moment Kenzo saw the man's face, his own face stiffened. He ducked into a patch of deep shade and waited for the man to pass.

The passerby was Gifu Inazawa, the manager of the company run by Kinue's common-law husband, Takezo Mogami. Fortunately he didn't notice Kenzo in the shadows. The first time they met, Inazawa had been very dapper and well-groomed, in a repellent sort of way, but on this morning he looked as if he had just fallen out of bed.

But whose bed? Kenzo thought, and his heart turned chilly.

Gifu Inazawa's face appeared oddly rumpled. His eyes were bloodshot and red around the edges, and his skin was as white as a sheet of calligraphy paper. Untamed by brilliantine, his sparse hair stuck up in all directions, giving him the look of an unkempt sea anemone. He was carrying a small package wrapped in a purple furoshiki cloth, and he kept nervously passing it from hand to hand. He was muttering something under his breath, over and over. It almost sounded as if he was chanting a Buddhist scripture. The overall effect was decidedly weird.

As Gifu Inazawa passed his hiding place, Kenzo was able to hear what the man was mumbling: "Oh, this is dreadful. This is really, really terrible." Kenzo's feeling of unease suddenly turned to jealous panic. He couldn't imagine that Inazawa would be out paying a social call at some other house in Kinue's neighborhood at this hour of the morning.

Oh my God, he thought, *don't tell me this man, this pig of a man, has just spent the night in the arms of my beautiful snake-woman!*

Kenzo was already finding it somewhat difficult to breathe because of the heat, and the worrisome encounter with Gifu Inazawa didn't help. Wiping his dripping face with a crumpled handkerchief, he set off in the direction from which Inazawa had come. Walking a few more blocks, he came upon a new-looking wooden nameplate bearing the calligraphed words NOMURA'S TEMPORARY RESIDENCE.

The house was the sort that, before the war, might have been built by a company section chief or an assistant professor who had saved up a good deal of money. Even in that refined neighborhood, Kinue's house was one of the more splendid. It was hidden from the street by a hedge and was separated from its neighbors on three sides by a high concrete wall. The lot itself appeared to be at least a hundred *tsubo*, slightly more than 3500 square feet.

The formerly elegant garden had been turned into a vegetable plot. Kenzo found it hard to imagine a glamorous woman like Kinue digging in the soil, but someone was evidently doing some gardening. The yard was a jungle of ripe tomatoes and glossy green squash with enormous leaves and spiraling tendrils. *What an amazing harvest,* Kenzo thought as he walked up the stone path that led to the entrance of the house.

The storm windows were closed tightly, and there was no sign that anyone in the house was awake. Kenzo rang the bell, but there was no answer. He rang again, but still there was no sound from inside the house.

"What on earth is going on here?" Kenzo said in a low voice. The vague sense of unease he had felt earlier began to take on an alarming shape, and his feelings of jealousy toward Gifu Inazawa were replaced by inchoate stirrings of fear.

Kenzo went around to the back of the house. One of the storm windows had been left partially open, leaving a gap as if a tooth had been extracted. Kenzo went up to the open window, stuck his head inside, and yelled, "Miss Nomura!"

That sounded rather foolish, considering their degree of intimacy. Just as he was about to call out "Kinue?" his eyes became accustomed to the murky light inside the house and the words died in his throat.

Kenzo was looking into a six-mat room—Kinue's bedroom. It was a terrible mess. Two *tansu* chests had been haphazardly pulled open and ransacked, and there was clothing scattered all over the floor. A long red kimono-tie had snagged on one of the *tansu*'s handles and lay stretched out across the tatami. Most shocking were three large splotches of blood, like the blowzy red flowers of a tree peony, which had seeped into the pale yellowish-green tatami mats that covered the floor.

Just then, someone took hold of Kenzo's shoulder. He wheeled around in terror. Of all people, it was Professor Hayakawa. He was dressed in pristine white linen with all the creases in place, and he was wearing his trademark Panama hat and carrying his rattan walking stick.

"What's this?" he said. "Young Matsushita? Hah, just as I suspected: you're an admirer of the tattooed temptress, too."

"Sensei," Kenzo stammered, "this is no time for that sort of talk. Something awful has happened! Look here!" Kenzo grabbed the professor's arm and pointed at the bloodstains on the tatami. Immediately the smile vanished from the doctor's face. He had just finished lighting a Peace cigarette, and it dropped from his lips.

"Matsushita, come on!" Professor Hayakawa shouted. He took off his shoes and stuck one stocking-footed leg into the house. "Be careful not to touch anything," he cautioned.

The floor plan of Kinue's house included one eight-mat room, two six-mat rooms, two four-and-a-half-mat rooms, and a three-mat entryway. The two men searched them all. Every room had been turned upside down, as if by a burglar looking for valuables, but there was no sign of any human presence.

The trail of splattered blood that began in the room where they had entered the house continued up the middle corridor, all the way to the back door. Kenzo and Professor Hayakawa rushed around, peering into all the rooms, but they didn't find anything. When they met back in the entryway, Kenzo let out a huge sigh of relief, for he had been afraid they might find Kinue murdered.

"Wait a minute," said the professor. "Do you hear that?"

Kenzo listened intently for a moment. "I hear it. What do you suppose it is?"

"It sounds like water. Somebody must have left a faucet on."

It was the faint but unmistakable noise of running water, at the end of the hall. Cautiously they went to investigate. It was coming from what appeared to be a bathroom. There was a solid door of dark brown wood, tightly closed.

Kenzo wrapped a handkerchief around his hand and tried to turn the doorknob. There was no keyhole, but he found it impossible to open the door. "Do you suppose someone might be inside?" he said.

Without replying, the professor got down on his knees in the hall. In the door of the bathroom there was a tiny crack, no bigger than a piece of string. It was an opening so minuscule that it hardly deserved to be called a crack at all.

Suddenly Professor Hayakawa turned around, his face an ashen mask.

"Oh, no," he whispered.

15

Kenzo's heart was pounding as he peered through the tiny opening in the bathroom door. It wasn't possible to view the entire room through such a narrow space, but he could clearly see what appeared to be a woman's severed arm lying on the white tile floor, its bloody stump like an overripe persimmon.

An ordinary person, confronted with such an appalling sight, would probably have screamed or fainted. Kenzo was deeply horrified, but he struggled to remain calm. He was a doctor, after all, and in his long years as a soldier in wartime he had seen enough dead and mutilated bodies to become inured to such things. This was different, though. *Please,* he prayed, *don't let it be Kinue. Don't take her away, just when we've found each other.*

"Matsushita, quick, go call the police! I'm sure there was a phone in this house, somewhere."

The professor's words brought Kenzo back to his senses, and he went to the entry hall and picked up the telephone. It occurred to him that he ought to go through the tedious process of placing a call to the local police box, which had probably never dealt with anything more exciting than a stolen bicycle. Instead, he dialed a number he knew by heart.

"Hello, is this Metropolitan Police Headquarters? May I have the first division of criminal investigations, please? I'd like to speak to the section chief." There was a pause as the call was transferred.

"Detective Chief Inspector Daiyu Matsushita speaking."

"Hello? It's me, Kenzo. I want to report a major crime. It's really terrible!"

"Just tell me what happened."

Hearing the strong, self-assured voice of his older brother, Kenzo calmed down a bit. "It looks like a burglary-murder," he said.

"Murder?" Daiyu Matsushita's tone changed in an instant from indulgent older brother to no-nonsense police chief. "Where's the place?"

"It's the house of Kinue Nomura, in Kitazawa 4-Chome."

"And is that woman the victim?"

"I don't know. We haven't been able to get close to the actual scene of the crime. The bathroom seems to be locked from the inside, and all we could see was what appears to be the fatal wound. It's really horrible."

"Get hold of yourself. You're supposed to be a doctor." Daiyu's voice was stern but not unsympathetic. "Tell me, who found the body?"

"I did, along with Dr. Hayakawa. You know, he's the professor at the university. The storm window was open, and the tatami is covered with blood, and there's stuff thrown all over the place."

"I'm on my way. I'll be there as soon as I can, so just wait for me, okay?" Wasting no time on pleasantries, the chief inspector hung up.

Kenzo stood in the dim entry hall, holding the buzzing receiver. The reassuring image of his older brother galloping down the stairs of headquarters, scolding several cowering subordinates on the way, floated before his eyes like a phantom. At the same time, thoughts about the necessity of concealing his secret relationship with Kinue Nomura were whirling around in his mind like a dark vortex.

Kenzo made an effort to pull himself together, then went back down the hall.

"Matsushita, how did you happen to stop by Kinue's house this morning?" Professor Hayakawa still looked pale and shaken, but his voice was strong.

"No special reason," Kenzo said glibly. "The other night at the meeting of the Tattoo Society, my old schoolmate Hisashi Mogami introduced me to Miss Nomura. When I said that I would be interested in hearing the story of her life, and of her spectacular tattoos, she said that she would give me a call and invite me over."

"The story of her life? When she had only just met you? That woman gives away her secrets much too easily." The professor was clearly jealous. Glaring at Kenzo, he said, "When did you receive that phone call?"

"Yesterday morning, in the research room." It suddenly struck Kenzo as suspicious that Kinue would have invited the professor to join their private rendezvous. "I'm a bit surprised that she would have called you at all, after your recent falling-out," he said.

"Not as surprised as I was," said Professor Hayakawa. "I mean, why would that woman call the two of us and suddenly ask us to come here? And why would we both get the calls around the same time yesterday morning? I wonder if she wanted to have some sort of joint medical consultation about her tattoos." The professor seemed to be recovering from the initial shock, for he was showing signs of his usual sarcasm.

"No matter how much your brother rushes to get here from Metropolitan Police Headquarters, it will take him at least thirty or forty minutes, don't you think?" he said, in a friendlier tone of voice.

"That sounds about right, since he's coming from the heart of Setagaya."

"Then let's go wait outside. This atmosphere of dissecting room and graveyard is just too depressing."

Professor Hayakawa immediately began walking around the garden in circles with his head bowed and his hands clasped behind his back. After a while he spoke. "Matsushita, look at this," he said as he peered at the bathroom window from outside.

"Look at what?"

"The iron bar is in place on the outside of this window. The window appears to be locked from the inside as well, and the glass isn't broken anywhere. And when you add the fact that the door to the bathroom is also locked from the inside, what do you have?"

"A locked-room murder," said Kenzo, after a moment's thought.

"Exactly." The professor pointed at the dry earth outside the bathroom. "What's that?" he said.

It was a fragment of black glass. There were several other shards scattered around; put together, they would have formed a pane about the size of a postcard. The pieces of glass were dark, with a distinctive sheen that identified them as the shattered remains of a photographic plate.

Professor Hayakawa picked up one of the pieces of glass. "It hasn't been here long," he said, turning it over in his hand. "Judging by the accumulation of dust, I'd guess that it was dropped here no earlier than yesterday."

Just then the quiet air was shattered by a shrill, piercing ring. "That's the phone," said the professor. He took two or three steps in the direction of the house, then stopped. "Matsushita, you answer it. I don't know who it is, but you'd better not tell them anything about this case."

Flustered by this new development, Kenzo ran into the

house and picked up the phone. As is the custom in Japan, the caller spoke first.

"Hello, Kinue, is that you?" It was a man with a low, muffled-sounding voice, but he still managed to give the impression of a certain amount of power and pride. Kenzo felt a surge of jealousy at the familiar way the stranger said "Kinue."

"I'm afraid Miss Nomura has stepped out for a while, but may I ask who's calling, please?"

The caller hung up.

16

Some moments later, a police officer from the local precinct ran into the garden, covered with sweat. His blue uniform was dark with perspiration, and he was panting slightly. Mopping his face, the policeman looked suspiciously at Kenzo and the professor. "What are you two doing here?" he said in an officious tone. "And why didn't you notify us immediately?"

Kenzo replied loftily, "We're both here because we had an appointment with the owner of this house, Miss Kinue Nomura, to discuss something of a scholarly nature. And since my brother works at Metropolitan Police Headquarters, I thought it would be quicker and more efficient to call them directly."

"And what does your brother do at headquarters?" The officer sounded skeptical, as he expected Kenzo to say, *He's an apprentice floor-mopper.*

"He's the chief of the investigative section," Kenzo said. "His name is Detective Chief Inspector Daiyu Matsushita."

The policeman's posture suddenly became rigid. Standing respectfully at attention, he said in a very formal tone, "I'm sorry, sir, I didn't know that. Please forgive my rudeness. I've been ordered to protect the integrity of the crime scene, so would you please stay in the garden for the time being?"

Kenzo sat down in a corner next to a late-blooming hydrangea bush and waited for his brother to arrive. Professor Hayakawa, meanwhile, continued to pace around the garden, his brow furrowed with thought. Just then a car from police headquarters stopped in front, its siren wailing. A tight-lipped Detective Chief Inspector Matsushita, followed by a large crowd of detectives and forensic investigators, burst into the garden.

"Kenzo, where's the body?" he called out in a loud voice.

"It's in the bathroom at the end of the hall," Kenzo replied, standing up. He felt dizzy, light-headed, and sick to his stomach. *Please, don't let it be Kinue*, he prayed again, to any god who might be listening. *Let it be anyone, but not my lovely snake-woman.*

"Right-o, show us the way." Daiyu Matsushita was all business, as usual.

With Kenzo shakily leading the procession, the new arrivals hurried to the scene of the crime. After listening to Kenzo's account of what had happened earlier, including his encounter with the distraught Gifu Inazawa, Daiyu tried pushing and pulling the door a couple of times. When it didn't move he issued an order to one of his subordinates. "You there, cut out this plank of wood, but be careful of the fingerprints." After a moment, a hole had been made in the bottom section of the door, large enough for one person to squeeze through.

One by one the men peeked through the crack, and one by one they gasped, or groaned, or made some exclamation: "Oh, no!" "This is too awful!" "Who could do such a beastly thing?"

There was a severed head, and two soft white forearms, and two long legs from the knees down, all laid out on the tile floor, with the hideous cuts of the saw clearly visible. The faucet was running, and the water had filled the bathtub and overflowed onto the floor. The long, luxuriant black hair on the bloated head twined and floated in the water like an undulant knot of snakes.

DCI Daiyu Matsushita, the first one in the room, looked at the locked door and moaned, "How on earth did the perpetrator get away?"

The key to the door was the old-fashioned bolt type. There was a horizontal bar which slid downward, and that bolt had been pushed firmly into place. Just as Professor Hayakawa had surmised, the window, too, was tightly locked from inside. There wasn't a crack an ant could have crawled through, much less a person.

When someone opened the door from the inside, Kenzo peeked in and gave an involuntary scream at the dreadful sight. "Kenzo, what's the matter with you?" said his brother, giving him a disgusted look. "You're a doctor, you should be able to handle this." Kenzo barely noticed that his brother was scolding him, for he was staring at something gray and viscous that was moving on the windowsill inside the bathroom. An animal that was shapeless, yet had a shape, unlike a human being, such an elusive creature could go in anywhere and get out again. The creature on the windowsill was a very large garden slug.

Professor Hayakawa appeared suddenly at his side, and Kenzo jumped. The professor's face was distorted with grief, and he spoke in a husky whisper. "It's just as I thought. But what on earth has happened to the torso? What's become of Orochimaru? Who stole that tattoo?" He sounded as if he was on the verge of hysterics.

"Tattoo?" said Daiyu Matsushita, stepping into the hall. "What tattoo?"

"Didn't you know? This woman had one of the most magnificent tattoos in all Japan on both arms and legs, and on her back. Oh, what kind of fiend could do such a thing?" Professor Hayakawa slumped wearily against the wall, looking as if he had been beaten by thugs.

The police searched the bathroom from top to bottom, but they couldn't find the body's torso. Both arms had been amputated above the elbows, both legs had been cut off just below the knees, and there wasn't a trace of a tattoo anywhere. There wasn't even that much blood; the water had washed most of it away.

The policemen and investigators gathered at the door. Stunned into silence, they stood staring at the sad, horrible scene. They were all accustomed to death and violence, but they shivered in spite of themselves when the professor began softly chanting, "The snake eats the frog. The frog eats the slug. The slug dissolves the snake."

17

The first thing Detective Chief Inspector Daiyu Matsushita did after seeing the corpse in the bathroom was to summon his brother. "Kenzo, come here a minute," he called in his curt official voice. With Kenzo following, he went into the large eight-mat room, which was the only part of the house that hadn't been messed up in the apparent burglary. Daiyu plopped down on the floor tailor-fashion and slowly lit a cigarette.

"What were you doing here, anyway?" he asked. "What sort of relationship did you have with the murdered woman?" The warmth and humor that filled his voice at home were totally absent, and his facial expression was severe.

Kenzo swallowed nervously. He had never lied to his brother before, but he didn't see any alternative. "Well," he said, "we were just… acquaintances, really. The murdered woman, Kinue Nomura, was the mistress of a man called Takezo Mogami who runs a big construction and engineering company. She was the daughter of a famous tattoo master named Horiyasu, and before the war she apparently persuaded her father to give her a full-body tattoo. Earlier this month there was a meeting of the Edo Tattoo Society, and she won the grand prize in the tattoo contest. At that meeting I happened to run into an old school friend, Hisashi Mogami, who is the younger brother of the contractor I mentioned. Hisashi introduced me to the woman, and we chatted a bit. Out of the blue, she told me she had a feeling that she was going to be killed. Not only that, but she had an unbearable premonition that after being murdered she would be stripped of the tattoo on her back. It was a rather startling conversation, to say the least. I'm sure the reason she confided in me is because she knew I had a brother in the police department. So anyway, yesterday I got a phone call in the research lab at the university, and it was that woman, begging me to help her. *Lend me your strength*, she said. I couldn't help sympathizing, so I stopped by here early this morning. You know the rest."

Kenzo felt satisfied that he had managed to make his story ambiguous, yet not suspiciously so. His brother had listened without interruption, nodding his head and blowing an occasional perfectly symmetrical smoke ring toward the ceiling.

"I see," he said. "Someone was saying that woman had a tattoo, right? But somehow the torso containing that tattoo has disappeared. With the primary identifying characteristic missing, how can you be sure the murder victim is Kinue Nomura?"

"Well," Kenzo said carefully, "I only met her once, but she wasn't the kind of woman you'd soon forget. I'm absolutely certain that the, um, head in there is that of Kinue Nomura." His stomach seemed to turn a back flip as he spoke those horrific words, but he managed to keep his face as expressionless as a Noh mask.

"Is that so." Daiyu Matsushita's expression was equally inscrutable as he closed his eyes and blew three leisurely oval smoke rings. His reverie was interrupted by the shrill, bloodcurdling sound of a woman screaming somewhere in the house.

"What on earth was that?" Daiyu asked a member of the criminal investigation team who had just entered the room.

"Oh," said the investigator, "that's the neighbor, a Mrs. Kotaki, wife of a government employee. When she saw the severed head she fainted dead away. What can I say, she's a woman."

"I don't know what it has to do with being a woman," Daiyu responded in a serious tone of voice. "I think anyone might faint at such a ghoulish sight. I mean, if this weren't our job, a few of us might be under a doctor's care right about now."

The investigator looked properly chastened, and Daiyu quickly asked, "Any luck in establishing the time of the crime?"

"Well, the body, if you can call it that, appears to have been dead for between twelve and seventeen, possibly eighteen hours. Of course, it's a bit difficult to perform a precise autopsy when the trunk of the body and all the vital organs are missing."

"I see. So if it's eleven A.M. now, then the crime probably took place last night between six o'clock and midnight, is that right?"

"Yes, that's the one thing we're sure of at this point."

"Cause of death?"

"I can't say for certain, but we found an empty whiskey bottle on the table in the sitting room, along with two cups."

"Hmm."

"There was some liquid left in one of the cups, and it smelled faintly of cyanide. We'll run some tests on it, but I'm pretty sure it will turn out to be potassium cyanide, or some similar type of poison."

"Potassium cyanide, huh. During the war the female volunteer workers in army factories were passing that chemical out to everyone, as a suicide pill, but you don't see it around much anymore."

The man from the Criminal Investigations Department shrugged. "Actually, Chief," he said, "this may surprise you, but I think this case is going to be quite simple to solve."

"Why is that?"

"Because anyone who would use something as obvious as potassium cyanide as a method of murder can't be very intelligent. I think it's just a matter of time before the murderer does something to give himself away."

Daiyu Matsushita closed his eyes and shook his head lightly, "I hope you're right," he said, "but somehow I don't think we're going to get out of this case so easily."

As the man from the CID took his leave, Detective Akita came in. He was a solemn-faced man with heavy-lidded eyes and a diagonal scar across one cheek, which emphasized his high Mongolian cheekbones. "Chief," he began, but then he noticed Kenzo and glared suspiciously in his direction.

"Ah, Akita," Daiyu said with an imperial wave of his hand. "Don't worry, that's just my younger brother, Kenzo. Have you finished canvassing the neighborhood?"

"Yes, that's what I came to report. Kinue Nomura has been living in this house with her maid. Apparently she didn't make an effort to conceal her tattoos, nor did she seem to be ashamed of them. People said that in hot weather she would wander around wearing nothing but a short chemise. Needless to say, she had quite a reputation around the neighborhood."

"That's not surprising, in a conservative residential neighborhood like this."

Akita nodded, then resumed his report. "Because of the sort of woman she was, she didn't form intimate friendships with any of the neighbors. There were delivery trucks from high-class stores coming and going all the time, and she didn't seem to have to worry about paying her bills. That didn't help her reputation, either. Anyway, they say that she used to be a low-level geisha in Yokohama, but now she's the mistress of a man named Takezo Mogami, who owns a successful construction company. So it all begins to make a little more sense."

"What about men? Did she seem to have a lot of lovers?"

"Evidently not. Aside from her patron, the neighbors said they didn't see any men entering or leaving the place. They seemed almost disappointed that there wasn't anything to gossip about on that score."

"You should know better than to take that sort of report at face value. If she had wanted to cheat on her patron, there are plenty of ways to do that in secret."

Kenzo had no reason to believe that his brother's words were directed at him, but he felt as if his heart had been scooped out with a sharp dagger.

"Kenzo, where are the offices of this Mogami?" Daiyu asked.

"In Ogikubo. And I remember hearing that Takezo Mogami lives in Nakano."

"Nakano and Kitazawa, huh? That's a suitable distance for a concubine's house. Okay, Akita, you and Yokoyama go to Nakano as fast as you can. If Takezo Mogami is there, bring him in for questioning."

There were now four uniformed policemen in the room, and Daiyu Matsushita turned his attention to the second pair. "Officers Takizawa and Noto, you'll go to Ogikubo and check out Mogami's office. I especially want to know what Gifu Inazawa, the manager of the company, was doing last night."

The four policemen rushed off to round up the possible suspects. As they left, a singular-looking man entered the room. This was Officer Ishikawa, a figure of great height and heroic bearing who held a total of twelve black-belt degrees in judo, kendo, and karate. Shrugging his massive shoulders like the mythological giant Atlas, he addressed his boss. "Chief, when we asked the next-door neighbor to check on the severed head she almost passed out, but she seems to be back to normal,

100

more or less. What shall we do now? She says that she definitely saw the deceased last night around eight."

"Eight o'clock, eh? Right-o, better bring her on in here." Daiyu Matsushita took a deep drag on his cigarette and issued four flawless circles of smoke.

18

A white-faced Mrs. Kotaki entered the room, led by a police officer. As she lowered herself to the floor in front of Detective Chief Inspector Daiyu Matsushita, she heaved a sigh so deep that her thin shoulders shook. She was a petite, disappointed-looking woman in her fifties, clad in a nondescript gray house-dress under a plain blue apron.

"I can't begin to say how sorry I am for the dreadful shock you've just had," Daiyu said. "It's really lamentable to meet under such circumstances, but allow me to introduce myself. I'm Matsushita, the chief of detectives. You're absolutely certain that the deceased was Kinue Nomura?"

"Yes…"

"And I gather that you saw Miss Nomura last night. Is that correct?"

"That's right. Last night around eight thirty she stopped by my house briefly, saying that she was on the way home from the public bath."

"The public bath? Why would she go out to the public bath when she had a bath in her own house? Did she do that often?"

"I don't think so. When she first moved in, I came over to extend my greetings, and of course I had no idea that she was tattooed. But sometime after that I met her at the public bath, and I was shocked. She was talking to me casually enough, but then some college coed said in a loud voice, 'Hey, look at the female bandit.' Miss Nomura got very angry, and after that she rarely went to the public bath. But yesterday her maid apparently had the day off. Miss Nomura said that she forgot to heat the water for her own bath ahead of time, so she went to the public bath instead."

"And where is this public bath?"

"It's about halfway between here and the station. It's called Asahi-Yu, the Rising Sun Bathhouse."

"And why did she stop at your house?"

"Well, I ran a little sewing business out of my home, and she stopped by to ask if I knew how to make a certain type of Western-style dress. She didn't come in. We just chatted in the entryway for ten minutes or so, and then she went home."

"What about after that? Did you notice anything unusual happening over here?"

"I don't know of anything myself. But from about nine until eleven, my husband's younger brother was playing guitar on the second floor of our house with some of his friends, and there's a perfect view of this house's gate from there. Shall I ask my young brother-in-law if he saw anything?"

"Yes, please do that. Can you think of any reason why something like this should have happened?"

"No, I really can't think of anything but... well, to be perfectly honest, I don't think an ordinary person like me can really understand the existence of a person who is covered with tattoos. I mean, who knows, perhaps there was some sort of argument with some of her yakuza friends."

A very slight change of expression flitted across Mrs. Kotaki's face, but it was enough to tell Daiyu Matsushita how Kinue Nomura had been perceived in Kitazawa. For a person like Kinue to try to fit into such a refined neighborhood must have been like mixing sesame oil with water. No doubt Mrs. Kotaki and the other women in the area felt a deep abhorrence for Kinue's tattooed body and the unconventional past it symbolized. They probably felt some resentment of her luxurious life, as well.

Yes, Daiyu thought cynically, *I wonder how heartbroken the neighbors will be when they learn that Kinue Nomura has been murdered.*

"Thank you very much for your help," he said out loud. "I'll be sending one of my subordinates over to your house a bit later, but for now you're free to go." Mrs. Kotaki bowed her head, then rushed from the room as if she were being pursued by wolves. Her thoughts seemed to be written on her rapidly-receding back: *I hope I never have to set foot in this den of immorality and horror again.*

As he watched her go, Daiyu smiled ruefully and shook his head. Before he even had time to take a deep breath, the next reports came in like a volley of machine-gun fire. "We have the address of the maid now," announced a police officer. "She lives in Kitatama County, at 263 Tanashi-cho, her name is Fusako Yoshida, and she's twenty-three years old. According to the talk around the neighborhood, she's been off for the past couple of days, but she filed a certificate for change of residence yesterday."

"We just spoke with Mr. Kotaki's younger brother," another detective said. "He seems certain that no one entered or left this house between nine and eleven last night."

The third reported, "The wall around this house is concrete. It's more than twenty meters high, and there are fragments of broken glass embedded in the top. Even if someone had a ladder, I don't think he could have escaped over the wall. The only way in or out would be through the gate on the main road, or by the small door into the garden."

A fourth detective: "According to the neighbors, around seven thirty last night a car stopped in front of this house,

104

carrying some sort of baggage. It wasn't a truck, just a passenger car, and the baggage wasn't particularly large or bulky. They thought it was some sort of package delivery service. Apparently Miss Nomura did a lot of shopping."

The fifth police officer looked a little paler than the others. "Regarding the method of dismemberment, the limbs were cut off with a sawlike instrument shortly after the time of death," he said. "The amputation seems to be the work of an amateur."

Finally, the sixth police officer added his report to the others. "I went to the Asahi-Yu public bath, and there is no question that Kinue Nomura was there last night. Since she had such conspicuous tattoos, the person who was sitting in the watcher's seat remembers very clearly. He said that she came in just before eight and left about twenty minutes later. The bathhouse was just about to close, and that's the reason he remembers the time so precisely."

After listening to the last report, Daiyu Matsushita blinked three times, as if to clear his head. "The estimated time of death is somewhere between six and twelve last night," he said. "Even if there were a slight discrepancy one way or another, it wouldn't be more than thirty minutes to an hour. However, we know for certain that this woman was still alive at eight thirty. So the crucial time is between eight forty and midnight, right? Starting now, the investigation will focus on this time period."

The search for fingerprints throughout the house evidently ended just then, for the person in charge of that part of the investigation, his face showing signs of strain, entered the room. "Chief, we've found five clear sets of fingerprints, not including those of the victim. There are three sets that appear to belong to males, and two sets that we believe may be female prints. They're all quite recent."

"Three men and two women, eh? If you assume that one set of male prints belongs to Takezo Mogami, and that one set of female prints belongs to the maid, that leaves two men and one woman. Kenzo!"

Kenzo had been sitting in a corner of the room, docile as a housecat, his mind awhirl with troubling thoughts. His brother's sharp tone of voice made him flinch.

"Surely you didn't leave any of your fingerprints around, did you?"

"Of course not," Kenzo said indignantly. "Professor Hayakawa warned me about that, and I was very careful. I think it should be all right. I even covered the receiver with a handkerchief when I telephoned the police."

"Just to be on the safe side, would you be so kind as to let us take your fingerprints?" said the white-coated technician. Reluctantly, Kenzo held out both his hands and submitted. A moment later the technician was shaking his head. "We didn't find these prints in the house," he said. He sounded almost relieved.

"You'd better get Professor Hayakawa's prints, too," said Daiyu Matsushita. "When you're finished, please send the professor in here."

19

Professor Hayakawa strode through the door. He seemed to have regained his composure, and behind the thick gold-rimmed lenses his cold, penetrating scientist's eyes glittered brilliantly as he gazed around the room.

"You're Professor Hayakawa? I'm Detective Chief Inspector Matsushita. Thank you very much for all you've done for my brother." Daiyu gave the most minimal of bows, just a slight forward motion of the head and neck.

"Ah, so you're Kenzo's illustrious older brother. I've heard a great deal about you." Using language that was almost too polite for the occasion, Professor Hayakawa one-upped the chief with a very low, elaborate bow.

"Please forgive me for not greeting you properly earlier," Daiyu Matsushita said, upgrading his level of politeness to match the professor's. "In all the confusion…"

"Don't worry about that," said the professor. "The last few hours have been confusing for everyone. By the way, your goons aren't very mannerly, are they? A while ago they insisted on taking my fingerprints in the other room. Isn't that an infringement of my civil rights?"

"We didn't mean to be rude, but since you and my brother found the body, we thought you might have accidentally left some around. As it turned out, neither of your prints was a match for the ones we found."

"Oh, I see. It's a matter of simple arithmetic: five minus x equals y, is it? That's the limitation of scientific criminology, right there. There's no way you're going to be able to solve this crime with such commonplace methods. I mean, elementary math just isn't going to be enough with a complex case like this."

"Well, Sensei, you may be hoping that some fictional mastermind detective will show up like Sherlock Holmes and solve all the riddles of this case, but I'm afraid it doesn't work like that in real life. We have to investigate meticulously, one step at a time. Even if we know from the start that leads are going nowhere, we have to conscientiously follow up. That may seem like a very roundabout approach, but it ends up being the most efficient way by far. In murder investigations, the shortest distance between two points may turn out to be a circle."

"Actually, the shortest distance between two points is a narrow mind," the professor quipped. "You might catch the perpetrator of a burglary or an unplanned murder with such an elementary approach. However, this crime was committed by someone who is a notch or two above us in intelligence, maybe even a genius. I don't think you can solve this case unless you take it to a higher level and bring in concepts like non-Euclidean geometry. There may be more here than meets the eye. Or, quite possibly, less."

"Are you saying we should add two and two and get five?"

"Sure, you might get five, but you also might get three, depending on the circumstances. Anything's possible in a world where parallel lines can converge in a single point."

"Perhaps so, but unfortunately we happen to be living in a world where parallel lines never meet. Or hadn't you heard?"

Ignoring the chief's sarcasm, Professor Hayakawa plunged ahead. "The one thing we know for certain is that the sort of fool who would leave behind his fingerprints would be incapable of committing such an artistic murder. I may be an old relic of a doctor, but I have done quite a bit of research into criminology, and I must say I find this case absolutely astonishing. To amputate a tattooed torso and somehow manage to escape with it from a locked room! That's a truly splendid scheme, don't you think? Whoever the culprit is, he certainly got the jump on me. I mean, first the older brother and younger sister die, and now the last of the family is gone, along with her beautiful tattoo. I'm sorry to say I've lost the chance to add a precious work of art to my collection."

"Sensei, you almost seem to be praising the murderer. I get the feeling you might even know the perpetrator's identity."

"I know a lot of things," the professor snapped. "And one thing I know for certain is that there's a big difference between good versus evil, and beauty versus ugliness. For example, you people tend to despise tattoos, as if they were an affront to your puritanical eyes. You seem to see anyone who happens to have a tattoo as a thief or a murderer or some sort of lowlife scum, and that simply isn't the case at all. In the so-called civilized countries of the West, even among royalty, aristocracy, and members of the upper classes, getting tattooed was a widespread fashion at the turn of the century. And all those people agreed that the Japanese tattoo was the absolute zenith of the art form, on a par with our famous *ukiyo-e* woodblock prints. If you people in the police department could just learn to look at tattoos with a slightly more artistic eye, I think you might be surprised to discover the strange beauty there. I don't mean to climb on my soapbox, but I really think Japan should use our defeat in that stupid war as a time for national rebirth. We need to repeal the senseless ban on tattoos, once and for all."

Daiyu Matsushita had listened patiently to this polemic, tapping his tented fingertips against each other with a piano-playing motion. "Sensei," he said in a coolly authoritative tone, "we have already been treated to a display of your erudition on the subject of tattoos, and I may want to solicit your expert opinion at some future date. What we would like to know right now, though, is why you came to this house this morning."

"If that's all you want to know, it's a very simple matter. The truth is, there was a tattoo contest recently. This Kinue Nomura took first place, and even though she didn't mind parading naked in front of a large crowd of people, she refused to give me her photograph. I was rather persistent, I must admit, but she was downright rude in her refusal. So rude, in fact, that I was very surprised when she called me yesterday morning, saying that she had changed her mind. She asked me to come here today at nine o'clock. She even said she would share some photos of her late brother and sister, who were both magnificently tattooed, of course. When I arrived I rang the bell at the gate, but there was no answer so I let myself in. Then I noticed that one of the rain shutters was open, and a young man had stuck his head inside. I thought it was a burglar, but when the man turned around I saw that it was young Kenzo here. I asked him what was going on, and he pointed to some bloodstains on the tatami. I peeked in and saw immediately that something was very much amiss. After searching the ransacked house and finding nothing, I noticed the sound of running water coming from the locked bathroom. When I peered through a crack in the door I saw a severed human arm. I realized then that it wouldn't be wise for an amateur to fool around with the scene of a crime, so I asked Kenzo to call the police. I think that's about it."

"Are you sure that's all?" asked Daiyu Matsushita sharply. He seemed to have taken a dislike to the professor, perhaps because he wasn't used to having potential suspects argue with him.

"Well, my primary purpose in coming here was to get the photographs, but there was something else on my mind. I was hoping to be able to buy the Orochimaru skin…"

"Buy the skin?" It wasn't that Daiyu Matsushita had no prior knowledge of the professor's penchant for collecting tattooed skins. But in this particular situation, something about that phrase caused the chief's already unfriendly feelings to explode.

"Incidentally, Professor," he went on in a chilly, magisterial tone, "I'd like to know what you were doing last night between six P.M. and midnight."

"Ho, so now you're asking me for an alibi?" Professor Hayakawa's voice was heavy with sarcasm. "What would happen if I were to refuse to answer that question?"

"I can't tell you exactly what would happen. What I can say is that if you'd be kind enough to answer the question it would be a lot more pleasant for everyone, yourself included."

"Yes, well, I think I'll refuse to answer." The professor's tone was defiant. "I have no direct connection with this murder case, and I really don't see why an upstanding citizen should have to tell a bunch of meddling cops every detail of his actions."

"An upstanding citizen, eh? I see. On the other hand, once a crime has been committed, it's *our* duty as upstanding citizens to devote all our energies to solving that case."

"That's what I'm trying to explain. If my actions last night had the slightest bearing on this case, I would be more than happy to share them with you. But since there is no connection whatsoever, I see no reason why I should be forced to divulge where I was or what I was doing."

"In that case, Professor, I'm going to have to ask you to come along to the station."

"Whatever for?"

"As a suspect in the murder of Kinue Nomura."

The professor didn't seem at all perturbed. On the contrary, there was a self-confident sneer on his face as he lit a fresh Peace cigarette.

"Detective," he said, deliberately using the improper term of address, "you have a reputation for being one of the most distinguished cops in the nation. However, it looks to me as if you're losing your touch. On exactly what evidence would you be arresting me? I have no possible motive and nothing whatsoever to gain from this murder, and there isn't a scintilla of evidence against me. Now, Miss Nomura's patron, Takezo Mogami, is the closest thing she has to a relative, so it wouldn't be illogical for you to suspect him even without any concrete evidence. But to think that someone like me, however passionate I might be about collecting tattoos, would go so far as to murder someone just to steal her skin? That's utterly ridiculous."

The professor took a long drag on his cigarette, obviously relishing the taste of the smoke. "In the first place, Officer," he went on, demoting the detective chief inspector still further, "do you really think you can solve a case like this by checking out people's alibis? If you do, you're totally off base. I mean, don't you think that the person who created this fiendish crime would have taken the trouble to create a sturdy alibi for himself while he was at it? I'll bet the culprit is having a good laugh at your expense, at this very moment. Instead of wasting your resources interrogating an innocent person like myself, why don't you and your cohorts spend your time doing something a little more productive, like learning about tattoos?"

Kenzo was startled by the caustic tone of Professor Hayakawa's voice. He could sense the professor's determination to flout authority, and it struck him as a strange and foolhardy thing to do. Daiyu Matsushita's face was flashed with the heat of battle as he and the professor glared at each other. The room was filled with tension, as if the two men might be about to leap up and unsheathe their swords.

"*Hahaha…*" Daiyu let out a sudden, hearty laugh, and in that instant the tension vanished completely. "No, seriously, Professor, I'm afraid I've been terribly rude. You probably figured this out already, but we think you might know more about the circumstances surrounding this case than you're letting on. We were just hoping you might spill a few beans under pressure, so to speak. Of course I never thought for a moment that *you* were the murderer. You're free to leave any time you like."

Wearing a triumphant smile, Professor Hayakawa got to his feet. He gave a small, satirical bow to the still-seated chief inspector, then turned on his heel and left.

20

"Ishikawa!" Even as he called "Black Belt" Ishikawa's name, Detective Chief Inspector Daiyu Matsushita was signaling with his eyes that the officer should follow Professor Hayakawa. "What a dreadful man," Daiyu mused a moment later, exhaling a string of miniature smoke rings. "There's a thin line between obsession and derangement, and I'm not at all sure the professor hasn't crossed it. I'm positive that he knows something about this case, but he didn't let anything slip at all." The chief inspector addressed these remarks to a nearby police officer, but he seemed to be talking to himself.

Just then Kenzo called from outside. Daiyu went into the garden, where he found his younger brother in a state of extreme agitation. "Look!" Kenzo said, pointing at the dirt. "The plate! The broken fragments!"

"What? What on earth are you talking about?"

"Just before you and the other officers arrived, we were walking around in the garden and the professor found a broken scrap of a photographic plate. There were some other pieces in the dirt."

"A photographic plate? What kind of photograph?"

"I don't know, because the phone rang and I went to answer it. Right after that a policeman came along, and it slipped my mind until just now."

"I see, and what was the professor doing during that time?"

"He was standing outside the whole time."

"So it looks as if the professor must have concealed those fragments somewhere while you were gone, because after we arrived on the scene neither he nor anyone else would have been able to do something so risky. And if the shards had been left in the garden, one of my subordinates would surely have found them."

"Are you just going to let him get away with stealing evidence?"

"No, I'm having the professor followed right now. If he did make off with something that could be considered evidence in this case, it may be that bad luck will turn to good," said Daiyu Matsushita, quoting an old proverb. He wore a faint smile, as if to say, *We'll see who gets the last laugh, Professor.* Immediately resuming his normal serious expression, Daiyu began barking out orders to his subordinates.

"Telephone one Kitazawa Station, also Shibuya and Shinjuku. Inform them that if they see Officer Ishikawa, they should tell him to get in touch with me immediately. It looks as if Professor Hayakawa left this house with pieces of a photographic plate concealed on his person. Those fragments should be seized as evidence in this case, and I want the professor taken to the station for questioning."

"Chief, look at this album." A detective came up carrying a well-worn photograph album, bound in handmade paper patterned with pine boughs. Peering curiously over his brother's shoulder, Kenzo noticed that the first page of the album had been torn out. The remaining pages were covered with a large number of priceless photographs of a sort that would have made Professor Hayakawa's mouth water. The photos recorded the process of creating several superlative tattoos, in sequence. First there was the plain, undecorated nude body, without a single mark on it. Next came the body with arms tattooed, then the thighs, the back, and so on until the entire body was covered with intricate designs.

As they were turning the pages, a letter fell out of the album. The stamp on the cheap brown-paper envelope had been postmarked five days earlier. Inside was a flimsy piece of paper torn from a notebook. The message was written in the crude hand of an uneducated male.

Kinue, it began abruptly, *Long time no see. I haven't forgotten what you did to me, and I intend to repay you as you deserve. Just remember one thing—one of these days I'm going to kill you and take the tattoo off your back.* The note was unsigned.

"This is evidence!" Daiyu Matsushita was handing the album back to the detective who had found it, when the telephone rang. It was Detective Akita, reporting on the results of his surprise raid on the headquarters of the Mogami Group in Ogikubo.

"Chief, Takezo Mogami left on a trip yesterday just after one P.M. and hasn't been seen since. We found a second-class ticket to Osaka and an express-train upgrade in his wastebasket, torn to shreds."

"What about Inazawa?"

"There's definitely something suspicious about his behavior. I'm certain that he's keeping some sort of a secret. Shall we take him to the station for questioning?"

"No, bring him here. We'll show him the corpse and see how that grabs him." Replacing the receiver, Daiyu left the room. Information seemed to be bombarding him from all sides, and he wanted to get it all arranged in a straight line. To separate the useless data from that which was relevant to the case, and then to decide upon the main thrust of the investigation— those were the official duties of the detective chief inspector.

At first glance, the case appeared to be chaotic. Daiyu tried to calm himself down by telling himself that stranger, more complicated cases had been solved in the past, but it didn't do any good. Chain-smoking one cigarette after another, he stomped around the garden in slow circles, his thoughts focused on one single point: whether the net he had thrown out would ensnare Professor Hayakawa, and if so, where. There had been no word from Kitazawa Station. No reports had come in from Shibuya or Shinjuku, either, and the chief inspector was beginning to worry.

Daiyu looked at his watch and sighed. No, he told himself, it's going to be all right. Officer Ishikawa is following the professor, and he's as tenacious as a hunting dog. He'll catch up with him for sure.

For sure, for sure, for sure. He chanted the words like a mantra. Daiyu Matsushita lit another cigarette and gazed up at the pale blue sky, which was teeming with soft summer clouds, like smoke rings with the centers filled in.

21

"What's this all about? Why have you brought me here?" Led by Detective Akita, a protesting, white-faced Gifu Inazawa entered Kinue Nomura's house in Kitazawa. His body was shaking with nervousness, and his eyes darted around uneasily. As Inazawa was removing his shoes in the entry hall he looked up and made eye contact with Kenzo Matsushita for a moment, then quickly looked away.

Detective Chief Inspector Daiyu Matsushita took his brother aside. "Kenzo, you're absolutely certain this is the man you brushed by a while ago?" he asked in a low voice.

"I'm positive," Kenzo replied.

In the living room, the interrogation of Gifu Inazawa had already begun. "You understand why we've asked you to come here, don't you?" a police officer was saying.

"Uh, yes, no, I mean…"

"State your name and age."

"Gifu Inazawa. I'm forty-five."

"Where are you employed?"

"I'm the manager of the Mogami Company. We do engineering and construction."

"I see. We'd like to take your fingerprints now, if you don't mind."

Inazawa couldn't hide his distress. He didn't say anything, but the nicotine-stained hands he held out for fingerprinting were shaking perceptibly.

The fingerprint technician took the stamp pad and stencil paper and went into another room, returning a moment later to whisper something in Daiyu Matsushita's ear. "Since this is the house of your boss's mistress, there's absolutely no reason why you shouldn't have come here, is there?" the chief inspector asked the trembling Inazawa.

"That's right, I sometimes came here to deliver money…"

"Is that why you came here late last night, to deliver money?"

"No, ah, last night…" Gifu Inazawa looked down at the floor, and blushed.

"So this morning you were on your way home after spending the night here?"

"God, no!" Inazawa shouted. He patted his pockets frantically, clearly looking for a cigarette, but when he came up empty no one made a move to offer him one.

"Well, according to what we've heard, a witness saw you leaving this house this morning, carrying a small bundle wrapped in a furoshiki cloth. The furoshiki was purple, and you were supposedly clutching it nervously in both hands. How do you explain that?"

Ishikawa was obviously struggling to appear calm, but the contorted expression on his face betrayed his growing panic. After a prolonged search, he had finally found a single, slightly bent cigarette in one of his pants pockets, but his hands were shaking so much that he couldn't get the end to catch fire.

"How about it," growled Daiyu Matsushita, "why don't you just admit it? You're the one who killed Kinue Nomura, right? What did you do with the rest of the body?"

Inazawa dropped his unlit cigarette on the tatami and, holding out his hands in supplication, looked up at the chief inspector's fearsome face. "No, no, it wasn't me!" he shouted in an anguished voice. "When I got here Kinue was already dead!"

"Okay, tell us your story," the chief inspector said, in a gentler tone.

Inazawa took a deep breath, stuck his damaged cigarette in the corner of his mouth, and accepted a light from the chief inspector himself. "The truth is," he said, blowing out a blue-gray ribbon of smoke, "I was in love with Kinue Nomura. You may laugh at such folly in a man my age, but I used to be sent here frequently on errands for my boss, and before I knew it I was head over heels, like some adolescent schoolboy. Then, one time I happened to catch a glimpse of the tattoo on her back, and something about that unearthly beauty made me lose my grip on reality. I mean, here I am, over forty, with a wife and kids, and on top of that the object of my affections is the mistress of my boss, of all people. I knew it was dangerous, and wrong, but no matter how sternly I scolded myself, all I could think about was how much I wanted to touch her. I really think I was a little off my rocker; it was as if my reason had flown out the window. Anyway, I began to court Kinue in earnest. At first, she just laughed in my face. 'What are you talking about?' she would say, 'You're an awful lech. I'm going to tell my old man!' Of course, her 'old man' was my boss, Takezo Mogami She rebuffed me time and time again, but I didn't give up. I realize this may sound like bragging, but based on my past experience with women, I felt there might be some hope. I just kept plod-ding along, one step at a time, and I noticed that her feelings toward me seemed to be thawing a bit. Yesterday I finally got a favorable answer to my pleas. My boss was supposed to leave last night by train for a business trip. 'Come by tomorrow night at midnight,' Kinue said to me. 'My old man will be safely off on his business trip by then, and I've fired the maid, so we'll be all alone.' Needless to say, I was overjoyed. To think that at last I was going to be allowed to touch that beautiful tattooed body with these hands…" He spread his trembling fingers and stared down at them wonderingly, as if they belonged to someone else.

Daiyu Matsushita and his colleagues exchanged a bemused glance which seemed to say, *Are we conducting a serious criminal interrogation or listening to a soap opera?* Still, Inazawa didn't appear to be lying, and everyone listened attentively as the nervous, unprepossessing little man resumed his story.

"So last night I was at the restaurant of an acquaintance of mine in Shinjuku, having a few drinks. I know it's childish, but I started to worry that Kinue might lose interest if I showed up drunk, so I left that place a little after eight. When I got to Kitazawa Station around eight thirty, I went into a coffee shop and ordered an iced coffee, thinking it would help sober me up and also cool me off because it was still very hot outside. I left that place after about fifteen minutes. When I got here all the lights were off, and the house was completely silent. I was several hours early for our appointment, and there were still a few people on the streets, so I decided to pretend that I was just out taking a walk. I wandered around the neighborhood, and at about ten thirty I came back to the front gate. It was still early, but I didn't feel I could wait any longer. I was just about to go into the house when I noticed some university students on the second floor of the house next door, playing the guitar and looking in my direction. I thought things might get complicated if they started asking me questions, so I decided to wait a while longer. When the lights next door finally went off, around eleven, I opened the garden gate and sneaked in."

"Wait a minute. While you were waiting, were you standing in front of the gate?"

"That's right."

"And during the time you were waiting, between ten thirty and eleven, you didn't see anyone coming or going through this gate?"

"Not a soul."

"Okay, let's hear the rest," Daiyu said, stone-faced.

"I found the front door locked, of course, but according to plan Kinue had left one of the storm windows at the back of the house unlocked. I opened that and called out, 'Miss Kinue!' but there was no reply. I thought she might have fallen asleep, so I crept into the house. But when I went into her sleeping room, there was no one there, and the futon wasn't even spread out. About that time I started to think I might have been tricked, and I was filled with rage. Then I heard a noise from the end of the hall, the sound of running water, and I felt so relieved. *Oh good,* I thought, *she's taking a bath. She's soaking in the tub with the water running, getting ready for our night together, and that's why she didn't hear me when I called.* While I was jumping to all these conclusions, I made my way to the bathroom door and called out Kinue's name again. There was no reply, and aside from the sound of the running water there was no sign that anyone was inside. I turned the doorknob, but the door didn't open. That seemed odd, and then I looked down and noticed that my socks were strangely sticky. That was when I realized that I had been walking through puddles of blood."

22

After a policeman had fetched him a glass of water, a visibly distraught Inazawa continued his narrative. He was breathing heavily and his eyes were wide, as if he were reliving that horrific moment.

"When I saw the blood I was so startled that I just wanted to run away, but then I started to worry about what might be in the bathroom. There was a tiny crack in the bottom of the door, and I could see a little light shining through, so I took a deep breath and peeked through the crack. What I saw was too horrible for words; it looked like the cut end of an amputated human arm, all bloody and awful. I must have passed out then, and when I regained my senses my only thought was to get out of that house as fast as possible. I don't even know what roads I took, but somehow I got back to my house in Omori around three A.M., after walking all the way. Even after I got home my head was in a muddle, and I didn't know which way was up. Every waking minute, the vision of that bloody, gleaming arm kept dancing in front of my eyes.

"I lay awake till dawn, and then I realized something truly alarming. The previous day I had bought a handbag in Shibuya as a present for Kinue, and it was wrapped in a furoshiki cloth. In my haste and confusion, I had left it behind when I fled. And to make matters worse, my name was printed on the furoshiki!"

Inazawa took out a white handkerchief and wiped the oily sweat from his brow. "I had no idea what I ought to do, but I realized that I had left something at the scene that might be misinterpreted as evidence of my involvement in the crime. I racked my brains for another solution, and finally decided that the only thing to do was retrieve the bundle. So without even eating breakfast, I rushed out and came back to this house. It was already after eight o'clock, but fortunately there wasn't anyone on the streets. Thinking that things were going my way so far, I went in the house. The night before everything had been in order, aside from the blood, but now it looked as if the place had been ransacked. The furoshiki bundle was still in front of the bathroom door at the end of the hall, where I had dropped it. Thanking my lucky stars, I grabbed the bundle and hightailed it out of there, through the garden. When I peeked through the gate, there still wasn't anyone on the street, so I headed for the train station with a great feeling of relief. I went to Nakano by way of Shinjuku, and I've been at the office until now." Inazawa took a deep breath, signaling that his lengthy confession had finally come to an end.

Daiyu Matsushita had been listening quietly, but now he asked a question. "So the light in the bathroom was on when you discovered the body?"

"That's right."

"Do you remember turning it off?"

"No, I don't."

"Kenzo, come here a minute." The chief inspector stood up and called Kenzo out into the hall. "Listen," Daiyu said in a solemn tone, "when you and the professor first discovered the body, was the light in the bathroom on or off?"

"I didn't notice."

"But you didn't switch it on?"

"I didn't touch the switch at all."

"What about the professor?"

"I don't know."

"When you went off to call the police, where was the professor?"

"Standing in front of the bathroom door."

"You can't see the bathroom from the place where the phone is, can you?"

"No, you can't."

"In that case, you really have no way of knowing what the professor might have been doing while you were off making that call."

"That's true."

"But when we came in, the light switch for the bathroom had been turned off from the outside," Daiyu Matsushita muttered, looking meaningfully at his younger brother.

"Does that have some significance?" Kenzo asked.

"Yes, it really bothers me. How shall I say this? I've spent so many years learning to do this job that I've developed a sort of sixth sense. Okay, we know that the criminal somehow managed to hide the remains in the locked room. Of course those remains are evidence of the crime, so the later they were discovered the better it would be for him, in terms of making a getaway. So naturally, he would have turned off the water and the lights. Yet they were left on. Is Inazawa telling the truth, and did the professor purposely switch the light off? These are the points we need to get straightened out."

After returning to the impromptu interrogation room, Daiyu shifted the focus of his questions to the relationship between Kinue and her wealthy patron.

"So what's the story on your boss, Mr. Mogami?"

"He was supposed to be leaving last night for a business trip to Shizuoka. Yesterday, around two P.M., I heard him get a phone call from someone. After he hung up, he came into my office and said, rather grimly I thought, 'I have to stop somewhere before I leave on my trip. I may end up taking a later train, so there's no need to come and see me off at the

125

station.' He left the office, alone, and that's the last I saw of him. Around five o'clock, I called his house, but they said he hadn't been there at all. I thought he might have gone straight to the station, but the person who was on duty at the office last night had some business with the boss, and when he called the inn in Shizuoka, where he was supposed to be staying, they said he hadn't arrived yet."

"And he hasn't been back to his house this morning?"

"Yes, we know that for sure." Inazawa's voice was trembling.

"How large is Mr. Mogami's fortune?"

"Somewhere around seven or eight million yen, at current prices. And then there's all his hidden wealth. I couldn't begin to guess at that."

"What about his family?"

"The boss has kind of a strange philosophy about that sort of thing. He often says jokingly that he doesn't exactly dislike women, and I myself have been involved in financial negotiations with a number of his mistresses. But he has never gotten married, or entered any woman's name in his family register. 'I'm inclined to get bored with women after a while,' he always used to say. 'And once you make someone your legal wife, you can't throw her out when she ceases to interest you.'"

"Would we be correct in assuming that Kinue Nomura was just another of those temporary distractions?"

"No, I think she was different."

"In what way?"

"Well, we call our boss Mr. Broom behind his back, because of his behavior toward women. You know, sweep them off their feet, then sweep them into the gutter? But Miss Nomura was something special. I mean there simply aren't that many beautiful, charming young women with magnificent tattoos all over their bodies. At the beginning, I think he was drawn to her just out of curiosity, but soon he was totally smitten. He used to tell me sometimes in a happy voice, as if he wasn't really complaining, 'It's that snake tattoo, you know. I feel as if I'm bound up in the coils of that giant snake, and I can't escape.'"

"I see. Can a tattoo really cast such a spell? I just find them grotesque," the chief inspector whispered, as if to himself, but Kenzo felt his own cheeks grow red with embarrassment.

"What about Mogami's family?" Daiyu Matsushita resumed the questioning.

"There's a younger brother, Hisashi. They're related by blood."

"And what is Mogami's relationship with Professor Hayakawa?"

"The professor is the younger brother of the boss's mother."

"So they're nephew and uncle, eh. And if something unfortunate were to happen to Mogami, who would inherit his fortune?"

"His younger brother, I assume. I really don't know the details. Mr. Sayama is the company's legal adviser, and he counseled the boss about his personal and financial affairs. You should probably ask him."

"What sort of man is Mogami?"

"It's difficult to answer that. He's a very good and generous person, very kind to his subordinates. But if you ever betray his trust, you'll be in really major trouble. I mean, when he gets finished with you, you won't even be able to blow your nose."

"If that's true, then you were putting yourself in serious jeopardy just to seduce a woman."

"Yeah, I guess I was…"

A complicated expression flitted across Daiyu Matsushita's face, a curious blend of pity, bewilderment, and sympathy. As far as Inazawa's statement went, it was too early to tell whether it was genuine or not, or to reach any conclusions about his guilt or innocence. But this fortyish man's tale of disappointed love had touched Daiyu's tough policeman's heart.

"And what about this woman Kinue, did she have other men?"

"As far as I know, she hasn't been seeing anyone else since she became involved with the boss. She once said to me, 'A tattoo is like an animal's warning colors, it tends to scare men off. They assume that I'm not an ordinary woman, or even that I'm some sort of female outlaw, and they don't want to get involved with me. The sort of men who are attracted to me usually have only one thing on their minds. That's why a tattooed woman can never lead a truly normal life.' Aside from that, she was also well aware of the boss's jealous nature."

"Do you know anything about her former lovers?"

"I don't know the whole story by any means, but I gather that she got tattooed to please a man. In the beginning, when I first learned that she was tattooed, I was shocked. I mean, the majority of men can't endure the tattooing process, so I was doubly impressed that a woman would be able to stand so much pain. When I said that to Miss Nomura, she laughed out loud and said, 'In Osaka slang, a tattoo is called *gaman*—you know, "patience" or "perseverance." There are two things about getting tattooed that seem to impress people, the money it costs, and the pain it causes. In my case, I didn't have to spend a fortune to get tattooed; my father was a tattoo artist, so it didn't cost me a cent. Once the process was begun, short of running away from home, there would have been no way to avoid seeing it through.' That's what Miss Nomura told me, and then she laughed again, throwing her head back the way she does... I mean, the way she used to do." Gifu Inazawa's narrow face suddenly contorted into a mask of grief, and his small eyes brimmed with tears.

"Hmm." Chief Matsushita nodded.

"Did you find the photographs?" Inazawa asked, recovering his composure. "There was a picture of Miss Nomura with no clothes on, standing next to a naked man."

"I haven't seen it."

"The man had a tattoo of Kintaro holding a carp, or something like that. He was Miss Nomura's first love. I heard that he was a photographer turned yakuza. Apparently she met him while he was passing through Horiyasu's house—that was where he got his tattoo—and for some reason they hit it off. He gave her such a hard time about not having a tattoo that she finally got one."

"What was this guy's name?"

"I don't know. I also heard that during her time in Yokohama—what she used to call her 'gambling-geisha days'—she was involved with some other yakuza. Whoever it was, I imagine he's probably in jail by now."

"Any other men in her life?"

"I heard that she was pretty wild when she first left home, but, no, I don't know of anyone else since the war ended."

"I see. So recently there was Professor Hayakawa, and Takezo Mogami, and that photographer, and the possible yakuza paramour, and you? Five men who were all infatuated with the same tattoo, you might say."

Kenzo realized that his own name wasn't going to be added to that list, and he heaved a huge sigh of relief. He also noticed that when his brother reeled off the names of the men who were infatuated with Kinue, he placed special emphasis on the name of Professor Hayakawa.

23

That bastard, where the hell is he going, and why? Officer Ishikawa had been assigned to follow Professor Hayakawa, and he was trudging along under the blazing summer sun in (quite literally) hot pursuit, swiping at his brow and muttering to himself.

There were two train stations near the crime scene, but the professor did not go to either of them. Instead, he crossed the Odakyu Line tracks, turned near some Quonset huts belonging to the Army of Occupation, climbed a narrow hill through a neighborhood of walled estates, and emerged into a deserted shopping area. He walked straight through Iki-no-Ue Station without boarding a train. Then he wound around and around on narrow streets. He passed through the basin between the former Aviation Research Institute and the train tracks, emerging next to the Japanese Folk Art Museum. Finally, at Komaba Station, he got onto a train for Shibuya.

That bastard! He's known all along that I've been following him! Officer Ishikawa thought unhappily. He scrambled onto the train as the doors whooshed closed.

Professor Hayakawa got off the train at the next-to-last stop, Shinsen Station. The neighborhood had once been a red-light district filled with attractive geisha houses, but it had been reduced to rubble by the bombing. Threading his way among the ruins, the professor finally stopped in a partially rebuilt shopping district halfway to Dogenzaka. After scrutinizing the plastic-food displays in the windows of a couple of shabby-looking noodle shops, he went into a Chinese restaurant called the Golden Duck.

Hey, I'll bet he's going to go out the back way, and then I'll have him cornered. Officer Ishikawa approached the building. Professor Hayakawa was sitting at a window table on the second floor, staring down at him. The policeman turned around and went into a shop at the end of the street, borrowed the telephone, and called Detective Chief Inspector Matsushita at the crime scene. Panting slightly from his long hike, Ishikawa reported the situation.

"Since we left you the blasted professor has led me on a merry chase, all over Tokyo. I'm totally drenched with sweat. At the moment we're in the Shibuya area, and the professor is in a Chinese restaurant called the Golden Duck having a leisurely lunch, cool as you please."

"Chinese food, eh? I wouldn't mind some dim sum, myself. Seriously, thanks for all your hard work, Ishikawa. And don't worry, your efforts won't be wasted. It turns out that the professor took what may be an important piece of evidence from the crime scene here. It's several fragments of a photographic plate. Do you think he might have disposed of it along the way?"

"No, he wouldn't dare try any funny business like that while I'm following him." Officer Ishikawa sounded a bit huffy.

"Take the professor to the nearest police station. See whether he has the plate fragments in his possession. I'll get your report later on."

Officer Ishikawa sprinted across the street, burst into the Chinese restaurant, climbed up the stairs to the second floor, and approached the window table. The professor was eating cold wheat noodles garnished with a colorful array of vegetables and bits of red-tinged *char siu* pork.

"Ah, it's you," he said in a friendly way. "It gets hot when you're walking, doesn't it? How about joining me for a bowl of noodles or something?"

Officer Ishikawa flinched as if someone had just blown poisonous gas in his face. "Professor," he said sternly, "why did you come all this way…"

"I felt like taking a walk."

"More like a hike. I'm amazed you can eat after witnessing such a terrible murder scene."

"It's because of the line of work I'm in. If I lost my appetite every time I saw a dead body, I'd soon die of starvation. Let's face it, tragedy and gore are an unavoidable part of both our jobs." Professor Hayakawa spoke quietly.

Officer Ishikawa threw his massive shoulders back and said in his most officious voice, "Professor, please accompany me to a nearby police station."

"Police station? Whatever for?" The professor paused, chopsticks in midair.

"You're under suspicion of having removed several potentially important pieces of evidence from the scene of a murder. My orders are to search you until those items are found. This is rather a public place. Being frisked here might be embarrassing for you."

"Fine, let's go." Professor Hayakawa threw his chopsticks down on top of his half-eaten meal and stood up.

When they entered the nearby police box, the professor immediately took off his white linen jacket. "Go ahead," he said. "Search me all you like."

The photographic plate fragments weren't in any of his pockets. There was nothing unusual at all, just a wallet, a handkerchief, a packet of tissues, and a small plastic comb in a brocade case.

"Where are the things you picked up, the pieces of photographic plate?"

The professor didn't reply. He just stood there in triumphant silence, dressed in nothing but a white dress shirt and his underwear, calmly fanning himself with a beige fan patterned with delicate medieval calligraphy.

"Wait here until I get back," Officer Ishikawa called out over his shoulder, as he left. The police box had no telephone. Returning to the shop where he had used the phone before, he placed a call to the murder scene.

"Check out the Chinese restaurant!" Matsushita's order was short and sharp.

Dripping with sweat, Ishikawa made his way back to the Golden Duck. At the top of the stairs he almost bumped into a Chinese-looking waitress, who was so startled that she nearly dropped the case of Tsingtao beer she was carrying.

"I'm from the police," Ishikawa said crisply. "The person who was just here is a suspect in a murder investigation."

"Yes," said the woman, nervously adjusting her red apron. She didn't appear to speak much Japanese, or perhaps she was just frightened.

"Did that customer leave anything with you?"

"Yes." After a moment's hesitation, the woman disappeared into the kitchen. She returned with a small bundle wrapped in a large paper napkin, which she handed wordlessly to the policeman. When he opened it, his heart gave a shout of joy. Nestled in the paper were several fragments of shiny black glass. At last, he'd gotten his hands on the elusive photographic plates!

One by one, Officer Ishikawa held the fragments up to the light from the window. The plates showed the rear view of a naked woman, without a stitch of clothes. Because it was a negative, the pattern didn't show up very clearly, but he could see that there was some sort of strange design dancing all over the woman's body, completely covering her back, her arms, and her legs.

"Thanks," the policeman said.

"Yes," the Chinese woman replied, and her round face broke into a radiant smile. Officer Ishikawa went downstairs to place yet another call to his boss. The chief inspector instructed him to take the professor down to Metropolitan Police Headquarters right away, adding that the crew from the crime scene would join them as soon as possible.

When he got back to the police box, Officer Ishikawa waved the fragments under Professor Hayakawa's nose. "Hey, Professor, look what I found at the Chinese restaurant! You can't play innocent anymore now, can you?"

"Fascist," the professor said under his breath, but he appeared quite calm. "I have a mania, you know, and I guess that makes me a maniac. A maniac doesn't choose the means to the end, he just follows his appetites. When I saw a photograph of a tattoo, I couldn't just leave it lying there. I had to have it."

To the policeman, those words sounded like the defiant song of a condemned man. "Professor, please accompany me to police headquarters."

"I don't seem to have a choice." The professor shrugged his shoulders and stood up. "By the way," he said, "do you think I could have those fragments back when this is all over?"

Cheeky bastard, Ishikawa thought, but he answered politely. "I really couldn't say. You'll have to ask the chief inspector. It'll depend on whether the negatives turn out to have any direct connection with this case."

"There has to be some connection, doesn't there? I mean, it's hardly likely that this *picture* of a tattooed woman would turn out to have no relevance whatever to the *murder* of a tattooed woman." The professor spoke in a patronizing tone.

"If this weren't a negative—if you could turn it into white on black—you could solve the mystery of this case in a minute, but because of the ungentlemanly way in which you people choose to conduct yourselves, I'm not going to help you out of this maze. Quite frankly…"

"Let's get going, Professor," Officer Ishikawa interrupted in an icy tone. "You'll have plenty of time to express your learned opinions down at the station."

24

By the time Kenzo Matsushita was allowed to leave the scene of the crime, it was nearly evening. A rodent-colored dusk had fallen over the troubled city of Tokyo. Kenzo was totally exhausted, and he nodded off several times on the crowded commuter tram. "*Tadaima...* I'm home," he said to his sister-in-law Mariko, a pretty woman in her mid-thirties. She greeted him at the entry of the modest two-story wooden house. Without even mentioning the murder case, Kenzo climbed the narrow stairs and flopped down on the tatami-matted floor of his bachelor room.

It was a small rectangular room, with a single frosted-glass window that looked out on what had once been an apartment building but was now a pile of charred rubble inhabited by a pack of stray dogs. It was strange, Kenzo often thought, how the firebombs could destroy one house and leave the next one untouched.

The room's only furnishings were a low table and some square, flat zabuton cushions. The bedding was folded up in a closet, behind sliding doors. There were no bookshelves, and Kenzo had medical texts and mystery novels piled everywhere, even (to his sister-in-law's consternation) in the *tokonoma* alcove that would traditionally have contained an elegant scroll and a simple but striking flower arrangement. The walls were unadorned except for a tattered calendar that stopped at December 1941, when the world changed forever. The picture on the calendar showed a maiden wearing the indigo-dyed costume typical of the Ohara area outside of Kyoto, against a backdrop of autumn foliage.

Kenzo was wide awake now. He felt numb yet agitated. After several cigarettes he could feel himself calm down. *Dead,* he thought. Kinue was really dead. He would never hold her close or talk to her again. The idea was like a room full of monsters he was afraid to go in, so he tried to pretend it wasn't there.

To distract himself from the nightmarish murder, Kenzo picked up the evening paper he had bought at the station. He hadn't expected to see any news about Kinue's death so soon, but on one inside page, at the top of the city news, a headline in large-point type caught his eye: TATTOO MURDER CASE. A brief story followed, no more than five paragraphs. The blunt headline was a perfect expression of the essence of the case. Whoever composed it had a journalist's instincts for going to the heart of a matter. They had stripped away the embellishments and with almost uncanny prescience, had identified the underlying reason behind the murder—the tattoos.

Kenzo wasn't thinking that coherently, though. No matter how hard he tried to concentrate on the printed page, he couldn't stop visualizing that naked, dismembered body—the woman he was so desperately in love with. Closing his eyes just made the image grow more vivid. Even as he grieved, he couldn't help wondering what had happened to the torso. Who had run off with the Orochimaru tattoo, and why?

He didn't have any appetite, and when his sister-in-law Mariko came upstairs to call him to dinner, he told her that he didn't feel like eating. His brother would probably have made some joke about Kenzo's famously prodigious appetite, but Mariko was always impeccably tactful and kind.

"You probably have a touch of the summer malaise," she said in her soft Kyoto accent. "You're looking rather pale, too. The best thing for you is to go to bed early tonight." Mariko had no idea what Kenzo was enduring, and her solicitous words only made him feel worse.

Shortly before sunset, the doorbell rang. Praying that nobody had come to call on him, Kenzo sat motionless in his darkened room. After a moment Mariko came up the stairs and said in a worried-sounding voice, "Kenzo, dear, what are you doing in there with the lights off?"

"I have some things on my mind, and I like it this way. I find it easier to concentrate in the dark," Kenzo replied.

"There's someone here to see you."

"Who is it?" Kenzo hadn't had a visitor since the war ended.

"Two people. They said their names were Hayakawa and Mogami."

"Hayakawa and Mogami!" Kenzo exclaimed in disbelief, thinking it must be the professor and his missing nephew, Takezo. Without even thanking his sister-in-law, he charged down the stairs to the entryway.

Hisashi Mogami was standing there, looking like an accident victim. One of his arms was bandaged, he had the beginnings of a spectacular black eye, and there were sticking plasters attached to his temple in two or three places. Next to him was a woman Kenzo had never seen before, long-faced, slender, about thirty-five, dressed in a tasteful copper-colored kimono. She was obviously a married woman from a good family, but her lovely face was swollen from crying, and there seemed to be an aura of distress about her.

"Ah, Hisashi. And who is this?" Forgetting his manners, Kenzo stared at the beautiful stranger.

"This is Professor Hayakawa's wife."

"Mrs. Hayakawa? To see me?" Kenzo felt a stab in his heart. He knew that the professor had been picked up in Shibuya and taken to police headquarters. Since it was he who had told the police about the photographic plates, Kenzo couldn't help feeling that he was the cause of this woman's suffering. He knew he had done the right thing but, even so, he felt guilty.

The woman said, "I wonder if it would be all right if we disturbed you for a few minutes?"

"Oh, please, do come in. The place is a mess, but…" Kenzo had recovered his manners sufficiently to utter the customary disclaimers. In fact, the house was always spotlessly clean. Kenzo led the way upstairs to his room, which was reasonably tidy aside from the books piled everywhere. He turned on the switch. A large yellow moth was resting on the lampshade. He watched the moth flutter around the lamp, leaving a trail of fine dust. A sudden chill passed though him at the thought that the moth might be a reincarnated human soul.

"Please forgive us for barging in on you at such an inconvenient time…" As she entered the room, Mrs. Hayakawa knelt politely on the tatami and bowed so deeply that her forehead touched the floor. Kenzo was moved by the vulnerability of the pale nape of her neck, but then the cloth of her kimono shifted and he caught a glimpse of skin tattooed in a pattern of dark and light, color and shadow. He was so startled that he momentarily forgot the proper response.

"Oh," he finally blurted out, "please make yourselves at home. As you can see, it's a miserable hovel."

Kenzo busied himself with setting out cushions for his guests, while his sister-in-law Mariko served green tea and crisp, seaweed-wrapped rice cakes. Apologizing for the absence of proper refreshments, Mariko closed the door behind her and went downstairs. A few minutes later she began to play a Chopin prelude on the piano, very quietly, with her foot resting firmly on the mute pedal.

"The truth is," Hisashi explained as they settled in around the table, "I got a sudden phone call from my aunt here. When she told me what had happened I naturally thought of you because of your connections with the police department. I mentioned that to my aunt, and she said she would like very much to talk with you. I thought I had better come along, so here we are." An unlit Peace cigarette hung jauntily from his lips, but Hisashi looked troubled.

"I see," Kenzo said. "So I gather you already know about the murder?"

"We have a general idea, but we haven't heard any details," said Hisashi, sipping his green tea.

Mrs. Hayakawa nodded in agreement. "This afternoon some people from the police barged into my house, saying they had a warrant to search. Of course, I was shocked. I asked if they would mind explaining what was going on. They said there had been a murder, and my husband was a suspect. My response was that there was no way my husband could possibly be involved in such a thing, but when I heard that the victim's tattooed torso had vanished, the world went black before my eyes."

"It's hardly surprising that the police wanted to ask him some questions and search the house," said Kenzo, feeling obliged to explain his brother's behavior.

"Anyway," Mrs. Hayakawa went on, "I was terribly upset, and I called Hisashi for advice. He mentioned knowing you, and I thought we might be able to get details of this terrible situation if we came to see you." Tears were glistening in the corners of her eyes.

"I'll be glad to tell you what I know about the case," Kenzo said. "But first I'd like to ask you something. Was the professor at home last night?"

"No…"

"What time did he come home?"

"It was around midnight, just as the last streetcar was passing by."

Kenzo had a sick feeling in his stomach. "Do you know where he went last night?"

"I have no idea. He never tells me where he's going."

"That isn't good. The police are estimating that the crime was committed between eight thirty and midnight last night. I don't believe the professor is the killer, but—" Kenzo proceeded to relate the facts of the case as he understood them.

"Now I understand," said Mrs. Hayakawa when Kenzo had finished. "Where tattoos are involved, he always behaves like a demented person." She spoke fondly, almost as if she approved of her husband's actions.

"If it were just a matter of his having walked off with the photographic plates, I don't think it would be a major offense," Kenzo said. "In fact, I don't even know whether the photographs were of a tattoo or not."

"They must have been; I'm positive of that." Mrs. Hayakawa seemed more resolute than she had at first. "It's very kind of you to take the time to talk to us when you are so tired," she said. "We'd better take our leave now, before we impose any further."

Hisashi exchanged a glance with Kenzo, then said easily, "If you don't mind, Auntie, I'd like to stay a while longer."

"That's perfectly all right. I'll be on my way, then."

As Mrs. Hayakawa bowed her gracious good-byes, Kenzo caught a glimpse of tattooed cherry blossoms in the secret recesses of her sleeve.

25

"This is terrible! This is really, really terrible!" Hisashi spoke in a voice that was close to a wail. His hands were trembling so violently that when he tried to take a cigarette out of the pack he ended up accidentally crushing it between his fingers.

"Why is that?" Kenzo asked rhetorically. The two men were upstairs again, facing each other across the low table.

"Why?" Hisashi sounded incredulous. "Because my brother Takezo has disappeared, and my uncle is a suspect in a murder! How could I not be upset? I always knew something awful would result when my brother got involved with that woman."

"Your arm is bandaged—what happened?"

"Nothing, really. Last night I stopped for a drink on the Ginza, got sloshed, and ended up staging a martial arts display on a couple of uncouth buffoons. I spent the night in jail. When I got out, I found everything in an uproar. All in all, it hasn't been what you'd call a really tiptop day."

"Where were you before?"

"At the Togeki Theater. The show ended around eight."

"And you got in the argument right after that?"

"No, I think that was closer to nine. I was drinking pretty heavily, so my memory isn't too sharp."

"A barroom brawl, huh. Thanks to that fight, you have a perfect alibi."

The two men's eyes met, and they shared a mordant chuckle.

"By the way," Kenzo said, "you may not understand this any more than I do, but I was wondering why your uncle, the professor, was behaving so strangely."

"Oh, the business with the photographic plates? Probably just as my aunt said: the images had to do with tattoos. If he found something he could use in his research or add to his collection, there's no way he would just leave it lying there."

"But to steal a piece of evidence from the scene of a murder…"

"What's so strange about that? An ordinary person can't begin to understand what it means to be in the thrall of an obsession. Actually, even my aunt."

"What about your aunt?"

"Well, she made a bad marriage, if you ask me. She was the daughter of a good family, a family that also happens to be very wealthy. As a condition of marriage my uncle insisted that she get tattooed."

Kenzo was shocked. "You aren't serious!" he said.

"Completely. It was a love marriage, not arranged. My aunt had quite a thing for my uncle and he didn't exactly dislike her, either. But after they got engaged, this is what he said: 'I'm sorry, but for a man like me, a woman without a tattoo has no appeal at all. If we get married with you in your present state, I'm afraid our married life would be a failure. So I want to ask you to promise me one small thing.' That was how he first broached the subject. The woman he was talking to was an inexperienced girl, the daughter of an attorney father and an aristocratic mother who had inherited a great deal of property. Naturally she was flabbergasted to hear such a thing before her wedding."

"Then what happened?" Kenzo said.

"My aunt asked for two or three days to think about her fiancé's request. She went into seclusion and discussed the matter with her parents. Needless to say, they were as surprised as she was. But her father seemed to have confidence

143

in my uncle. He said, 'Now that the betrothal gifts have been exchanged, your body belongs to the House of Hayakawa. When a woman becomes a bride she must subjugate herself to her husband.' So my aunt made up her mind to do whatever it took to satisfy her husband-to-be. She really did love him."

"And she got tattooed—all over?" Kenzo was thrilled, and horrified.

"No. At first she just had a single peony tattooed on the inside of each of her upper arms, hidden away where only her husband would see them. The wedding took place. By all accounts, their married life got off to a splendid start. But after a while my uncle said, 'A tattoo is the embodiment of carnal desire and, once she's had a taste of the needle, a woman—much more than a man—will feel herself aroused and wanting more. At first the process may seem frightening, but that's just the same as the fear a maiden will feel on her wedding night. It's soon forgotten in the discovery of pleasure.' He kept harping on this theme, and finally my aunt went back to get some more tattoos. Just as my uncle predicted, the more time she spent in the world of sharp needles and vermilion ink, the more tattooing she wanted. She now has tattoos all over her back and arms, and I gather she's in the process of getting them on her thighs as well. Have you ever heard of anything so stupid?" Hisashi's voice was filled with scorn.

"I don't really know," Kenzo said evasively.

Hisashi shrugged. "I was trained as a chemist. I look at everything from that point of view. To me, the relationship between a man and a woman is just a matter of chemical reaction. If I understand what my uncle was trying to say, a tattoo was a necessary catalyst for him to feel sexually aroused. In fact, it was absolutely indispensable."

"I see the logic of what you're saying. But what does all that have to do with this murder case?"

"I'm not trying to imply that my uncle has any direct connection with the murder. I'm just saying that if there was something about his behavior that mystified you and the police, it was probably the product of this strange quirk of his. That's all."

While he was listening to Hisashi's words, Kenzo's mood was growing increasingly gloomy. He was fond of Professor Hayakawa, and he had a feeling that the cloud of suspicion hanging over the professor was growing darker by the minute. "What on earth has happened to your brother?" he asked, hoping to change the subject.

"I don't have the foggiest," Hisashi said, shaking his head. "Since I've been living alone, I don't talk to my brother that often. The first I heard about this was this afternoon. A policeman came knocking on the door asking whether my brother was at my house. At first I thought he might be in trouble for his black-market operations, but then the cop started asking about my alibi for the night before. I still thought it had to do with business, since I knew my brother was being investigated by the Office of Land Reclamation. Then I got a phone call from my aunt, who was in hysterics. You know me; I'm usually pretty easygoing, but I didn't feel I could just sit around the house and do nothing, so I went to my brother's house in Nakano to find out what was happening, and after that I went to my aunt's house in Yotsuya. We discussed the situation, and then we ran around all over town, to the police station and the lawyer's office, and we finally ended up here."

"So who's at the house in Yotsuya now?"

"Just the housekeeper."

"Is your brother married?"

"No, he's practically made a religion out of staying single, though certainly not in the sense of celibacy or abstinence. He's just someone who vowed never to get formally married. His bachelorhood is a very feudal and opportunistic sort, strictly for convenience. That tattooed woman is the first mistress who's made him think about making a commitment."

"Your brother must have loved that woman a lot."

"You know what they say—there's no accounting for taste. But she's the first woman I ever saw who could lead my brother around by a nose ring. He had even started the paperwork to make her his legal wife. He's incredibly jealous, and she was a woman who liked men, so I guess he thought he might lose her if he didn't bind her to him legally. I gather she didn't see herself as the wife type, though. She was putting up a struggle."

"I guess a woman like that must have had a lot of affairs," Kenzo said guilelessly. "Putting the past aside, do you think she was fooling around lately?"

"I wouldn't know. But even if she felt like cheating on my brother, I doubt that she would do anything so reckless. She was well aware of his jealous nature, and his violent temper."

"But what about the manager of your brother's company, Gifu Inazawa? I was amazed to hear that he had a major crush on that woman. He thought she liked him, too."

Hisashi pursed his lips. "I find it hard to believe that she would invite that little weasel over for a midnight rendezvous. He wasn't exactly a Don Juan, except in his imagination. If my brother had found out, Inazawa's goose would have been cooked but good. I really can't imagine that he would have risked my brother's wrath. Dead women tell no tales, so we have no choice but to believe what Inazawa tells us about Kinue."

"Are you saying you doubt his story?"

"I'm saying that I don't trust a single human being on this earth, with the possible exception of myself." A smile flitted across Hisashi's face.

Kenzo said, "When I met your brother for the first time at that tattoo contest, I noticed something strange. You may laugh, but during the war I used to see a sort of death shadow on soldiers who were about to be killed in action. I saw the same look on your brother the other night."

"Oh, so now you're an aura reader?" The words sounded facetious, but Hisashi's demeanor was totally serious. "What about that woman," he said, leaning across the table and staring into Kenzo's eyes. "Did you see the same look on Kinue?"

"I didn't notice anything like that. Her body made a much stronger impression than the face… because of the tattoos," Kenzo added hastily.

"This is really incredible. Matsushita the Soothsayer. So what about Inazawa?"

"He looks rather mousy, yet he gives the impression of being a complete hedonist. I could see that at a glance."

"And my uncle, the professor?" Hisashi said.

"He's obviously totally consumed by his interest. In medical terms, I'd call him a monomaniac."

"What about me?" Hisashi's tone was almost coy.

"You?" Taken by surprise, Kenzo blurted out the first thing that came into his head. "You have the mark of a genius. You're highly intelligent. Also lazy. You don't make any effort to do work that doesn't appeal to you. But once something engages your interest, you apply yourself wholeheartedly to solving that problem. The trouble is that you rarely find an objective that seems worthy of your attention. In this postwar mess of a country, I would guess that you're having a hard time finding a practical application for your genius. It's a shame, but—"

"Thanks ever so much for the lovely eulogy," Hisashi interrupted sardonically.

Kenzo said, "If only I had a fraction of your intellect. How about it, don't you feel like playing detective?"

"Detective? Me? Why don't you ask your brilliant friend, the Boy Genius!" It was clear from Hisashi's sarcastic tone that he resented the fact that his own schoolboy nickname had been the Black Sheep, with no mention of the intellectual brilliance he took such pride in.

"Mainly because the last time I saw the Boy Genius, as you insist on calling him, was in Peking in 1944. I haven't heard a word from, or about him, since. I just hope he's all right. Anyway, never mind. It was just a thought."

Hisashi said, "You were a big fan of detective novels back in middle school. Why don't you solve the case?" Hisashi laughed, but not unpleasantly. "Actually, I wouldn't mind playing Sherlock Holmes, but the problem with this murder is that it involves my relatives. I'm just too close to the whole thing. It wouldn't be proper for me to meddle in it."

"If there's anything you can think of that would help my brother, please let me know."

"I certainly will. I'll do anything I can to help. Please feel free to ask any questions you like."

"Well, about these photographs…" Impulsively, Kenzo opened a drawer, took out the photographs he had received from Kinue, and passed them to Hisashi.

"The three tattooed siblings," Hisashi muttered as the color drained from his face. "How did you come to have these photos?"

"That woman, Miss Nomura, gave them to me at the tattoo contest. They were sealed in an envelope. She said that if something happened, I should open it and look at the contents."

"I wonder what she was thinking of?"

"Have you ever seen these photographs before, Hisashi?"

"Yes, I have. She showed them to us one time when I was at her house in Kitazawa with my brother."

"Were they pasted in an album?"

"Yeah, on the first page."

"Did she say anything about the pictures? Or was there any sort of an explanation written on the page? According to what she told me, there was some sort of secret surrounding those three tattoos."

"A secret about the tattoos? I haven't heard anything about that. But wait a minute..."

"What is it?"

"I remember now that she didn't show us the back of that page. In fact, she was hiding it kind of nervously." Hisashi was silent for a moment. "This really is a frightening case," he mused. "The actual murder was remarkably brutal, right? People are saying it was like a scene from hell. Weird as this may sound, to me the single most terrifying thing you told us was about the slug that was crawling on the windowsill."

Kenzo nodded. "I agree, absolutely. When I saw that awful slug, I got goosebumps all over."

"This will probably sound strange too, but to me, the killing is reminiscent of those gory picture books from the Edo Period. It's almost like a murder in old-fashioned clothing, and that just makes it more difficult to figure out. It's just like a chess problem."

"A chess problem?" Kenzo said.

"Right. If you play it perfectly, there should only be one order in which you can arrive at checkmate. If you do it any other way your opponent will end up escaping from you. However, the more complicated a problem becomes, the more you get tangled up in confusion. This criminal has obviously been very prudent and thorough in his preparation. He's basically getting away with murder, and flaunting it. I would guess that the person who committed this crime is feeling pretty invincible right about now, and I doubt if he thinks he has much to fear from the people who are investigating the case."

"I see what you mean. So our job is to get rid of the confusion he's created, to clear the board of the extraneous pieces, so to speak. The problem is, how do we tell which are the irrelevant elements?"

"I have no idea. As you know, I'm a dreamer. I enjoy playing around with theories. Putting them into practice isn't really my forte." With a sad little laugh, Hisashi stood up and said good-bye.

Kenzo took a long hot bath, then threw his bedding on the floor and climbed between the rough muslin sheets. He fell asleep immediately. A few minutes later he was wide awake, heart pounding. His eyes were wet with tears. He had dreamed he was making love to Kinue. It was blissful at first, but when he took Kinue's hands and stretched her arms above her head, his lover's tattooed limbs came off at the shoulders.

26

Detective Chief Inspector Daiyu Matsushita didn't get home until well after 10 p.m., but it was still nearly as warm as it had been at noon.

"God, it's hot out there. You could fry an omelet on the sidewalk," Daiyu said as he handed his briefcase to his wife in the entry hall. He headed straight for the bathroom and Mariko followed a minute later.

"Were you working on a case, dear?" she asked her husband, who was standing under a cold shower. There was a worried look on her sweet face.

"Did Kenzo say something about it?" Daiyu said, over the sound of the water.

"No." Mariko unfolded a bath towel and stood ready to hand it to her husband.

"That's strange," Daiyu said, emerging from the shower and shaking his wet head like a hunting dog emerging from a river. Mariko wiped the drops of water from her face and handed her husband the towel. "Is Kenzo in some kind of trouble?" she asked.

"You might say he's involved in the case. He discovered the body. Fortunately he was drinking with me last night, and there's no better alibi than, 'I was having a few drinks with a police chief,' right?" Laughing heartily, Daiyu allowed his wife to help him into a crisply starched *yukata*. He wound the striped-rayon sash around his big-boned body and pushed it into place, low on his hips.

"Please tell Kenzo to come down here," he said as he sauntered into his study. "And bring me a cold beer while you're at it," he added, over his shoulder.

After receiving his brother's summons, Kenzo dragged himself out of bed, splashed some cold water on his sleep-swollen face, and shuffled down to his brother's study. Not knowing what to say, he stood rooted to the spot, staring at his feet.

"No need to be so formal," Daiyu said casually, taking a swig from a frosty brown bottle of Sapporo beer. "Go ahead, have a seat. By the way, thanks for your help today."

"I didn't really do much, but you're very welcome."

"So, what do you think about this case so far?"

Timidly, Kenzo produced the envelope he had been hiding behind his back and laid it on his brother's desk. "I'm not sure, but I think this might be relevant," he said.

"What's in here?"

"Photographs. It's pictures of the tattoos of the murdered woman, Kinue Nomura, and her older brother Tsunetaro and her younger sister Tamae."

Daiyu spread the photographs out on the desk, then picked up the photo of the Tsunedahime tattoo and stared at it intently. "This is it!" he said. He nodded vigorously, then caught Kenzo's eye and said, "How did you come to have these in your possession?"

Kenzo tried to sound nonchalant. "It's really nothing which is why I had forgotten about them until now. What happened was, when Hisashi Mogami introduced me to that woman at the tattoo contest, I mentioned casually that I wouldn't mind having a picture of her tattoos. I thought for sure she would refuse because the newspaper photographers were pestering her for the same thing, and she gave them the brush-off. To my surprise, she took this envelope out of a silk furoshiki cloth and handed it to me. She said she had a feeling that someone might try to kill her, and she would feel safer if these photographs were in the hands of a person she could trust." Kenzo had broken out in a cold sweat while he was spewing forth this stream of lies. He was just about ready to drop the charade and make a clean breast of things, but Daiyu seemed to take his wild story at face value.

"Take a look at this," the chief inspector said. He took a photograph out of his briefcase and laid it on the desk. The photo showed the rear view of a totally naked woman, and although the surface of the print was disfigured with tiny cracks, it was clearly a picture of the tattoo known as Tsunedahime. In fact, the photo was an exact duplicate of the one Kenzo had just showed to his brother.

"Where did this picture come from?" Kenzo was bewildered.

"This is a print made from those fragments of photographic plate. The original was evidently made many years ago, but we were able to make this print by piecing together the fragments that the professor made off with."

"And what is the professor saying about this?"

"He's saying that after you went to answer the telephone, he wrapped his hand in a handkerchief to avoid destroying any fingerprints and picked up the pieces of the photographic plate that were lying on the ground in the garden. When he saw that it was a picture of a tattoo, his collector's mania kicked in and he furtively stuck it in his pocket. We needled him a little, saying, 'So, is stealing a potentially important piece of evidence from the scene of a murder your idea of doing your duty as a virtuous citizen?' He apologized, in his sarcastic way, but he still refuses to tell us anything at all about his activities on the night of the murder. He just keeps saying that his movements have absolutely nothing to do with the crime. We're just going to let him sit in jail and stew in his own juices for two or three days. That goes against my usual policy, but with an adversary like Professor Hayakawa, there's no other way to handle it."

"Did you check out the professor's house?"

"Yes. Both his wife and the maid said that he went out around six and came back around midnight. Those times correspond exactly to the hours for the murder, so we really would like to know what he was up to during that time block."

"What about Inazawa, what's going on with him?"

"Nothing new to report. After being taken to police headquarters he got more and more excited and finally refused to talk at all, so we decided to leave him alone for the time being. The serious investigation will begin tomorrow."

"Did you manage to locate Takezo Mogami?"

"Not yet. We've staked out his house and his office, and we've got the dragnet spread as far as Osaka. So far no word. It's possible that he's flown the coop, maybe even gone abroad. I mean, if he is the murderer, he wouldn't have any reason to hang around here, waiting to be captured."

"What about you? Do you think Mogami's the murderer? The newspapers seemed to be leaning toward that theory."

"I really don't know yet. He seems the most likely suspect. The thing I can't fathom is why the torso disappeared. What on earth was the point of that? This is the strangest case I've ever seen, in all my days as a cop."

"Were you able to identify the fingerprints?"

"Yes, thanks to the fingerprints, we've been able to cast a little bit of light on this mystery. Of the three sets of male prints, one belongs to Takezo Mogami, as we thought. We were able to match them to prints at his home and his office. Another set belongs to Inazawa. Our search turned up his prints on the outside of the bathroom doorknob and in several other places as well. The third man we figured out much more quickly than we expected. While going through the files at the station, we discovered that the third set of prints from the scene matched those of a convicted felon named Ryokichi Usui. He's your basic lower-echelon yakuza, with a police record as long as your arm. He did hard time for killing a man during an argument. When he got out of prison a couple of years ago, he ended up in Yokohama. He ran into Kinue Nomura there. Apparently they had been lovers before, when she was younger, but in Yokohama she wouldn't give him the time of day. After a while Takezo Mogami appeared on the scene and a rivalry ensued. I imagine it was like a sumo champion and a very small grasshopper. Mogami was rolling in money and had a certain amount of social status. The way we see it, Usui wasn't about to stand by and watch another man horn in on what he still considered his territory, even though Kinue had made it clear he didn't have a chance. Maybe it was a matter of yakuza's honor or fear of losing face, or maybe it was just stubborn male pride. Usui followed Kinue and Takezo around, harassing them incessantly. Kinue finally reported him to the police, and he ended up back in prison. So Ryokichi Usui has plenty of motive for murder."

"And you think this Usui sneaked into Kinue's house some time last night?"

"It certainly looks that way. The problem is, Usui has shown absolutely no indication of having the kind of intelligence required to commit this crime. We can't know for sure until we arrest him, but I suspect that if Usui had wanted to kill Kinue he would have simply stabbed or strangled her. That would probably be the best he could do. My intuition tells me this is going to be a very difficult case to solve."

"What about the maid? Did you find her?"

"Yes, we checked at her family home, and they said she had gone to the country. She should be back in two or three days."

Kenzo looked somber. "Actually, I had a couple of unexpected visitors today: Professor Hayakawa's wife and Hisashi Mogami, Takezo's younger brother."

"Professor Hayakawa's wife, eh? I see. According to the police officer who went to her house, she's quite an intelligent woman. Attractive, too. I didn't meet her myself, but she came to the police station. I imagine she came to see you because she was unbearably worried and wanted to find out what you knew about the case."

"That was my impression, too. She evidently dragged Hisashi Mogami all over town with her."

"Hisashi Mogami, huh. I can't say I don't find him a bit suspicious, too." Daiyu bit his lip.

"But he has a perfect alibi. He went to see a play at the Togeki Theater with some woman, and afterward he got in a big brawl on the Ginza and spent the night in jail in Tsukiji or somewhere. That can easily be checked out, right? Kinue was seen alive in Kitazawa around nine o'clock, which is just about the same time Hisashi was being thrown in jail, so that pretty much puts him out of the picture."

"We can check. The Togeki Theater is a different matter. The quality of the ushers isn't what it used to be. Unlike the old days, they no longer have any recollection of who was sitting in which seat."

"The Togeki lets out around eight o'clock, right? So that portion of his alibi really doesn't have any bearing on the case."

"Yes, I suppose that's true." Daiyu took a deep drag on his cigarette, lost in thought. A parade of wobbly, oblong smoke rings emerged from his mouth. Then he spoke. "Why on earth did the murderer run off with the torso? I really think that's the key to solving this case. Did Hisashi Mogami say anything about that, by any chance?"

"Not really. Except when I mentioned having seen a garden slug crawling on the window of the bathroom, he turned very pale."

"Sounds like he's more superstitious than you might think. I wonder if he thought the slug had fallen off the Orochimaru tattoo? That's the most ridiculous thing I ever heard." Daiyu's hearty laugh resounded through the thin-walled house, momentarily drowning out the sound of his wife, Mariko, struggling valiantly with a difficult passage in Rachmaninoff's Second Piano Concerto in the adjoining room.

Kenzo decided not to bother explaining that it was the Tsunedahime tattoo that featured a slug, not Orochimaru. Instead, he gave voice to a question that had been on his mind all day. "What sort of motive could a murderer possibly have for chopping up a body and making off with one of the parts?"

"Usually it's to keep the victim from being identified. The most common practice is to hide the head of the murdered person, or burn off the fingerprints. In this case, because there were tattoos on the body, I can understand why someone would have wanted to hide the torso, but you'd think he would have taken the head away with him as well. It's strange to go to so much trouble to disguise the identity of a murder victim who is killed right in her own home."

"Isn't it possible that the murderer cut up the body to make it easier to carry and then hid the pieces in the bathroom, intending to take them away a few at a time?"

"You've got to be joking. It's not like carrying a bag of vegetables home from the market. You can't just toss severed heads and sawed-off limbs around a murder victim's house and then wait two or three days to cart them off. If the perpetrator was going to take the rest of the body away, he would have done it the night of the murder."

"But the fact is that the murderer locked the body parts in the bathroom. Maybe he thought they wouldn't be discovered for another two or three days."

"Your reasoning is really amateurish sometimes, you know that? If that were the case, why would he have left the light on in the bathroom? Assuming that Inazawa's telling the truth about finding the light on, then you have to wonder why, if the perpetrator wanted to hide the body, he wouldn't at least have turned off the light. After all, the switch is right there in the hall. Looking at it from this perspective, you have to conclude that the perpetrator had no intention of hiding the body." He slapped the desktop in frustration.

Kenzo said, "Okay, let's say that the killer didn't particularly care about disguising the identity of the victim. What other reason could he have for hiding just one part of the body?"

"I think what we're dealing with here is an abnormal mentality," Daiyu said. "You remember the famous case of O-Sada, the one who cut off her dead lover's penis and carried it around in her pocket for several days? In this case, don't you think it's possible that the perpetrator has a peculiarly obsessive attachment to tattoos?"

"If that's the case, then Professor Hayakawa would seem to be the prime suspect."

"Of course. But Professor Hayakawa wasn't the only person with an abnormal attachment to that tattoo. For all we know, there could be some other person we don't even suspect, someone who is just as obsessed as the professor but whose irrationality isn't so readily apparent."

Kenzo nodded thoughtfully. "Whoever the killer was, do you have any idea how he got out of the locked bathroom?"

"One possible scenario is that the perpetrator somehow sneaked into the house between eight and nine while Kinue was out, committed the murder between nine and eleven, then hid somewhere and left while Inazawa was in the house, or else ran away himself after Inazawa fled. I checked it out. It doesn't look possible to climb over the concrete wall. So the perpetrator must have left either by the front entrance or the garden gate. But that area was under surveillance from nine to eleven, by the people next door. Kinue came home around quarter of nine. It would hardly have been possible to commit such a complex murder in ten or fifteen minutes. So no matter where you start, you end up back at the same conclusion."

"Is it possible that the killer hid himself in the bathroom until the next morning?"

"That doesn't make sense. Suppose Inazawa had called the police instead of running away. The killer would have been a sitting duck, if he was still hiding in the bathroom. Of course, this is all based on the assumption that Inazawa was telling the truth. If Inazawa were actually the perpetrator, that would change everything."

Kenzo gave a big sigh and hesitated for a moment before he finally addressed his brother. "Tell me, do you really think the dead woman is Kinue Nomura?"

"Well, if it isn't Kinue Nomura, then who the hell is it?"

"This is just a thought, okay? Suppose that her younger sister Tamae, whom everyone has been assuming was killed by the bomb in Hiroshima, was really alive all along, and that she was the one who was murdered?"

Daiyu began to shake his head no. "Please, spare me the convenient solutions," he said in a withering tone. "You've obviously been reading too many detective novels. The two women may have been sisters, but these photographs clearly show that Tamae had tattoos below her elbow and below her knees. The arms that were found had been cut off above the elbow, and there was no trace of a tattoo at all. Same with the legs. If it was a simple tattoo, that would be another matter, but surely such an elaborate tattoo couldn't simply be erased?"

"Oh, that's right," Kenzo said dejectedly. "I forgot. It's been a long, strange day and a lot has happened. With the heat and everything… I'm sorry."

"It's no wonder. Even for me, this bizarre case is a first," Daiyu muttered, exhaling as he spoke. With the same breath, he blew a parade of perfectly circular smoke rings toward the ceiling. "It seems unlikely that Tamae Nomura survived the bomb," he said thoughtfully. "According to our information, she was living right in the center of Hiroshima. But if she did survive by some fluke, I wouldn't be looking at her as a possible victim, since the photos prove that's impossible."

"What do you mean?"

"I mean that if she were alive, which I doubt, I would want to interview Miss Tamae Nomura as a Person of Interest, or even a possible suspect in this case."

"But surely she couldn't have done something so horrible to her own sister? I mean, moral considerations aside, a woman wouldn't have the strength, would she?"

"No. She would need a male cohort to do the heavy lifting, and probably the butchering as well."

Kenzo winced at the thought of Kinue's beautiful body being hacked to pieces like a side of beef, but he quickly resumed a poker face. "What could her motive have been?" he asked. "Theoretically."

"You name it," Daiyu said. "Jealousy, resentment, a long-simmering grudge. Hardly a month goes by that we don't see a truly heinous case of family members killing each other, often over the most trivial things. Of course, many of those cases are murder-suicides. Just the other day I heard about a case in Kyushu where a divorced mother threw her two tiny children into the mouth of a volcano. The man she wanted to marry didn't want to be a stepfather, and she had no relatives to farm the kids out to. I like to think I'm unshockable, but that really made my blood run cold. Whoever said that erotic love was a form of insanity hit the nail on the head. This case is a disturbing one, too. I have to admit I was knocked for a loop by the gruesome scene in that bathroom."

Unable to hold back any longer, Kenzo blurted out, "Please let me help with this case. My involvement could be completely unofficial and off the record, and I promise not to do anything to mess it up."

"Let you help?" Daiyu sounded incredulous.

"That's right. I wouldn't be able to contribute very much, but by some strange karma, I seem to have been dragged into this from the beginning. And in terms of the scholarly aspect, I can't help thinking there's a possibility that some of my medical knowledge might be useful. After all, my specialty is forensic medicine."

Daiyu Matsushita nodded. "Okay," he said slowly. "You can help, but be careful. This isn't one of your sanitized mystery novels. We're looking for a nasty killer, and it could get very dangerous."

27

On the day after the murder, the saw that had presumably been used to dismember the corpse was found in a bombed-out building about two hundred and fifty yards from Kinue's house. There were dried bloodstains clearly visible on the saw's blade, and the blood type matched that of the victim. No fingerprints were found, and the saw itself was a very ordinary, well-used tool with no distinguishing features of any sort. So in the end, this dramatic discovery didn't yield a single useful clue.

Day by day, the investigation moved along. Kinue Nomura's former maid, Fusako Yoshida, returned to Tokyo after visiting her family in the country. She was fingerprinted and interviewed. The technicians were able to confirm that one of the sets of fingerprints found at the scene belonged to her. The police showed her the bloody saw. She had never seen it before. From this they deduced that the murderer didn't impulsively grab the nearest saw and cut up the body after the murder.

One thing surprised the official in charge of the examination: the revelation that she had not left the job by choice. Kinue had fired her. Evidently several days prior, a letter in a brown paper envelope had been delivered to the house. When Kinue read it, all color had drained from her face. "Immediately afterward," said the maid, "she sentenced me to my fate."

This aroused a certain amount of suspicion among the officers in the investigation. If the letter was the same one that was stuck between the pages of the photo album, then it contained a terrifying death threat. Given that Kinue was frightened and feared for her life, one would think that rather than firing the maid and leaving herself unattended, it would be natural to have surrounded herself with as many people as possible, for comfort and protection. Most of the officers assigned to the case found Kinue's behavior incomprehensible.

However, there was one dissenting opinion, from an out-spoken junior detective. "That woman, Kinue Nomura, seems to have had an almost excessive amount of confidence in her own appeal," he theorized. "Hate is the flip side of love, and it's possible that the man threatening her life was someone who was once in love with her. Perhaps she thought that if he were actually in her presence, she could use her feminine wiles to defuse his anger and recapture his heart. The maid might have gotten in the way of such a scenario, and that's why Kinue Nomura made a point of letting her go. At least that's the way it looks to me." The theory sounded reasonable, but there was no way of knowing whether it was right or wrong.

Kinue's personal effects were examined carefully. Many of her clothes were missing and there was no trace of any cash, gemstones, or precious metals. According to the maid, Kinue had had her assets frozen once before and didn't trust banks. She kept large amounts of cash in the drawer of a chest in her sleeping room. That drawer had been emptied, and there wasn't so much as a one-yen coin left in the house.

There was something old-fashioned about the maid. She was dressed in traditional Japanese style, and the only modern touch in her appearance was the somewhat frizzy permanent wave in her short black hair. When asked to describe Kinue's usual conduct, Fusako Yoshida replied in this way:

"It's been about six months since I began working for the missus... for Miss Nomura. During the war my father became obligated to the master—you know, Mr. Mogami—and that

163

was how I got the job. At first I didn't know about the tattoos. When I found out, I was really shocked. Even the missus said, 'Because of these tattoos, every time I find a new maid she gets scared and runs away.' In fact I wanted very much to quit that job at first, but after a while I got used to seeing the tattoos, and they didn't bother me so much anymore. Most of the time the missus was a very pleasant, generous person. She gave me all sorts of nice things, like some really beautiful kimonos that hadn't been worn more than two or three times. If I admired something of hers, she would simply give it to me, without hesitation. But when she was in a bad mood, it was a different story. She would snap at me about the most trivial things and find fault with everything I did, so I really suffered a lot. Anyway, the master used to come over almost every evening, and he would usually spend the night. At that time the missus didn't go out at night at all. During the day she would go shopping, or to a play or movie, and the rest of the time she was at home. Then she got involved in opening a bar on the Ginza—I gathered it was some sort of membership club catering to businessmen. Until the beginning of this month she was working there in the evenings. Lately, though, she seemed to have quit that job. Oh, you were asking whether she got along with the master? At first they seemed to be getting along very well, although even then I couldn't have sworn that she loved him with all her heart. It wasn't that there was another man around. Nothing like that. But about ten days ago the missus entered a tattoo competition, and ever since then the master seemed to be in a really foul mood. Whenever he came over they would get into loud, nasty arguments, and he would storm off in a huff. And then the missus suddenly told me she wouldn't be needing my services anymore."

Having run out of things to say, the maid began to gather up her things. When one of the detectives asked her whether she had noticed any unusual occurrences in the Nomura household recently, she sat right down again.

"Now that you mention it, there was something around noon, three or four days ago. I had gone out to buy some tofu, and when I came home there was a suspicious-looking man standing in front of the house. He was trying to peer inside. When he noticed me, he glared really hatefully, then turned and walked away very fast. He wasn't bad-looking, but he had a scary look in his eyes and a scar on his chin, and his hair was cropped so short that his scalp looked almost blue. I'd guess he was about five foot three or four, and fairly well built. He was dressed in some filthy trousers and a ragged shirt, khaki-colored, like an old army uniform. I couldn't tell whether he had any tattoos or missing fingers, but there was definitely something gangsterish about him."

Here, at last, was a major clue. Ryokichi Usui was known to have gone to visit his brother-in-law in Mito after being released from prison in July, but after that he seemed to have vanished. When the maid was shown a photograph of Usui, she immediately identified him as the man she had seen loitering outside Kinue Nomura's house. There was a sample of Usui's handwriting on file at the central police station, and it turned out to be a perfect match for the writing on the threatening letter Kinue Nomura had received.

The house of Takezo Mogami was thoroughly searched. The most interesting thing the police detectives found there was an empty pistol case hidden away in a chest of drawers. According to the housekeeper's statement, two or three days before he disappeared, she had been startled to see Takezo polishing his pistol. He had what she called "a terrible look" on his face.

The investigations of Professor Hayakawa and Gifu Inazawa made no progress at all. Inazawa kept repeating the same statement over and over, while the professor continued to refuse to account for his own activities on the night of the murder.

It took all of twelve minutes to verify Hisashi Mogami's alibi. He had been incarcerated behind iron bars from nine fifteen P.M. until nine the next morning. The woman who had accompanied Hisashi Mogami to the Togeki Theater was the owner of Mona Lisa, a fashionable dress shop on the Ginza. Her name was Kyoko Kawabata. She testified that she had been with Hisashi at the theater from three thirty until eight o'clock. After that, both the waitress and the bartender of Linden, a notoriously rowdy Ginza tavern, corroborated that at around eight thirty he had been drinking there and had gotten into a violent brawl.

The investigation into Kinue Nomura's background revealed that her original family home had been in the Honjo district of Tokyo, an area reduced to cinders by the Allied bombing. Fortunately the detectives were able to locate an elderly man who had lived all his life in the neighborhood and had been evacuated to a country village during the war. Thanks to his lively memory, they were able to gather a fair amount of material about Kinue's background.

The old man told them that Horiyasu had been a fine man and a respected tattoo artist. His wife, however, was a notoriously wicked woman who caused the honest, hard-working Horiyasu a great deal of anguish. Eventually she became involved with a younger man and ran off with him, and her life went downhill from there. Horiyasu was left to raise three young children alone. He did his best to bring them up properly, but it was an enormous struggle.

The oldest, a boy, helped his father with his work and even did some of the actual tattooing himself but, since tattooing was illegal, they couldn't very well advertise their wares on a signboard outside the house. As a front, they put up a sign that read DEALERS IN SECONDHAND GOODS. By the time the boy, Tsunetaro, went to take his conscription exam, his entire body was covered with elaborate tattoos. Not wanting to be outdone, his sister Kinue began getting tattooed herself. The old man remembered seeing her coming and going in the street. Sometimes, when the weather was warm, she would nonchalantly let her sleeves flap open and he would catch a glimpse of the designs that adorned her upper arms. He seemed to recall that Tamae, the youngest of the three children, had also embarked upon the tattooing process. About that time, the family moved away, so he had no idea what the pattern of Tamae's tattoo might have been.

"I'm sure the younger one would have gotten an even showier tattoo than her sister had," the old man told the police. "Those two were competitive from the time they were small, always trying to outdo the other. They fought like cats and dogs, too; I often heard them screaming at each other. I used to close the windows, so my wife—God rest her soul— wouldn't have to hear the nasty language they used. I always thought sisters were supposed to have a special bond, but apparently that wasn't the case with the Nomura girls. They were both lookers, that's for sure, just like their mother. The talk around the neighborhood was that they took after their sinful mother in other ways, too."

*

167

The police were very interested in seeing Takezo Mogami's last will and testament, but Takezo's attorney refused to unseal that document. His position was that since there was no conclusive proof that Mogami had murdered Kinue Nomura, there was no way he could break the seal on the will without Takezo's permission. Speaking off the record, the lawyer was quite open about discussing his missing client with the police. He told them that about a month earlier, Takezo Mogami had said that he wanted to add Kinue Nomura to his family register, thus making her his legal wife. Several days before the murder, though, Takezo had met with the attorney and told him that he wanted to postpone that process for a while. In addition, he had mentioned that he was thinking of disinheriting his freeloading younger brother, Hisashi.

The police also turned their attention to Serpent Bar. There were strict regulations governing night life—the so-called "water trade"—and in the Ginza area alone there were innumerable bars like Serpent operating on the sly. Illegal gambling was rife at many of these outlaw bars. Whether Kinue had been afraid for her life or had merely feared a police raid, Serpent had been closed just before the murder. The place had evidently been scrubbed down, for there were hardly any fingerprints to be found.

That was the full extent of the information that Daiyu Matsushita and his team of investigators had gathered in the three days since the murder.

Daiyu Matsushita was not the sort of policeman who used violence, intimidation, and torture to extract confessions from suspects. He preferred to let reason and systematic detective work do the job. His philosophy reflected the New Constitution of 1946. He tried at all times to show respect for a suspect's human rights, and he would only send a case to the prosecutor if there was direct evidence to back up the accusations. Nevertheless, his patience was being sorely tried by Professor Hayakawa's use (or abuse) of the right to remain silent. There were times when a cold anger swept through Daiyu and he felt a strong urge to punch the professor right in his uncooperative mouth.

28

It was the first day of September, a sizzling Sunday. Detective Chief Inspector Daiyu Matsushita was exhausted from working day after day in the fierce heat. He didn't drag himself out of bed until after nine o'clock. Dressed in his rumpled blue sleeping robe, he was eating a late breakfast of rice, fermented soybeans, miso soup, and grilled sardines when the telephone rang.

"Hello?" Daiyu said, still chewing audibly. "Yes. Yes. Okay."

Daiyu threw his chopsticks onto the table and stood up. Kenzo, who was sitting across from him reading the morning paper, gave him a quizzical look. His brother said, "Damn, they've just found the body of my prime suspect, Takezo Mogami. I hate it when that happens. Do you want to come along?"

"I do," Kenzo said. As soon as they had thrown on their clothes, the two men piled into the police car sent from headquarters and headed west on O-Umemachi Street at top speed. In the backseat of the car, Kenzo turned to his brother. "You said they'd found Mogami's body. How?" he asked.

"I have no idea. They didn't tell me any details on the phone."

"Where was he found?"

"In some sort of warehouse that belongs to Mogami. No one was living there, and the house was registered under a false name." That was all Daiyu Matsushita had to say on the subject. No matter how many questions Kenzo asked, his older brother just sat there in silence chain-smoking, blowing half-formed smoke rings, and absentmindedly dropping cigarette ashes in his lap.

They drove rapidly through Ogikubo, Nishi-Ogi, and Kichi-joji, where the tattoo contest had been held. With each passing mile, the scenery became a bit more rural. In the vicinity of Mitaka Station, just after crossing the railroad tracks, they spotted Officer Akita standing in front of a police box. He raised his hand in greeting and, when the car stopped, he climbed in.

No sooner had Akita closed the door behind him than Daiyu Matsushita was demanding, "Who found the body?"

"An employee of the Mogami Group."

"How did he happen to find it?"

"The place is known around here as the Haunted House because of some weird things that have happened there. Mogami bought it in foreclosure, and he had been having trouble getting rid of it because of its reputation. He finally decided to tear the house down and rebuild it in another location, and the construction and demolition work were scheduled to begin tomorrow. The employee had come out to inspect the site, and he found the body in the storeroom."

"What was the cause of death?"

"One shot to the head with a pistol. He appears to have died instantly."

"Where was the gun?"

"The victim was grasping it in his own hand."

"So it was suicide?"

"It's too early to say for sure, but it certainly looks that way."

"Hmm." Daiyu Matsushita nodded, but his face wore an expression of extreme displeasure. The car pulled up to a rusted iron gate and came to a stop.

"This is as far as we can go by car," Officer Akita said. "We'll have to walk the rest of the way."

"Right-o," said the chief inspector, suddenly cheerful again. He climbed out of the car, tossed away his half-smoked cigarette, and stood staring straight ahead. The place they were in was about a thirty minute walk north-northeast from Mitaka Station, and the scenery retained something of the aura of the old Musashino Plain. Things had changed quite a bit since Kunikida Doppo had written his masterpiece *Musashino*. In the hazy distance the tall towers and chimneys of modern factories rose above the trees. At eye level, though, there was a certain timeless pastoral appeal in the forest and the clear, murmuring brook.

At that particular moment, Daiyu Matsushita was completely oblivious to the bucolic charm of the scenery. The only reason he was looking around so intently was because he knew his first impressions could end up being useful in solving the crime.

"That's the place over there. It's the house in that grove of trees." Officer Akita pointed toward the end of a road that meandered along for sixty yards or so, closely following the curves of the small river.

"Is this road the only way in, or out?"

"That's right. But if you wanted to cut through the fields and the forest, you could escape in any direction."

"How far is it to the nearest inhabited house?"

"At a guess, I'd say three or four hundred meters."

"Right. Let's go!" Chief Matsushita set off at a brisk pace. The weather had been clear for days on end, and the surface of the road was hard and dry, so there was no need to worry about disturbing any potential footprints.

They walked for several minutes and came upon a crumbling mud wall. A policeman who had been snoozing in its shade hastily snapped to attention and gave them a smart salute. A few steps farther along they came to the main gate, which was bolted from the inside.

"How do you open this thing?" Daiyu Matsushita asked Officer Akita, as he had tested the gate's resistance at several places, without success.

"There's a service entrance on the other side."

Leading the way, Daiyu walked along the mud wall and around two corners. A service gate in the rear wall led to an enclosed area of three hundred *tsubo*—eleven thousand square feet. The men stepped through the gate and found themselves waist-high in luxuriant grass and flowering weeds. In the heat and humidity, the tall summer grass gave off a heady aroma. The buildings consisted of an L-shaped residence of fifteen hundred square feet and, at the rear, a single storehouse whose whitewashed walls had long since begun to crumble into dust, like the earthen wall that surrounded the property.

"What sort of state is this place in?" Daiyu gestured toward the main house.

"All the tatami mats and the other furnishings have been ripped out. There's nothing left. These are such hard times that they even stole the glass from the windows. The place has been emptied. It looks as if tramps have been using it as a flophouse."

Daiyu nodded as he lit yet another unfiltered cigarette, then set off toward the storehouse. When the door was opened, the musty odor peculiar to storehouses assailed their nostrils, mixed with the unmistakable stench of a dead body.

"Open all the windows," the chief inspector ordered. One of his subordinates leaped into action, and in a moment brilliant sunlight was streaming into the dismal space. A huge cloud of blowflies was flying around inside. Attracted by the blood, they whirled in frenzied circles like a small tornado.

In the middle of the room, an empty beer crate was lying on its side. On the floor in front of the crate lay the sprawled body of Takezo Mogami, covered with flies.

29

That's the end of Mr. Broom, Kenzo thought melodramatically. While Takezo was alive, Kenzo had perceived him as a romantic rival, but he felt no satisfaction in seeing him dead. He remembered with a chill that the woman they had both loved was dead as well.

The corpse of Takezo Mogami was clutching a pistol. The barrel was pointed at Takezo's head, and a small hole was clearly visible above the right ear. A rivulet of reddish-black flowed from this entry wound onto the floor, where it had congealed and mingled with the fine dust that blanketed all the surfaces of the neglected storeroom. The portly cadaver was well on the way to decomposition, and the powerful aroma was nauseating.

"How long has this man been dead?" the chief said.

"I'd say between three and four days," the white-gloved forensics specialist replied.

"So that would make it the day of the Kitazawa murder, or the day after."

"That's right."

"And the cause of death was this pistol?"

"Yes, the bullet entered above the right ear and penetrated the brain on a diagonal trajectory. He would have died instantly."

"Is there any evidence to suggest a struggle or a fight of any sort?"

"We haven't come across any."

"What about personal effects?"

"There was a wallet containing a little more than two thousand yen in paper notes. And there's this gold watch, which at current prices would be worth seven or eight thousand yen."

"What about this distorted expression on the face? It almost looks as if he's smiling. Is it anguish? Pain?"

"Mmm, quite a bit of time has elapsed. It's really hard to tell…"

"And the pistol?"

"It's a Browning, made in 1936, with a silencer attached."

"Does the pistol match the case that was found at Mogami's house?"

"Perfectly."

"Any fingerprints on the gun?"

"Only those of the deceased."

"Is there anything to suggest murder?"

"Nothing to speak of."

"Assuming it was suicide, he must have sat on this empty box, pointed the gun at his head… pulled the trigger. The momentum of the blast could have caused him to tumble onto the floor."

"That sounds reasonable," the specialist said.

"What about the bullets in the gun?"

"It's a six-bullet chamber and it was fully loaded, except for the one fired into the victim's head."

"Does the bullet match the entry wound?"

"We won't know for sure until we remove the bullet, but I strongly suspect it'll be a match."

"Since there was a silencer attached to the gun, even if a shot was fired in here it wouldn't have been heard outside. Is that correct?"

"Yes. This sort of thick-walled storehouse has a natural tendency to absorb sound and, besides, this place is quite far from the outside wall. I think it's safe to say that unless someone was actually on the premises, no one would have heard the shot."

"Okay. Now, would you bring me the worker who discovered the body?"

Daiyu Matsushita knelt down and peered at the corpse. Taking another long look around the storehouse, he left and returned to the main house. He sat down on the filthy veranda. A young man in his mid-twenties, trembling visibly from the shock of finding his boss, was brought before the chief.

"My name is Ichiro Yoshioka." The young man bowed his head respectfully. "I'm twenty-six years old, and I'm employed by the Mogami Group."

"You're the one who found the body, right?"

"That's right."

"And there's no question that the body is that of your boss, Takezo Mogami?"

"No… no question at all." The young man closed his eyes.

"Could you please tell us in detail about how you happened to find the body?"

"Well, about three months ago our company bought this property. Our boss—Mr. Mogami—took it in foreclosure on a personal debt, just for the value of the land. The buildings aren't much to speak of, as you can see, and the place has a bad reputation. They say when you pass by here at night, you can hear voices groaning. Personally I think ghost stories are a lot of nonsense, but I have heard that the person who first built this house went bankrupt and hanged himself in the storeroom. The next person who owned this property supposedly went mad, and his successor got into some sort of trouble with the law and is now in prison. So when this property fell into his hands, the boss wasn't sure how to deal with it. Because the place truly seemed to be jinxed, or at

177

least unlucky, the best course of action seemed to be to tear down the buildings. The demolition was scheduled to begin tomorrow, and—"

"Wait a minute," the chief interrupted. "When was that decision made?"

"About two weeks ago."

"So everyone who worked for the company would have been aware that this house was going to be demolished in the near future."

"Everyone who was involved would have been aware of that, yes."

"Would your manager, Mr. Inazawa, have known about it?"

"Of course."

"Okay, let's hear what happened next."

"Well, because of the murder of Miss Nomura, everything was running behind schedule, but we couldn't just let this place sit forever, so I came out here to survey the situation. One of my colleagues was supposed to meet me at the station. When he didn't show up, I went ahead on my own. I wasn't particularly nervous about being alone. I figured that even if this house really was haunted, the ghosts wouldn't be around in broad daylight. As I was making the rounds of the property, I noticed the door of the storeroom was ajar. I thought that was strange, but I didn't see any signs of an intruder. When I threw open the door, the first thing I noticed was an extremely unpleasant smell, so strong that I had to hold my nose to keep from being sick. When my eyes got used to the dim light, I saw a dead body lying over there, dressed in a suit that I remembered having seen the boss wear. I was so shocked that I just wanted to flee, but I knew that wouldn't be right, so I ran to the nearest police box…"

The young man paused.

"All right, Mr. Yoshioka, I think I've got the picture. Thank you very much for all your help." Daiyu Matsushita wrapped up his questioning and immediately began conferring with the public prosecutor, who had just arrived.

30

Kenzo, meanwhile, was rambling aimlessly around the over-grown jungle of a garden, thinking about this latest death. The main question, of course, was whether the death of Takezo Mogami was suicide. At first glance, there didn't appear to be any reason to think it might have been murder.

But what could have driven Takezo to commit suicide? Had he destroyed his beloved Kinue Nomura, and then decided to take his own life in despair? Or was he simply unwilling to face the almost inevitable consequences of arrest, trial, and lifelong incarceration—even death? Kenzo had problems with both hypotheses.

If Takezo wanted to commit suicide, why did he choose this godforsaken place? Kenzo found that impossible to compre-hend. *If I were going to commit suicide,* he thought, *I would choose the place with care.* Kenzo wasn't merely theorizing. He had given considerable thought to the matter during the worst of his "black dog" depressions.

As far as he could tell, suicidal people were often in a strangely romantic mood. It was part of the reason why people still flocked to famous suicide spots as Mount Mihara and Kegon Waterfall—the lure of tradition, and the desire to decorate one's last moments with a bit of beautiful scenery. Why would Takezo deliberately choose such a gloomy place? His own home or Kinue's place in Kitazawa would have been much more comfortable and convenient.

"Why was the gun loaded with six live bullets? People who are about to commit suicide are sometimes oddly frugal, just as those who went to Mount Mihara, intending to fling themselves into the volcano, were always terribly careful to buy a one-way ticket. Perhaps Takezo had kept the gun fully loaded at all times; after all, saving money was the least of his worries.

And, if Takezo did kill Kinue, why did he dismember the body and cart off just the torso, leaving the bathroom locked from the inside? If Kinue's missing torso had been discovered along with Takezo's body, everything would have made sense, but that hadn't happened.

In spite of his reservations, Kenzo found himself leaning toward the theory that Takezo had committed suicide. The gun was Takezo's, and it was hard to understand how someone could have been killed so easily with his own gun. After all, if he brought a gun for purposes other than suicide, he must have been expecting some sort of trouble. Yet there were no signs of a struggle, and it was difficult to imagine that a conscious person would docilely sit down and allow a foe to place a gun in his hand and fire a bullet into his brain.

If you embraced the murder theory, however, it was conceivable that Takezo had come to the house with someone he trusted, and had been attacked by his companion. Surely Takezo wouldn't have come to such a remote place to meet a stranger, or an enemy. But if he were with a trusted friend or colleague, why would he bring a gun in the first place?

Or maybe Takezo was killed somewhere else, then brought here? No sooner had that thought crossed Kenzo's mind than he ruled it out, for there would have been no way to place a body already stiffening with rigor mortis in such a natural-looking position. And there wouldn't have been so much blood. It was truly maddening. Every possible hypothesis had an undeniable counterargument.

"You're concentrating awfully hard on something." A hearty voice suddenly boomed and Kenzo jumped. The voice belonged to the heroic-looking Officer Ishikawa, master of the martial arts.

Kenzo laughed weakly. "I was just thinking about this latest case," he said. "What do you think, Officer Ishikawa? Did Takezo commit suicide, or could he have been murdered?"

"It's really too soon to make that determination. I'm just an old-fashioned, by-the-book, physical-evidence sort of cop. You'll have to rely on your brother for the more cerebral stuff." Pointing a large-knuckled forefinger at his own oversize cranium, the policeman gave a self-deprecating smile.

"But you must have some idea," Kenzo persisted. "Even if you don't fully understand the case, don't you have some sort of intuition about it?"

"Oh, if you just want a hunch, here's one. It may look like suicide, but I think this was a perfect murder."

"What makes you think so?" Kenzo asked excitedly.

"The dust inside the storeroom."

"The dust? What about it?"

"Well, this storehouse hasn't been used for many months, right? So you would expect to see a much greater accumulation of dust on the floor. But instead it appears as if a great many people have trampled over this floor, so that any individual footprints have been obliterated. It wasn't the police who stomped around in here; it was like this when we found the body. So even if we wanted to compare Takezo's footprints with these, we wouldn't be able to lift a single clear footprint from the entire place."

"I see. I never even noticed." *A true expert really is a thing apart,* Kenzo thought, looking at Officer Ishikawa with renewed respect and admiration. "So you're saying that the murderer deliberately trampled all over the dust, to erase his own footprints?"

"That's how it looks to me. Oh, excuse me. Duty calls." Someone was shouting Officer Ishikawa's name, and he ran off toward the main house.

Looking around for someone else to talk to, Kenzo spotted the young employee of the Mogami Group, who was loitering about nearby, evidently wondering whether to stay or go. "It's really terrible that you've lost your boss now, on top of everything," Kenzo said in a sympathetic tone. "That must be disheartening."

"Oh, thank you very much. I'm deeply grateful for your concern." Ichiro Yoshioka looked a bit startled when Kenzo addressed him, but he answered in a very polite way. *Maybe he thinks I'm a police officer,* Kenzo thought, suppressing a smile. He did nothing to dispel that erroneous impression.

The young man went on in an agitated manner: "I just wish I knew what really happened. Was my boss murdered, or did he kill himself? Do you suppose the same person who killed Miss Nomura might have committed this crime as well?"

"It's too soon to make that determination," Kenzo began, shamelessly recycling the words of Officer Ishikawa. "Right now we're wondering about the state of the dust in the storeroom, as it relates to potential evidence, footprints and so on."

Ichiro Yoshioka looked bewildered. "There's no significance about the dust," he said. "Until recently, we were using that building for storage, so there's been a lot of traffic in and out."

"What?" Kenzo was dumbfounded.

"We had put some building supplies in there—sheets of galvanized iron, barrels of nails, bags of cement, stuff like that—but recently we began moving them elsewhere. So there would be no reason to expect the dust to have piled up undisturbed."

"What are you saying?" Kenzo felt as if he had been hit on the head with a nightstick. *So much for the perfect-murder theory,* he thought. Ichiro Yoshioka excused himself and Kenzo was left staring up at the brilliant summer sky, shaking his head in confusion.

All that day, officers combed the property and poked around the surrounding neighborhood. They didn't find a single thing that would qualify as a direct clue. Takezo's body was taken away to the forensic medicine lab of a university, where an autopsy was performed. The results of the autopsy merely served to reconfirm what had already been deduced. (1) The time of death was either the twenty-seventh or the twenty-eighth of the month; (2) the bullet removed from Takezo's brain was a perfect match for his gun; and (3) the sole cause of death was the bullet, which had penetrated the skull of the victim.

Meanwhile, at Metropolitan Police Headquarters in Setagaya, detectives were choosing sides on the theoretical question of murder versus suicide. The most popular theory was that Takezo had killed Kinue in a fit of jealous anger and then decided to flee. Holing up temporarily in the abandoned storehouse, he had gradually been overcome by feelings of guilt and finally, unable to stand the qualms of conscience, he had turned his pistol upon himself.

Daiyu Matsushita kept up a bluff, cheerful front, but his heart was filled with cold despair. Whether Takezo was the murderer or not, Chief Matsushita had been clinging to the belief that the mystery of Kinue Nomura's death would be solved once Takezo was found. Now he felt as though his main line of hope had been severed.

The following day, Counselor Sayama opened the seal on Takezo Mogami's will. Like the autopsy, the contents of the will did not produce any great surprises. Takezo had left half his property to his younger brother Hisashi, and one-third to Kinue Nomura. If either of those two parties should die before Kinue bore children, that person's share would go to the surviving party. The remaining one-sixth of Takezo's fortune went to his uncle, Professor Hayakawa, earmarked for research funds.

With those simple lines, Hisashi Mogami became the possessor of an enormous fortune. If finding Kinue's killer had been a matter of motive alone, Hisashi would most certainly have been a person of interest. However, Hisashi had an unshakable alibi, and Daiyu Matsushita had no choice but to cross him off the list of possible suspects. Unfortunately, Takezo Mogami had died before the police could question him about Kinue's murder… *Too bad there's no way to deliver a subpoena to the afterworld,* Daiyu thought ruefully.

There appeared to be ample reason to suspect both Gifu Inazawa and Professor Hayakawa, but the police couldn't hold them without concrete evidence. Reluctantly, Daiyu Matsushita placed his signature and stamp on the forms that would secure the release of both. Of the possible threads, four had been cut along the way. Not a single clue had turned up as to the whereabouts of the two remaining threads—Ryokichi Usui and the unidentified woman whose fingerprints were found at Kinue's house.

Short of having the mystery woman waltz into his office, the elusive yakuza seemed like his last, best hope. "Where the devil is Ryokichi Usui?" Daiyu muttered.

31

Three doors away from the Matsushita house lived a firefighter who was extremely colorful, in every sense of the word. He was a young man in his late thirties, a true Edoite, Tokyo born and bred. As was customary for men in his outdoor, dangerous type of work—firemen, roofers, high-altitude construction workers—he had a splendid tattoo on his back. The tattoo was a portrayal of Benten Kozo, a tattooed transvestite robber celebrated in Kabuki drama, who had such a beautiful face that he was able to masquerade convincingly as a woman. The fireman himself had a rough, manly, rather squashed-looking face. His name was Katsuo Goto, but he was known around the neighborhood as Chokatsu, "Tattooed Katsu," or Katsu for short.

On a bright Sunday morning Chokatsu stopped Kenzo on the street. They exchanged bows, and Chokatsu immediately began chattering away. "Hey, what's the deal with that mutilation murder case in Kitazawa? Have they caught the killer yet?"

"Not yet," Kenzo replied.

"It must be hard on your brother, having such a tough case to solve. And it's really nasty the way the murderer cut up the body and then ran off with the trunk. That gives me nightmares." Chokatsu stuck his hand inside his kimono as if to make sure his own tattoos were still intact.

"That's right, Katsu, you'd better be careful! The next time you break some poor woman's heart she might cut you up, too, and cart your tattooed torso away." Kenzo was in his manic mode, but he was glad to hear himself making a joke about something that had caused him so much misery.

"Don't be ridiculous," Chokatsu replied. "I'm not that much of a ladykiller... oops, pardon the pun. But seriously, what's the story? Why would anyone dismember a body and carry away the tattoo like that?"

"Ah, that *is* the question."

"Anyway, I'm glad I ran into you. I've been thinking about stopping by your place to say that I might have some information about the case. Why don't you come inside?"

Feeling as if he were boarding a ferryboat, Kenzo stepped across the raised threshold of Chokatsu's quaint little house. The entry hall was adorned with a large *matoi*—a sort of tubular banner carried aloft by firemen on parade. Inside the cozy, well-built cottage was a Shinto-style altar, replete with zigzag paper streamers and porcelain statues of foxes, which dominated the main room. The overall effect was like something out of a folk tale.

Kenzo mumbled the customary courtesies and Chokatsu replied in ritualistic kind, saying, "The place is a foul sty, but please make yourself at home."

Kenzo took a seat on the proffered cushion in front of an oblong hibachi brazier. Without wasting any more time on small talk, he said lightly, "I've seen your Benten Kozo tattoo plenty of times at the public bath, but I was wondering, when did you get it?"

"Let me see," mused Chokatsu. "I think it must have been fifteen or sixteen years ago when I got this tattoo from Horiuno the Second, over in Kanda."

"I've noticed that your tattoo doesn't have the artist's signature on it."

"Yeah, unfortunately, I ran out of funds shortly before the work was completed. After that my body forgot the taste of the needle, and the longer I waited the harder it was to go back."

"So you're saying you couldn't stand the pain?"

"Oh, sure, I won't pretend that wasn't part of it. I mean, you're letting someone poke your flesh with sharp needles, and shove pigments under the raw skin. No anaesthetics are used, so it isn't exactly a day at the beach. And during the entire process you're about half sick all the time, feeling nauseated and weak and running a fever for months at a time. I was still young in those days, and when I did get hold of some more money, instead of spending it inflicting pain on myself, I decided it would be a lot more enjoyable to use it to have some fun, if you know what I mean." Chokatsu held up his little finger in a gesture denoting romantic liaisons, then added, "The truth is, it wouldn't have taken that much more money or suffering to add the artist's signature, when I had come so far already, but in those days the authorities were being really strict about busting tattoo parlors. After a while it was just too much trouble to go back."

The fireman gave a carefree laugh, and Kenzo chose that moment to cast his line into the waters. "Say, Katsu, what is the information you mentioned?"

"Well, as you may know, Horiyasu, the father of the murdered Kinue Nomura, had two other children, and they were all tattooed. The eldest was a boy, Tsunetaro, and he had Jiraiya tattooed on his back. He became a tattoo artist himself, but he was fighting in the south and is listed as missing in action. Right?"

"Yes, I'd heard that," Kenzo said.

"Wait a minute," Chokatsu said. "Hey, O-Kané, come here!"

Wiping her hands on her apron, Chokatsu's wife O-Kané emerged from the kitchen. She was a plump-cheeked, white-skinned beauty in her late twenties who looked as if she might have been a geisha at one time. Given the whimsical folk-tale

188

atmosphere of the Goto household, Kenzo wouldn't have been surprised to discover that Chokatsu's wife had turned into a talking fox. He stole a surreptitious peek at her kimono hem, but there was no sign of the bushy russet tail that was the hallmark of fox-possession.

"Why, Mr. Matsushita, welcome," O-Kané said in a soft voice. "Please forgive me, I haven't even served you tea."

"Forget the tea, that can wait till later," Chokatsu snapped, in the time-honored manner of Japanese husbands. "Hey, listen, it's about the tattoo artist you've been going to in Shibuya."

O-Kané looked embarrassed by this sudden question. "Why, dear, what on earth are you thinking of, bringing up such a thing out of the blue, in front of Mr. Matsushita?"

"Hey, relax, all right? This is no time to be putting on airs. Remember that dismemberment murder in Kitazawa? Mr. Matsushita's brother is a police inspector, and he's having a lot of trouble trying to solve it."

"Is that so?" Looking first at Chokatsu, then at Kenzo, O-Kané pulled up a green zabuton cushion and sat down at the end of the low table. "Well, the tattoo artist I've been going to is called Tsune. I don't know his last name. He was in combat in the Philippines or somewhere, and he was recently repatriated. I believe he's only been back in Tokyo for about a month. He has a spectacular tattoo on his back of Jiraiya, the sorcerer."

When he heard those words, Kenzo felt like leaping to his feet and dancing around the room. He couldn't be absolutely certain that it was the same person, but the name fit, the tattoos matched, and tattoo artist wasn't exactly a run-of-the-mill occupation.

"Where is that tattoo artist now?" Kenzo asked eagerly. "Won't you please introduce me to him? If I could talk to him for a few minutes he might provide a clue to this case." He was so excited about the possibility of talking to Tsunetaro Nomura that he was practically shouting.

Chokatsu exchanged a worried look with his wife. "Well," he said slowly, "the thing is, from his point of view, business is business. I have a hunch that if you stage a frontal attack like that, he might simply refuse to talk."

"But why would he? I mean, his sister's been murdered!"

"That may be so, but that sort of fellow tends to be a bit paranoid about anything having to do with the police. Tattooing is still illegal, as you know. To tell the truth, that's why I've been hesitating about giving you this information. Look, how about this? How would it be if you went to see this guy as a private citizen, secretly, without saying anything to your brother at all?"

"Fine," Kenzo said, "let's do it that way. I'll just go on my own and see what happens. But I'll need the address."

"If you promise not to tell your brother, I'll be glad to take you there myself," O-Kané said, but Kenzo could hear the reluctance in her voice.

"I promise," Kenzo said. "Are you getting a tattoo as well, O-Kané?"

"Well, there's a design called Akaeboshi that my husband is very partial to. He's been bugging me forever to get that tattoo, and I always refused, but he finally just wore me down." O-Kané gave an embarrassed laugh.

"Actually," said Chokatsu, "the way it happened was, someone told me that this guy Tsune had only been back in Tokyo for a month or so, and he was already so sought after that he was turning potential clients away. Apparently his house burned down in an air raid, and he wasn't able to locate any of his relatives, so he's staying with a friend—a comrade-in-arms, as they say—who was with him on the southern front. He started doing tattoos as soon as he got settled, and pretty soon the word spread that his talent was something special. I happened to see one of the tattoos he had done. It was really spectacular. So I dragged O-Kané to his studio and asked him to tattoo her, and he agreed."

"I suppose it could be a case of mistaken identity, yet the similarities just seem too uncanny," Kenzo said. "In any case, I would be very grateful if you would take me to meet this man, this Tsune." He bowed so low that his eyebrows brushed the tatami, thinking all the while, *This is too good to be true.*

32

Kenzo and O-Kané took an express train to Shibuya, where they changed to the electric line for Aoyama. Outside Aoyama Station they turned onto a charred street where hastily built barracks sat right on top of the bombed-out ruins of homes and apartment buildings. Amid these makeshift dwellings were five or six simple eating-and-drinking places, lined up side by side. In front of one of the shabby little restaurants was a hand-lettered sign reading PEONY.

O-Kané stopped before the sign and whispered in Kenzo's ear. "It's in the rear of this building," she said. "Please wait here for a moment, okay? I'll go check out the situation." She went into the building, and returned several minutes later. "It's all right," she said. "He's working on a tattoo at the moment, but we can wait inside."

Nearly panting with excitement, Kenzo took a deep breath and ducked under the curtain of braided rope that hung above the entrance. Kenzo followed O-Kané through a small restaurant, crudely furnished with unmatched tables and chairs. Behind a muslin-curtained door at the rear was a step leading up to a dark, narrow hall. On one side were two medium-size sitting rooms, and on the other was a room with a closed door.

"Please, come in." A dark-complexioned woman who appeared to be the mistress of the house spoke to them in a friendly way, but Kenzo thought she cast a suspicious glance in his direction. He didn't care. He was as nervous and elated as if he had been on his way to a marriage meeting with the woman of his dreams.

Kenzo followed O-Kané into the larger of the two sitting rooms and sat down at the low table that was the room's only furnishing, aside from a vase of flowering weeds stuck into a rough alcove in one corner. From the other side of the flimsy paper doors, he could hear the *para-para* percussion of sharp needles perforating tender human flesh. There was also a rhythmic *haa-haa* sound, which he recognized after a moment as the shallow breathing of the person who inhabited that unanaesthetized flesh.

"He's tattooing a young woman right now," O-Kané said, leaning across the table to whisper in Kenzo's ear. "Shall we take a peek?"

"Wouldn't that be an intrusion, especially since it's a woman?"

"No, she won't mind. I know her quite well and believe me, she isn't the modest type." Laughing merrily at her little dig, O-Kané called into the closed room, "Sensei, hello! I'm going to peek in now, okay?"

A deep, pleasant male voice came from behind the closed doors. "Ah, O-Kané, you're early. I'm almost finished here. I'll be with you in a few minutes."

No sooner had the door slid open than Kenzo, in a state of extreme agitation, stuck his head through. As he had anticipated, the scene before him was so strange and wonderful that it nearly took his breath away.

One wall was hung with dark oil paintings, ambiguous Western-style landscapes in shades of green and bronze and lacquer-black, and in front of that moody backdrop a large number of cushions had been piled up to make an impromptu operating table. Lying face down on the cushions was a young woman of twenty-five or twenty-six. There was an underlying design of fish scales on her arms and back, which gave her the look of a two-legged mermaid. The pattern for those background tattoos was fully sketched in, and the shading phase had just begun.

The design was a magnificent rendition of the traditional pattern known as "The Mountain Road to Yoshino," the most famous blossom-viewing area in Japan. The woman's breasts, hips, and thighs were covered with delicate cherry blossoms. On her right shoulder the medieval dancer Shizuka Gozen was shown holding a small hand drum, while on the left shoulder was the folk hero Kitsune Tadanobu, "Tadanobu the Fox." Both designs were drawn with exquisite precision, and Kenzo could tell that he was looking at an exceptional work of art in the making.

This day's tattooing session was concentrated on the area of the right buttock. The woman had a blue polka-dotted bandanna in her mouth, like a gag, and she was biting down on it to keep from crying out. She was hugging a tubular pillow, while another pillow had been placed under the lower part of her body to elevate the work surface. Her eyes were closed as if in sleep, and she didn't seem to notice when Kenzo and O-Kané entered the room.

The tattoo artist sat cross-legged on a single cushion on the floor, his back to the door. Kenzo couldn't see the man's face, but he was able to observe the subtle movements of his hands. The artist used his right thumb and index finger to stretch the skin taut, and he held the brushes with his left index finger, middle finger, and ring finger. Using the widest part of his thumb as a lever, he pumped the bunch of fine needles in his right hand like a piston. Up and down they went, penetrating the skin and then popping out again. The motions made an almost train-like sound: *chaki-chaki, chaki-chaki, chaki-chaki.*

Each time the needles punctured her skin the woman would let out a strangulated gasp. Her entire body would twist and turn in pain, undulating from head to toe like a wave. The woman's naked body glistened with sweat, and every few moments a groan of agony escaped through the gag in her mouth.

Kenzo looked with interest at the tattooing tools. The bundle of thirty or so silk needles was held together by strips of pliable bamboo. Periodically the artist would dip the tips of the needles in ink and then continue tattooing without breaking the rhythm. He never went over the same spot twice, and it was clear even to an uneducated eye that to apply the shading so evenly required a phenomenal degree of technical skill and artistic finesse. Sometimes the excess ink overflowed the tiny perforations made by the needles and spread over the woman's milk-white skin. The artist would reach for a nearby cloth and blot the ink. As the area injected with blue-black ink grew larger, the flesh around the perforated skin began to swell and turn red.

Other parts of the woman's body, where the tattoos had already been completed, were covered with thin scabs. After four or five days this tissuey layer would peel off, and when the process had been repeated several times, the colored pigment would finally settle into the skin. The newly drawn lines on the woman's buttocks turned immediately into vivid red welts, while the entire shaded area was puffy and swollen. As a doctor, Kenzo knew that the woman would already be running a slight fever.

For thirty minutes Kenzo watched in fascination, hardly daring to take a breath. *Kinue went through this same process,* he thought, and his breathing quickened as he pictured his lover squirming in agony under the invasive needles. Kenzo couldn't help thinking that it was wasteful to expend so much effort on decorating one's mortal skin, but at the same time he felt there was something sublime and even awe-inspiring about a woman who would voluntarily endure so much pain.

Finally the tattooing session ended, and the young woman lay totally immobile, like a corpse. It wasn't until the tattoo artist placed a hot, wet towel on her fresh tattoos that she finally screamed, softly. A head-to-toe shudder animated her beautiful flesh, but she remained prone.

"That's it for today," said the tattoo master, as he smeared some soothing oil over the freshly tattooed area, which was about ten and a half centimeters, four inches square.

"Oh," said the woman limply. She raised her head for the first time and noticed that Kenzo was in the room. "O-Kané, you really are a rat sometimes," she muttered in an embarrassed tone of voice, but still she lay as motionless as a lavishly painted sculpture.

"We're finished here," the tattoo artist repeated. Slowly and painfully, the woman forced herself into a standing position. She was obviously not overjoyed to have an audience, but she bowed politely to Kenzo and O-Kané. Then, facing away from them, she pulled on a light kimono of blue-and-white cotton printed with a bamboo-leaf design. She sashed it loosely with a bright red obi, wincing as the crisp material brushed against her tender skin.

The tattoo artist wiped the sweat from his forehead with a polka-dotted *tenugui* bandanna. "I'm sorry to have kept you waiting," he said to O-Kané. He turned around at last, and Kenzo couldn't help gasping in amazement.

33

The tattoo artist was haggard from the suffering of war and internment, but Kenzo could see a clear genetic echo of Kinue's lovely face in the still-handsome features of this weary survivor. There was absolutely no question about it, this was the man from the photographs, the man with the Jiraiya tattoo. Kenzo swallowed, hard. He could hardly believe that he was standing face to face with Tsunetaro Nomura, in the flesh.

"This gentleman is Mr. Matsushita," O-Kané said, by way of introduction. "He has been very kind to my husband on many occasions. When he mentioned that he would like to see a tattoo artist at work, I brought him along."

"Oh, I see," said Tsunetaro brusquely. "Getting tattooed can be poison for a young person, you know." He glared at Kenzo.

"My name is Kenzo Matsushita," Kenzo said, "and I'm not really a candidate for a tattoo. I'm a graduate student at the medical school of Tokyo University. I just thought that I would like to observe a tattooing session, from the point of view of a scientist."

"You don't want to get too caught up in this world." Tsunetaro's voice was stern, but his facial expression had relaxed perceptibly. "I've seen it a hundred times. You may start off as an impartial observer, but tattooing is like narcotics. You become fascinated, then addicted, and the next thing you know you're ruining your own skin with ink and dyes." The tattoo artist's voice was filled with self-contempt.

"I'm certain I've seen your face before," Kenzo said, pursuing his own agenda. "Are you by any chance the son of the Horiyasu who used to live in the Honjo area?"

"That's right," said Tsunetaro warily. "I'm Horiyasu's son. Why?"

"You had a sister named Kinue, is that correct?"

"Yes, I do. Do you know where Kinue is now?" Tsunetaro asked almost breathlessly, not seeming to notice Kenzo's ominous use of the past tense.

"You haven't heard?" Kenzo said gently. "Kinue was murdered about two months ago, in Kitazawa."

Tsunetaro's mouth dropped open, and he stared at Kenzo in shocked amazement. The stick of sumi ink he had been grinding fell into the inkstone, and his eyes were filled with fear and disbelief. "Murdered? Kinue? Is that really true?"

"I wouldn't dream of joking about something like that," Kenzo replied.

"I see," said Tsunetaro slowly. "I've only been back in Tokyo for a month, and I haven't read the newspapers at all. I've been searching for both my sisters in my spare time, but with no luck at all. If you know any details, please tell me."

Kenzo knew all the details, of course, but he tried to be brief as he told Tsunetaro what had happened so far. In keeping with his agreement with Chokatsu, he omitted the fact that his brother was a police chief. As Kenzo spoke, Tsunetaro's face gradually clouded over with a curious expression of suspicion mixed with terror. "Those photographs that Kinue gave you—do you still have them, or were they confiscated by the police?" he asked when Kenzo had finished his narrative.

"The police made copies," said Kenzo. "I have the originals right here." He opened his briefcase and handed the envelope to Tsunetaro. As the tattoo artist looked at the photographs, his face was once again contorted with strong emotions.

"The three siblings of Jiraiya," he murmured, as if to himself. "The three tattooed children." After staring at the photographs for quite some time, Tsunetaro raised his bloodshot eyes. "Mr. Matsushita," he said, "this is a truly terrible crime."

"I know. It's so terrible that I sometimes think I can't bear it." Kenzo froze, hoping he hadn't given away his private feelings about Kinue, but no one seemed to have noticed.

"Still," said Tsunetaro, "I have a feeling that what I mean by 'terrible' is considerably different from what you mean when you use the same word. There's a lot more to this case than meets the eye. You people are only seeing what's on the surface. To put it bluntly, you've been conned."

"By the murderer?"

"Of course. In this case, there are layers upon layers of deception. If you persist in investigating only the apparent circumstances of the case, you'll never get anywhere."

"What do you mean by that?"

"The problem is with the patterns of the tattoos on the three of us, my two sisters and me. If I'm right about what happened, it's just too horrific to think about at this point. However, I will set you straight on one thing. Takezo Mogami didn't commit suicide. He was killed by the same person who killed my sister. There's absolutely no question in my mind about that."

Kenzo was flabbergasted and strangely excited, too. "How about it, Mr. Nomura, won't you consider telling me what you know about this case? I'm not asking out of curiosity, or personal ambition. The truth is, I didn't mention this earlier, but my brother is the chief of the investigative division of the Metropolitan Police. I can promise you that if you cooperate, nothing will happen to affect your business or your livelihood. I'll take full responsibility for that. Even if you don't get personally involved, the information you share with me could still result in the capture of your sister's enemies. Surely that's what you would want. Not only that, if you help us find the killer, then Kinue's soul will be able to rest in peace at last."

"I'll be glad to do what I can," Tsunetaro said. "But first there are a couple of things I need to check, just to make sure I'm not on the wrong track. For the next few days, would you not tell your brother about me?"

"I don't mind doing that at all. I just hope you'll keep in mind that you're dealing with a fiendish killer. On second thought, I really think it's too dangerous for you to do this alone. Won't you please let me go with you, and help?"

"No, I appreciate your offer, but please just leave this to me for a while. In return, I promise that the minute I'm able to confirm my suspicions, I'll let you know."

"Will you really be all right by yourself?"

"I just survived a major war," Tsunetaro said. "I'll be fine." His tone of voice made it clear that the discussion was at an end. Without saying another word he picked up his ink stick and continued grinding it on the wet, gleaming inkstone.

O-Kané was slipping out of her green plaid kimono. Kenzo didn't want to stare at her naked body, but out of the corner of his eye he could see that both arms were covered with stylized, shaded Chinese-style clouds, among which red-scaled dragons wound their way up and down her plump, rounded arms. Clearly she was nearing the end of the tattooing process. O-Kané lay down on her back and Tsunetaro bent intently over her, grasping his bundle of needles.

The previous client hadn't yet gone home. She stood off to one side, fully dressed, smoking a cigarette and staring at O-Kané's tattoo-in-progress. Kenzo timidly started a conversation. "Even though I'm a doctor, I can't help thinking that even a small tattoo would be very painful," he said. "I can't even imagine what it must be like to get tattooed over your entire body?"

"Mmm, the truth is, there are times when I just want to jump up and run away, it hurts so much. The first time I felt the ink going into my virgin skin I thought, 'I simply can't go on with this,' but recently I've pretty much gotten used to it. In fact, I've felt more pain at the dentist's when he drilled my teeth without an anaesthetic." The woman made a face. She wasn't a beauty by any means, with her moon-shaped face and stubby nose, but she had an engaging smile and an amiable, vivacious manner.

"It must take a lot of time to get elaborate designs like these," Kenzo said, gesturing vaguely around the room. He still felt a little shy about having seen this attractive stranger with all her clothes off.

"You can say that again," said the woman. "I had the lines drawn on during the war, but I had to quit halfway through. Everyone who saw my unfinished tattoo at the public bath said that it looked really ugly and pitiful, so recently I decided to start again. If I had stuck with it without interruption, the process would probably have taken about three months."

"Oh, really? It must be a big decision to choose the design, since it isn't like a kimono that you can take off when you want a change. And you can't see the major part of the design yourself, unless you look in a mirror."

"That's true," said the woman. "But the really crucial thing with a tattoo is to find a skilled and talented artist, like Tsune here, to do the work. How about it, as long as you're here? Won't you get a tattoo, too, just a teensy little one?"

"Don't be absurd!" Instinctively, Kenzo crossed his hands across his chest, as if to protect his unsullied skin from the dreaded needles.

The woman burst out laughing, covering her open mouth with her hand. "I'm only joking," she said. "That wasn't in very good taste, was it? The truth is, I'm so fervent about tattoos that I want everyone to get one. When I see a woman with a beautiful body at the public bath, I can't help thinking that she'd look even better if she were completely covered with tattoos. Isn't that awful? As if it was any of my business."

Kenzo had taken an immediate liking to this outspoken tattooed woman. Quite aside from his ulterior motive of hoping to learn something more about the intriguing world of the art tattoo, he found her frankness refreshing, and he was disarmed by her sunny disposition.

"I don't think it's so awful, at all," said Kenzo. He suddenly realized that he was flirting for the first time since that enchanted evening with Kinue. "But of course there's a big difference between painting on canvas or paper and painting on living human skin. Even if you carved the same design onto two people, it would turn out differently depending on whether they were fat or thin, squat or lanky. There really are a lot of factors to consider in creating an individual design. And if the artist makes a mistake on a tattoo, he can't very well go back and do it over!"

"I suppose that's where the tattoo artist proves his mettle," the woman said. "And there are some preliminaries. First you choose the design from the flash—the designs drawn on paper—and then the artist sketches it on your body with erasable ink. He doesn't start to put the ink under the skin until you're absolutely certain that's the design you want." There was a folio filled with rough sketches for tattoo designs lying nearby. She picked it up. "Take a look at this," she said, handing the book to Kenzo.

It was oversized, bound in the Japanese style, and filled with sheets of translucent rice paper on which were drawn innumerable designs for tattoos. They resembled *nishiki-e,* the colorful genre paintings called "brocade-pictures." Viewed as individual works of art, the sketches were nothing out of the ordinary, more like *art naïf* than the work of a professional draftsman. Looking at the flash for the first time, Kenzo found it astonishing that such mediocre sketches could be transformed into designs that seemed to take on a vivid, animated life of their own when applied to living skin.

"Still," Kenzo said, trotting out his favorite black-humor joke, "it might be better if your tattoo doesn't turn out to be *too* gorgeous. Someone might try to steal your skin."

The woman looked a bit shocked but showed her even, white teeth in a polite little laugh before remembering to clap her hand over her mouth. "You're right, I suppose," she said slowly, from behind her fingers.

Just then, O-Kané's tattooing session came to an end. "I'm sorry to have kept you waiting," she said. Unlike the other woman, O-Kané didn't appear to be in any pain as she shrugged into her green kimono and belted it with a mustard-yellow obi.

Kenzo felt reluctant to say good-bye to Tsunetaro. Finally, after repeating over and over like an overprotective mother, "Please don't take any unnecessary risks," he allowed O-Kané to drag him away from the tattoo studio. Just before they went their separate ways at Shibuya Station, O-Kané warned Kenzo once again.

"Mr. Matsushita," she said politely but emphatically, "Tsune seems to know something about who committed this crime, and it would certainly be fine if he could be of some help in the investigation. But please remember that his tattoo business is the only thing he has. Please do as he asked and keep this a secret from your brother until the very end. If the police find out about him, he would be in really big trouble."

"Don't worry," said Kenzo solemnly. "A promise is sacred, and until Tsunetaro gives me the go-ahead, I won't say a single word to my brother about him." Thinking about how pleased his brother Daiyu would be when he learned about this break in the case, Kenzo couldn't help smiling in anticipation.

34

A few moments after Kenzo and O-Kané had departed, the woman with the Shizuka Gozen tattoo slipped into her wooden *geta* clogs and left the tattoo studio. She turned at Shibuya Station and walked for a while along the electric-train tracks, then slipped down a narrow alley next to the police station. A ramshackle rooming house stood alone among the burned-out ruins of the neighborhood. The woman pushed open the latticework gate and went clattering up to the second floor, with her clogs making a *ton-ton* sound on the wooden stairs.

"Is that you, O-Kimi?" a rusty-sounding male voice called out. The woman slid open the tattered paper door. Inside, a half-naked tattooed man of about forty lay sprawled on the tatami-matted floor, reading a tabloid newspaper.

"Hello, sweetheart," said the woman happily. "I didn't think you'd be home yet."

"Where've you been?" the man asked in his rough voice. There was a scar on his chin, like an off-center cleft, and his hair was extremely short.

"Oh, I've just been taking off my clothes in front of strange men," she teased.

"Really?" growled the man.

"Yes, really. Are you jealous? You're such a silly man." The woman laughed, showing her dazzling white teeth. "I've only been to my tattoo session. Didn't we agree that the only men who get to see me naked, besides you, are my doctor and the tattoo artist?"

"Oh, right." Sulkily, the man sat up. "So what part of your body did the great artist work on today?"

Gingerly the woman got down on one knee, then eased her sore body into a sitting position on the floor. "I'll show you in a minute," she said. "Just let me catch my breath."

From below there came the sound of the wooden gate creaking open, followed by muffled conversation. After a moment, the landlady's voice called out, "O-Kimi! Can you come down for a minute?"

"I'm coming," said the woman. She slowly got to her feet and descended the staircase with tentative, shuffling steps. A few minutes later, she limped back into the room. "Darling, there's a strange man who wants to see you."

"Who is he? What does he want?" The tattooed man looked alarmed.

"His name's Heishiro Hayakawa, and he claims to be doing research about tattoos. He says he heard that we both had marvelous tattoos, and that's why he stopped by. He called us an 'honorable couple,' isn't that a scream? Anyway, he says he'd like to have a few words with us about preserving our tattoos for posterity."

"Heishiro Hayakawa, huh? He's the one they call Dr. Tattoo, because he's always sniffing around, trying to buy people's skins before they die. I've heard that he's obsessed with getting his hands on a Horiyasu, like mine. Aside from my parole officer, I really can't think of anyone I'd rather talk to less right now. Tell him this..." The man began talking in a comical high-pitched voice, using feminine language and an impudent tone of mock-politeness: "'I'm terribly sorry, kind sir, but both my husband and myself are totally inarticulate, so there's really no point in talking to us. We went through a lot of pain and suffering to obtain our marvelous tattoos, and we don't have the slightest interest in showing them off to some snoopy stranger. So while we're greatly honored by your gracious visit, we'd appreciate it very much if you'd put an egg in your shoe and beat it.' Is that polite enough, do you think?" the man asked, lapsing into his normal raspy voice.

The woman giggled. "You're awful," she said adoringly. "But listen to this—he wants to know who did our tattoos! He asked me at least three times, 'Who were the artists who carved your tattoos?'"

"There's no reason why you should give him that information. Go back down and tell him to get lost, and then throw some salt on the doorstep to purify it after he leaves."

"All right," said O-Kimi. A few minutes later, she returned to the second-floor apartment, still brushing the salt from her fingers. She opened the glass window and peered down at the street.

"You know, sweetheart," she said, "that guy really gives me the creeps. He's still standing there, right where I left him."

Just then the professor, who was indeed loitering at the entrance to the narrow alley, looked up, caught O-Kimi's eye, and gave her a jaunty, purposeful little salute.

O-Kimi banged the window down. "He's up to no good, that one," she said.

"Shut up and show me your new tattoos," ordered the man with the scar. O-Kimi obediently unsashed her kimono and let it drop to the floor, wincing slightly as the cloth brushed her newly embellished buttocks.

35

Kenzo spent the next few days on an emotional roller coaster. Sometimes he felt on the verge of solving the case, and his heart would swell with hope. Other days he would think it was the height of hubris to imagine that he, Kenzo Matsushita, could solve a case that had stumped the detectives of a great police force, and he was consumed with despair. He moped about, reading mystery novels and snacking compulsively. Every time the telephone rang he would leap to answer it, only to slink back to his room in disappointment when it turned out to be one of his sister-in-law's pupils calling to reschedule a piano lesson.

On the morning of the tenth day, Kenzo began to think that Tsunetaro might have forgotten their agreement. Unable to sit still, he made two or three trips to the Peony Restaurant in Shibuya, but the tattoo artist was invariably out. Then, late that same evening, as Kenzo was lolling glumly about in his room eating black-market Hershey Bars and reading *The Three Coffins* by John Dickson Carr, the phone call finally came.

"Mr. Matsushita, this is Tsunetaro Nomura. I know the truth now." Tsunetaro's voice was so filled with emotion that it was frightening. Kenzo couldn't believe his ears.

"What did you say?" he asked.

"I said, I know who killed my sister and Takezo. It's just as I thought, after all."

"Really?" Kenzo had been so caught up in his own fantasies about solving the case by himself that his first reaction to this stunning revelation, oddly enough, was a sense of disappointment. "That's really good news," he said halfheartedly. "Really, it is. But tell me, who is the murderer?"

"I can't talk about that right now." Tsunetaro sounded nervous, as if someone might be listening in.

"Why is that? Oh, I see, now that you mention it, this really isn't the sort of thing you can discuss on the telephone. Where are you now, at Peony? I'll come to meet you right away."

"No, there's no point in doing that. Even if you came over here, I couldn't tell you any more than I have already."

"But you said…"

"Please wait for three more days. If those three days pass without incident, I'll tell you everything I know, I promise. But until that time, no matter what happens, I can't say another word on this subject."

"Why is that? Why do you want me to wait three days? Why can't you just tell me right now?" Kenzo hated the way his voice sounded, high-pitched and boyish and hysterical, but he had no control over himself at that moment.

"It simply isn't possible. I can't explain now, but it's taken a lot of effort to get this far, and I just have to ask you to respect my wishes. I'm begging you, please wait three more days." Tsunetaro hung up abruptly, without saying good-bye.

Kenzo stood stunned, still holding the receiver to his ear. He could sense a vague feeling of unease rising in his chest, filling his heart with dread. Why did Tsunetaro want him to wait three more days? Why couldn't he have told him right now? Was Tsunetaro plotting vengeance?

Tsunetaro's behavior was like Kinue's—full of secrets and foreboding. Her life had ended before Kenzo had a chance to make love to her again, or to be the protector she had asked him to be. And now her brother Tsunetaro was acting exactly the same way.

Kenzo's heart was pounding as he recalled his first glimpse of Kinue's dismembered body, and he trembled with fear at the thought that a similar fate might await her likable, talented brother. *Oh dear,* he thought, *this is a real mess. Maybe I should just go ahead and tell my brother the whole story, and ask for his advice.* But then he decided that he would have to keep it to himself, after all.

Still holding the telephone receiver, which was now emitting an indignant beeping sound, Kenzo took a deep breath. "You have to stop stewing about this," he ordered himself sternly. "You need to assume that Tsunetaro knows what he's doing. It's only a matter of waiting three more days. Unlike his poor defenseless sister, Tsunetaro should be able to protect himself."

Having convinced himself that there was no cause for concern, Kenzo hung up the telephone. He went into the narrow, immaculate kitchen and helped himself to a bottle of Kinn beer and a bag of dried shrimp, then climbed the steep stairs to his tiny bachelor room.

36

"Banzai! Banzai! Banzai!" Late the following night, in the usually solemn war room of the Metropolitan Police Department of Investigation, a great cheer went up from the detectives who were working overtime, as they learned of an unexpected harvest. The prime suspect for whom they had been searching, Ryokichi Usui, had finally fallen into their hands.

Just after 11 P.M., in Chihaya Town in the Toshima district, Usui—Kinue Nomura's former lover, the photographer turned small-time crook—had been spotted leaving a private house after a break-in. An emergency police squad was summoned to the scene by a silent alarm. They gave chase on foot and ended up cornering Usui in the Ikebukuro black-market area, where they made the arrest and recovered the cash stolen from the house.

At first, the arresting officers thought they had just caught an insignificant and not terribly competent sneak thief. They were surprised and excited to learn that Ryokichi Usui was on the national Most Wanted list, being sought as a possible suspect in the now-famous Tattoo Murder Case. The prisoner was transported to the Metropolitan Police Headquarters without delay, and the questioning began the next morning.

When Detective Chief Inspector Daiyu Matsushita saw Ryokichi Usui's face, he couldn't help feeling disappointed. Usui was handsome in a brutish way, with sharp features, thick eyebrows, piercing eyes, and a knife scar across his chin. Until then the chief had seen only Usui's mug shots and he had thought those glittering eyes might denote intelligence, but now that the man stood before him in person

Daiyu knew instinctively that he wasn't looking at a criminal mastermind.

Assistant Inspector Shinohara undertook the interrogation with his usual thoroughness. He explored every angle and connection, and obtained a lengthy statement from Usui. By the time he was finished, Shinohara had unearthed a number of potentially useful facts.

When Usui was released from prison, he had begun searching for Kinue so he could carry out the plan of revenge he had been formulating during his years behind bars. Eventually he heard from an underworld contact in Yokohama that Kinue had split up with Takezo after Usui went to prison, and had subsequently ruined herself with dissolute living. Of course, that bit of grapevine intelligence was completely inaccurate, but at the time Usui had no way of knowing this.

Disappointed, he returned to Tokyo, where he supported himself by buying and selling American goods on the black market. After a while, an intriguing rumor reached his ears. Someone told him that Kinue Nomura had been seen plying her trade among the women of darkness somewhere around Yurakucho or Shinbashi. He immediately rushed over there, taking with him an old photograph of Kinue which he had taken just after she got her tattoo. One or two of the prostitutes said they remembered the face, although no one had seen any tattoos. The woman evidently had worked the streets for a short time, then disappeared without a word to anyone. That sort of behavior was nothing unusual in the floating world of prostitution, and she was soon forgotten.

The trail was stone cold, but Usui wasn't giving up yet. His obsession with finding Kinue was fueled half by desire, half by anger at her for sending him to prison, and he became almost demonic in his single-mindedness. (He did, however, find

212

time to strike up a relationship with a young tattooed woman named O-Kimi, who worked in a bar near his apartment.) In his spare time, when Usui wasn't engaged in burglary or in some shady moneymaking scheme, he searched for Kinue all over the city.

In the latter part of August he finally found her. Usui had gone to Shibuya to deliver some black-market watches purportedly made by the American company Timex, although for some mysterious reason the name on the watch face was spelled "Timox." He was loitering around the station when he spotted Kinue passing by, carrying several shopping bags from an exclusive kimono shop.

Usui followed his prey, being careful to stay in the shadows of the buildings and war ruins along the way. Fortunately the streets were very crowded, so Kinue didn't notice him creeping along a few paces behind. She boarded a train, and Usui actually managed to follow her all the way home to Kitazawa without being detected.

Watching the house every day, waiting for the chance to wreak his revenge, Usui bided his time. His anger was intensified by seeing Takezo Mogami coming and going with easy familiarity, and he resolved to beat the stuffing out of the so-called informant who had told him that Takezo and Kinue were no longer an item. Finally, on the night of August 27, Usui was ready. When darkness fell, he hid in the shrubbery near Kinue's house and assessed the situation. He knew from long years of experience that he would have a better chance of success if he broke into the house in the early evening rather than waiting until late at night.

Around 8:40, Kinue emerged from a neighbor's house dressed in a casual summer kimono and carrying a small wooden bucket, from which Usui deduced that she was on her way home from the public bath. Then, as if she had noticed that something was wrong, she stood for a moment with her hand on the garden gate and glared in the direction of Usui's hiding place before going inside. At that inopportune moment a policeman approached on foot from the opposite direction. Usui was startled but, affecting a casual demeanor, he left his hiding place and walked around the neighborhood for twenty minutes or so.

At around nine o'clock he returned to his former spot, only to discover a new hitch in his plans. The second floor of the house next door was now a blaze of lights. Some university students were sitting by the open full-length windows, playing the guitar and looking down on the area directly in front of Kinue's gate. Usui wandered around impatiently for the next two hours, watching the neighbor's house from a distance. Around eleven o'clock the upstairs lights were finally turned off, but just as Usui was about to act, a man came walking along the street and vanished into Kinue's house. It was pitch dark and there were no streetlights, so Usui couldn't see the man's face clearly—although he did get the impression that he wasn't all that young.

By then, Usui was sorely tempted to call it a night. Fate did not seem to be smiling on his little enterprise. Not once but three times he had gotten an unlucky break, and he was beginning to think this night might be jinxed. Usui was a superstitious man and he hadn't rushed into his plan without first checking the omens. Everything had indicated that today would be a lucky day for him, and the extremely auspicious fortune-paper he had bought at the Asakusa Kannon Temple earlier that day, which practically guaranteed success in anything short of a trip to the moon, had further bolstered his confidence.

So he wasn't quite ready to give up. For another hour he waited, concealed in the thick shrubbery across the street. Suddenly the other man came rushing out of Kinue's gate, his face as pale as if he had seen a ghost, and went charging off in the direction of the train station. There was nothing in the man's hands, so he obviously wasn't a rival burglar. His behavior was very strange, though, and Usui wondered what had happened inside.

If I fail this time I may never get another chance, he thought as he crept quietly into the garden. The storm shutters had not been closed. He found that a bit surprising but figured that Kinue had left them open on purpose because it was so hot. "Finally, a stroke of luck!" he muttered as he slipped into the house through an open window.

There was no sign of activity inside, and Kinue Nomura was nowhere to be seen. Usui ran feverishly through the rooms, searching for the object of his love and his hatred. He couldn't find her anywhere. At last he gave up his fantasy of seducing Kinue by force and reverted to being a sneak thief. He ransacked the *tansu* chests, drawer by drawer, filling a large furoshiki cloth with garments that could be resold to foreigners—mostly American soldiers—who were living in Japan. The truth was, rather than such troublesome, easily traceable goods, he had been hoping to find some hard cash lying around, but he didn't find so much as a five-yen coin.

He noticed that the light was on in the bathroom and the water running. He knocked on the door, and when there was no response, he assumed no one was inside, so he switched off the light from outside. Usui left then, carrying his sack of stolen clothes on his back. When he read in the newspaper the next day that Kinue's body had been found in the bathroom he was so surprised that his mouth dropped open, and, as he

215

put it, it was a very long time before he could get it properly closed again.

When he had finished reading through the thick folder containing Usui's sworn statement, Daiyu Matsushita raised his eyes and looked at Assistant Inspector Shinohara. "What do you think?" he asked. "Is this guy on the level?"

"I believe so," Shinohara responded in a confident tone. "He may be a lowlife scum-of-the-earth burglar, but I don't think he's a liar. In fact, he's been unexpectedly docile and cooperative. If I had thought he was lying, I wouldn't have prepared his statement." Shinohara gestured at the bulky file that lay on the table in front of the chief. "The only problem is, we're not certain what he was doing at eight o'clock, but since Kinue was still alive at that time, it isn't really a crucial point. From then on his testimony is in complete accordance with that of Gifu Inazawa. No discrepancies at all."

"That's certainly true. In fact, their testimonies are so identical that it bothers me. It could mean that they're telling the truth." Daiyu gave a wry smile.

Shinohara smiled back at the chief. "Well," he said, "fortunately we caught Usui in the act of committing larceny and we can bind him over for that. So at least we don't have to worry about him slipping through our fingers."

"Yes, but I really doubt that he's our man in this murder. I simply don't think he'd be able to pull off anything as clever as that locked-room trick. If we had found the body strangled or stabbed with a knife, then Usui would definitely be a suspect, but frankly, I think he's more of a dim bulb than an evil genius."

"There's one rather interesting thing in his statement," Inspector Shinohara said. "What do you make of this prostitute who supposedly resembles Kinue Nomura?"

216

"One thing seems certain, it wasn't Kinue. True, she was a rather licentious woman, but she was busy with other things."

"Suppose Kinue's sister survived somehow, and returned to Tokyo?"

"Most likely it was just someone who happened to look like the Nomura sisters. I mean, we've all seen strangers who look like someone we know, right?"

Shinohara nodded. "That's probably it," he said.

"Still, we can't afford to leave any lead unexplored," Daiyu said. "Assign someone to check it out, would you?" Inspector Shinohara saluted and left the room.

Daiyu Matsushita looked at the Tattoo Murder Case folders scattered on his desk and let out an enormous sigh. "What a mess," he said. "What a bloody, blasted mess."

37

It was just past six thirty, and the ruined city of Tokyo was already wrapped in the dark cloak of a moonless night. Outside the small Shibuya eatery called Peony, an unusual-looking woman was pacing back and forth. Two or three times she started to enter the restaurant, but each time she hesitated at the door, then withdrew.

Finally, with an air of resolution, she ducked under the braided rope curtain that covered the top part of the sliding doors and called out in a low voice, "Excuse me, but do you by any chance have a person by the name of Tsunetaro Nomura living here?"

The woman was quite well dressed. She wore a black kimono, and a black shawl was draped around her head and shoulders, even though it was a bit early in the autumn to be wearing such a dark color. When she raised her arms to push aside the rope curtain, it could be seen through the openings in her kimono sleeves that both her arms were wrapped in white surgical bandages from below the elbow to the wrist.

"Tsunetaro? He's here, all right," the owner of the restaurant answered casually. She was busily wiping the tables with a damp cloth, although the place had no customers at all. "He's been away for the past ten days or so, but he finally came back last night. He said he was making some house calls, or something." The proprietor lowered her voice confidentially. "Did you want to have something done, too?"

Surely there was only one reason why a woman would come alone to call on a tattoo artist. The restaurant owner prided herself on being a good judge of character, and of appearances, and she could tell from her costume and bearing that this woman didn't live in the straight world. The bandages, she was sure, must be covering a multitude of tattoos.

"No," the stranger replied coolly, "I just came to talk to him about something."

"Well… he's in the back right now, so please come in."

"I'm sorry to trouble you, but could you kindly ask him to come out here?"

What a strange request, thought the landlady, but she asked politely, "And what is your name, please?"

"That's not important. If he sees me he'll understand right away."

The landlady found the woman's behavior rather odd, but since it was getting close to the hour when her restaurant would suddenly be mobbed with customers, her mind was on other things. She called his name into the back of the shop, and Tsunetaro appeared.

"A female visitor? For me?" he asked. With an air of agitation, he slipped on his *geta* and rushed outside. Standing near the alley, Tsunetaro had a brief whispered conversation with the mysterious woman in black. Then, his face gone suddenly pale, he hurried back into the building and went straight to his own room.

A few minutes later he emerged again, and the landlady noticed that he had changed into the khaki-colored uniform of a demobilized soldier. "Are you going out again?" she asked.

"Mmm-hmm," he said distractedly.

"Are you going to make a house call?" Even as she asked that question, she realized that he wasn't carrying any of his tattooing tools. "Oh, I see," she said coquettishly, "you're going out to have a good time."

"Don't be ridiculous," Tsunetaro said sharply. He looked suddenly as if he might be about to cry. "It isn't something frivolous like that. This is really a terrible world, you know that? I mean first we got our asses kicked in the war, and even though I was happy to come back to Japan in one piece, things have turned out pretty miserably since then. You know the old Confucian saying, the one about divided loyalties? Well, I'm living the truth of that right now, and it makes it difficult to try to do the right thing. Whoever invented the term *ukiyo*— floating world—knew what he was talking about. It's like they say: Life is hell."

On the shelf above the counter was a row of whiskey bottles, each bearing the name of a customer. Tsunetaro reached up and took down a bottle of Castory whiskey with his name on it, poured a shot into a small glass, and drained it in one gulp. Then, without saying another word, he went outside and walked away with the woman in black, so close that their shoulders were almost touching.

38

Later that same night, Daiyu Matsushita returned home from work to find his younger brother grinning from ear to ear. This was a surprise, since Kenzo had been downcast for the past week and a half.

"You're looking absurdly cheerful, for a change," Daiyu said. "Did you find a wallet full of cash on the way home, or what?"

"Actually," Kenzo said, smiling even more broadly, "something rather good seems to have happened."

"What's that?"

"Unfortunately, it's a secret, and I've sworn on my honor not to reveal it."

"So, what? Did the daughter of a millionaire fall in love with you or something?"

"Hardly! Who would fall in love with a bum like me?" The brothers looked at each other and laughed out loud. After a moment Kenzo said with a suddenly serious face, "By the way, whatever happened with Usui?"

"Oh, yeah, speaking of bums. Well, we just finished the preliminary investigation." Daiyu proceeded to summarize the interrogation of Ryokichi Usui.

"So that's his story," Kenzo said when his brother paused.

"Kenzo, tell me honestly, what do you think?"

"Well, on the surface at least, Usui's story seems to hold together. He sounds like a nasty piece of work, and I'm sure he wouldn't hesitate to stab someone to death or strangle somebody with a kimono sash. I don't think he would be capable of anything much more sophisticated than that, though

I certainly don't see him pulling a stunt like dismembering a body and then leaving parts of it locked in a room."

"That's exactly the same conclusion I came to. But the really maddening thing is that Usui was our prime suspect. Now that we've pretty much eliminated him, we don't have a clue who the murderer really is."

"Why is that?"

"Well, Takezo Mogami is dead, and there isn't a shred of hard evidence that he killed Kinue Nomura. Hisashi Mogami has a perfect alibi from nine o'clock on. Gifu Inazawa was seen leaving the house empty-handed, so he couldn't have made off with the torso. The most suspicious person would seem to be Professor Hayakawa, because we know he didn't get home until just before midnight. However, no one left the Nomura house between nine and twelve. Damn. Oh well, at least we found out why the light was off in the bathroom. Usui switched it off.

"There seems to be no problem with Inazawa's statement. So the question becomes, when did the killer escape? Somehow, in the very small gap between eight forty and nine o'clock, the murderer managed to kill someone, dismember the body, and escape with the torso, leaving the bathroom locked behind him. Even if we're talking about some evil genius, that simply doesn't seem possible. So let's assume the killer was Takezo Mogami, and he was hiding somewhere in the house after killing Kinue. Then when Usui came sneaking in, Mogami grabbed the torso and made his escape while Usui was prowling around in the dark. I really don't see any other possible explanation, do you?"

Kenzo felt trapped. Even when confronted by Daiyu, who combined the authority of an elder brother with that of a chief of detectives, he still couldn't persuade himself that it would be all right to break his promise to Tsunetaro. Not knowing what else to do, Kenzo gently nudged the conversation in another direction. "What about the prostitute who was seen in Yurakucho? Who on earth could she be?" he asked.

"Well, the only thing we know for sure is that she wasn't Kinue," his brother replied, exhaling a smoke ring shaped like a *hyotan* gourd.

"So what does that mean?"

"Oh, I see, you're trying to drag Kinue's dead sister into the picture again. Even if she managed by some miracle to survive the A-bomb, my instinct tells me she isn't involved in this case."

"Then who was the mystery woman? What about the photographic plate with a picture of the Tsunedahime tattoos on it and the pictures in the envelope Kinue sent to me before she died? They must have some significance."

"What on earth are you getting at? Surely you aren't going to tell me that the two tattoos, Orochimaru and Tsunedahime, got into some sort of a supernatural battle, and the slug melted the snake?"

"No, I'm not saying anything of the sort. Never mind. It's just that I have a feeling everything will be revealed in the next few days."

"Hey, hey, hey! Don't talk so big! What are you trying to do, show me up in my own line of work? Seriously, though, do you have some sort of clue, or is it just a hunch?"

"A little of both," Kenzo said cagily.

"What is it? Tell me!" His brother leaned forward across the table with an intense expression on his face. His cigarette hung from his lower lip, momentarily forgotten.

"It's that… you know." Laughing as if it had all been a joke, Kenzo pointed at the framed calligraphy that was hanging from the lintel joist. The characters had been written by the prewar home minister, Kenzo Adachi, in a facile, fluent hand.

Kyakka Shoko: "The answer is right before your eyes."

39

Kenzo woke up very early the next morning in a highly optimistic mood. He felt certain that the Tattoo Murder Case would be solved in the next day or so, and he would be a hero. As he lay in bed savoring this feeling of anticipation and well-being, Kenzo heard his brother shouting on the telephone downstairs.

"Hey, what is this, some kind of a lousy joke? You're telling me that the victim is a naked male, and his skin has been peeled off? This is too much." Daiyu put his hand over the receiver and let out a groan. Then, snapping into super-efficient detective-chief-inspector style, he said, "Right, I'm on my way." As usual, he slammed the telephone down without saying good-bye.

"What's going on?" Kenzo stood in the hall, sleepily rubbing his eyes.

"Mmm," said his brother distractedly, as he lit his first cigarette of the day. "They've just found the body of a man in a burnt-out building in Yoyogi. The weird thing is that the skin has been removed from his torso, and his arms, and his thighs."

"Do you think that could be because he was tattooed all over?" Kenzo asked, struggling to remain calm. After all, Tokyo was full of tattooed men.

"I hadn't thought of that," Daiyu said. "Maybe this could have something to do with the other case. Do you want to come along?" His tone was oddly urgent.

Kenzo's mind was in turmoil, but he nodded his assent. The two brothers rushed back to their respective rooms and quickly jumped into their street clothes, then set off for Yoyogi.

The place where the body had been found was a ten-minute walk from Yoyogi Station. After leaving the main street and walking for five minutes or so along a narrow alley, the brothers came to the crime scene. It was a half-collapsed building of red brick, set back fifteen or sixteen feet from the curb. The concrete walls made it difficult to see inside, but some urchins playing hide-and-seek had stumbled upon the body by the first light of morning. If not for the children, the crime might have gone undiscovered for weeks.

The naked corpse was lying face down on the dirt floor inside the ruined building. It was wrapped in straw matting, with the head sticking out at one end. Trembling with fear and dread, Kenzo bent down to look at the face. "Oh my God," he moaned, "it's him." He staggered off to the other side of the building and slumped against a wall, feeling as if he might vomit.

"Kenzo, what's wrong? Pull yourself together." Daiyu Matsushita grabbed his brother by the shoulders and shook him roughly. "Kenzo!"

Kenzo stood up straight and struggled to compose his face, but Daiyu continued to glare at him. "What's with you, anyway? For God's sake, you're supposed to be a forensic doctor, not some squeamish schoolboy! Doctors aren't supposed to fall apart at the sight of a dead body! If you're feeling ill, why don't you go home and get some rest?" The words sounded solicitous, but Daiyu's tone was devastating.

"Don't give me that condescending bullshit!" Kenzo bellowed. All the police officers and forensics experts stopped what they were doing and looked up in surprise. "You don't understand," Kenzo went on in a small voice. "Something really terrible has happened here. I know who this is. This man... this corpse... this is Kinue Nomura's older brother, Tsunetaro Nomura!"

225

40

Everyone in the building gasped and stared at each other in astonishment, as if they had heard Kenzo's words but couldn't quite grasp the meaning. In the next instant, the chief of detectives turned on his younger brother, his face flushed with anger.

"How the hell do you know this is Tsunetaro Nomura?" Daiyu demanded, shaking Kenzo's upper body with so much force that his teeth seemed to rattle. "Quickly, quickly, tell me everything you know."

As Kenzo tried frantically to marshal his thoughts, he was acutely aware that this was one of the lowest, most miserable moments of his life. He took a deep breath and blinked back his tears. Then, making the story as concise as he could, Kenzo related his experiences with Tsunetaro in a trembling voice. When he had finished, his brother exploded in such violent wrath that Kenzo felt as if he had been struck by a thunderbolt.

"You stupid idiot! What the hell did you think you were doing! How dare you withhold something so important from me! Goddamn son of a bitch! Stupid little brat! Thanks to your incompetent interference, this case is even more screwed up than it was before! Damn, damn, damn!" Daiyu Matsushita pounded the nearest wall with all his might, and loose plaster flew in every direction.

"I'm sorry, I'm sorry, I'm so very, very sorry," Kenzo cried, involuntarily throwing himself on the ground at his brother's feet. "I was completely wrong, and I don't know how to apologize. I wish I were dead." Kenzo burst into tears of grief and shame. After a few minutes, as he continued to grovel in the dirt begging incoherently for forgiveness, the tears turned into dry heaves.

For a moment or two, Daiyu Matsushita stared at the abject form of his younger brother with a stupefied expression. A second later, though, he seemed once again to be filled with his usual dauntless fighting spirit, and he turned to Officer Akita and began barking out orders. "Go check out Shibuya! Find out everything you can about the victim's movements until now!"

Without pausing for discussion, Officer Akita gave a quick salute and dashed out the door. Daiyu immediately turned his attention to the forensics expert in charge of the crime scene. "How many hours has it been since the time of death, can you tell?" he asked in a calm, professional manner.

"We're probably looking at fifteen or sixteen hours," the forensic pathologist responded. He was a thin, sober-faced man in a white lab coat.

"So that means the crime was committed last night around six or seven P.M.?"

"That would appear to be the case."

"And what was the cause of death?"

"The body has the symptoms of some sort of prussic acid poisoning, but we won't be able to verify that until an autopsy has been performed."

"There probably isn't much traffic in this area at night, is there?"

"Almost none, apparently."

"And would an amateur be able to remove the skin this way?" Daiyu Matsushita tweaked aside a corner of the straw matting that covered the desecrated body of Tsunetaro Nomura, and winced in spite of himself.

"I wouldn't go so far as to say that one would have to be a professional to remove the skin from a body like this. However, I don't happen to think this crime was committed by a sheer amateur. I would guess that the person has some degree of basic scientific training, and I also think he must have better than average digital dexterity and hand-eye coordination."

"And how long do you think it would have taken to strip off the skin?"

"Probably about an hour."

"In that case, the victim was probably poisoned somewhere else. The dead body was then brought to this burned-out building, where the skin was removed. It hardly seems likely that the skin would have been removed at another location and the body brought here afterward, does it?"

"That's correct. If they had tried to move the body soon after such a radical operation was performed, there's no way they could have coped with all the blood."

"But why on earth would the killer have wanted to take the tattooed skin? The face is completely unmarked, so it wasn't to disguise the victim's identity. It looks to me as if this criminal has some sort of preoccupation or obsession with tattoos." Daiyu Matsushita seemed to be growing more chagrined by the moment. While they were still trying to figure out what had happened to the tattooed torso that vanished from the scene of the first murder, the killer had issued a brazen challenge by murdering Tsunetaro Nomura, who very probably held the key to the case. Just to make the crime more egregious, he had stripped off Tsunetaro's tattooed skin right under their noses.

Three hours went by in a blur of activity. At the end of that time, Officer Akita returned from his mission to Shibuya and gave an account of the events of the previous evening. "Just after six o'clock yesterday evening, the victim went out with

228

a woman dressed entirely in black… The proprietor thought she must have come to discuss getting a tattoo… Her forearms were covered with white bandages…"

Just to make sure he hadn't missed anything, Daiyu Matsushita had Officer Akita repeat his report twice. Then he once again shouted orders at his subordinates.

"Professor Hayakawa, Gifu Inazawa, Hisashi Mogami: find out what these three men were doing last night, and check out their alibis under a microscope. After that, find the prostitute who disappeared from Yurakucho, the one who looked like Kinue Nomura. I'm serious, I want you to canvass all the red-light districts. Look under every American GI in Tokyo, if you have to. It's a long shot, but we can't afford to leave anything unchecked. I'm going to solve this case if it kills me!"

Kenzo cowered in a corner while his brother rampaged around the building in a frenzy, like the Hindu-Buddhist demon Asura. There was no way he could have brought himself to look Daiyu in the face at that moment. If Kenzo had said just one word to his brother before all this, a human life could almost certainly have been saved. Reeling under his unbearably heavy load of regret and guilt, Kenzo felt a new storm of tears welling up. He crept behind a pile of crumbling bricks, put his face in his hands, and wept as if his heart would break.

41

The police detectives spent a busy day pursuing leads and interviewing suspects. Toward evening Detective Chief Inspector Daiyu Matsushita called a press conference and released some information regarding the alibis of the three prime suspects in the grisly murder of Tsunetaro Nomura. The reporters scribbled furiously, while flashbulbs popped.

The first suspect was Hisashi Mogami, brother of the late Takezo Mogami. Hisashi went to visit a female friend in Yokohama and stayed there until around five o'clock. After that, he said, he ate dinner at a Chinese restaurant, went to a movie, and took a stroll around Isezaki-cho. Around eight thirty he checked into the White Swan Hotel in Honmoku and spent the night. Both the proprietor of the hotel and the woman he was with until five o'clock confirmed this account. To go from Honmoku to the scene of the crime in Yoyogi would have taken an hour and a half at least, even if Hisashi had been very lucky with changing trains. It would have been all he could do to make the round trip from Honmoku to Yoyogi. There was simply no way he could have committed the murder, stripped off Tsunetaro's skin, and disposed of the remains in such a short time.

The second suspect, Mogami Group manager Gifu Inazawa, claimed to have spent the entire evening at a dance hall in Shinjuku called the Red Jewel. He wasn't a regular patron, and there wasn't a single person who had noticed his presence that night, so there was reason to doubt his story. Inazawa could easily have ducked out of the dance hall, committed the murder, and sneaked back in. It was only a fifteen-minute walk from the dance hall to the scene of the crime.

Suspect Three was Professor Hayakawa. He had been with a friend in Shinjuku until around six o'clock. He took a look at the hospital his colleague was managing, and then the friend treated him to a dinner of shabu-shabu. After leaving the restaurant, he claimed to have walked around the Ginza until about nine o'clock, and then returned home. The question was whether the Ginza in its present state of disrepair had sufficient charm to move a middle-aged man to stroll aimlessly around for three hours on a chilly late fall evening. Professor Hayakawa's behavior was definitely suspicious, nor did he lack for motive. However, there still was no direct evidence to tie him to the case.

While the suspects were being interviewed, there had been one small development on another front. A team of detectives had discovered that the name of the streetwalker the chief had them search for was Sumiyo Hayashi. Because of the shady sort of business she was in, though, there was no way of knowing whether that was her real name or an alias, a *nom de nuit*. More than half a year had passed since Sumiyo Hayashi had last been seen in the Yurakucho area, so her trail was seriously cold.

No real leads, no viable suspects. The investigation seemed to have run aground as all the formerly promising threads of the case were snipped, one by one. The murder of Tsunetaro Nomura, and the attendant loss of valuable clues, seemed to be the straw that broke the detectives' already sagging spirits. No one was more disappointed than Daiyu Matsushita, but he took this latest setback like a man. After his volatile blow-up at the crime scene, he didn't say another critical word to Kenzo.

In the days that followed, the investigation went idly around in circles like a dog chasing its tail. One rather interesting bit of information did surface, however. While it cast some light on the complex background of the case, it couldn't by any means be called a direct clue.

In the course of investigating Horiyasu's past, the detectives found out how Horiyasu's wife—that is, the mother of Tsunetaro, Kinue, and Tamae—had spent the latter part of her life. After abandoning her husband and children, she became a notorious female burglar. The lover who lured her away was a much younger man, a career criminal whom she had met when her husband was doing the man's tattoos. She was eventually sentenced to life imprisonment for her part in a sensational robbery-murder case, a crime for which her partner received the death sentence. After serving many years in a women's prison in Tochigi, she fell ill and died in her cell, alone and unmourned.

After hearing that story, Daiyu Matsushita thought he understood what Professor Hayakawa meant when he told Kenzo that Horiyasu appeared to have inked his children with those unlucky tattoos as a way of expressing his festering anger toward their mother. When the chief of detectives reviewed the mother's unwholesome life, he seemed to gain a clearer understanding of how two of the siblings could have met their deaths as the victims of such appalling murders. The third child being in Hiroshima was not exactly a stroke of luck, either. Police detectives are supposed to be relentlessly rational, but Daiyu couldn't help thinking that the Nomuras had been a singularly ill-starred family.

Meanwhile, Kenzo was in his own private hell. His grand ambitions of solving the case had been completely pulverized, and he felt as if he had fallen from the heavens into the bowels of the earth. Cheerful no more, he languished in his room in an unleavened state of depression and self-loathing. He tried rereading *The Maltese Falcon* and *Farewell, My Lovely*, but the translated words blurred before his eyes.

Again and again, Kenzo went over what had happened since he first met Tsunetaro, torturing himself with guilt and recriminations. He always ended up at the same excruciating realization that because of his own shallow-brained thinking, a gifted artist had been murdered and mutilated. As a result, Kenzo had lost his brother Daiyu's trust and respect, his brother had lost face in front of his subordinates, and the investigation had been thrown into a tailspin. Kenzo wanted desperately to redeem himself somehow, but his self-confidence was gone.

Hour after hour, he sat staring despondently at the wall, chain-smoking like a junior locomotive. Between meals he munched on dried squid and American candy bars, washed down with endless glasses of cold tea brewed from roasted barley. He racked his brain for ways to atone for his mistake and advance the stalled investigation. He made elaborate lists and time lines, but he always seemed to end up with a headache from thinking in circles.

Kinue's shocking death had broken his heart, but this was different. Tsunetaro would almost certainly still be alive if Kenzo had not approached him in the first place, and Kenzo felt that the perpetrator had somehow killed a part of him as well. To survive the war and then to die like that... The murderer had already touched Kenzo twice, indirectly. Now a genuine fear for his own safety was mingled with the feelings of grief, anger, and remorse that had consumed him since Tsunetaro's death. Theoretical thinking was all very well, but Kenzo had lost faith in his own judgment, and he lacked the courage to put his plans into action.

As he was sitting in his darkened room, wallowing in his own impotence and despair, there was a knock on the door.

"Kenzo, dear, I'm worried about you," said his sister-in-law Mariko's sweet voice. "You haven't been out of the house in days. Are you sure you aren't ill?"

"I'm just getting ready to go for a walk, right now," Kenzo said. The words were a fib when they came out of his mouth, but then an idea struck him. Grabbing his jacket and briefcase, he ran down the stairs. Without a word of explanation to his astonished sister-in-law, he jumped into his combat boots and dashed out the front door, with his untied shoelaces trailing behind him like baby snakes.

"It's late for a stroll," Mariko called after him, anxiously. "Please be careful."

42

When Kenzo left the house around ten thirty, the starless sky was the color of charcoal and the air was heavy with the promise of rain. He hadn't thought to bring an umbrella, but he decided that someone who had managed to return alive from the hellish jungles of the Philippines should be able to survive a few raindrops. After a brisk five-minute walk through quiet residential streets, Kenzo found himself at the back entrance to the train station.

A number of vendors had set up mobile food stands in the narrow, crooked alleys behind the station, and they were doing a lively business. Customers perched on wooden stools, their upper bodies hidden by flapping canvas curtains that bore decorative ideographs advertising fried noodles, sake, and roasted rice cakes. Kenzo could hear the clink of glasses and the murmur of tipsy conversation, mixed with an occasional off-key snatch of song. Ordinarily he might have been tempted to stop for a quick snack, but on this night he was galvanized by a welcome sense of mission.

The Yamanote Line train wasn't terribly crowded. In Kenzo's car there were only a few bleary-eyed office workers heading home after an evening of mandatory drinking with colleagues and clients, three black-uniformed students reading paperback novels, and a rosy-cheeked peasant woman with a mouthful of gold teeth and an immense cloth-wrapped pack on her permanently stooped back.

Unsold vegetables, or some sort of farming supplies, Kenzo speculated, his amateur detective's brain going full speed as usual. He settled into a blue plush seat in the corner of the car and resumed his ruminations. There were so many questions, and so few answers.

Why did Horiyasu etch three unlucky tattoos on his own children? Did Kinue really ask Professor Hayakawa to come to her house that morning, or was he lying? Why was Kinue's torso cut off and taken away, and how was that done? Who was the mysterious woman in black who lured Tsunetaro out? What was the meaning of the bandages on her arms? Could she have been Tamae, covering up her tattoos? Speaking of tattoos, why did someone peel them off Tsunetaro's body? What was the motive for his murder?

And the question that had catapulted Kenzo out of his smoky depressive's lair and onto this late-night train: What was the true identity of this woman who called herself Sumiyo Hayashi, and where did she disappear to?

"Otemachi," the conductor announced sadly, as if he were the bearer of tragic news. The train stopped and two attractive young women dressed in expensive kimonos got on. One of them looked exactly like Miss Ogi, the young secretary at Kenzo's research lab. Kenzo had occasionally caught Miss Ogi staring at him, and she always went out of her way to bring him coffee and green tea before he asked. If he hadn't been so wrapped up in the case, and so busy carrying a torch for Kinue Nomura, Kenzo might have noticed that he had made a conquest.

He was halfway out of his seat, beginning to bow, before he realized that the woman on the train was a stranger. From a distance the resemblance had been striking, but at closer range Kenzo could see that this woman had slightly fuller cheeks and a more prominent chin. Aside from those physiognomic details, her hairstyle, build, coloration, carriage, gestures, and expression were startlingly similar to those of Miss Ogi.

"Doppelgänger," Kenzo said softly, under his breath. He had taken three years of German as part of his premed studies, and had always been fascinated by that word. Doppelgänger— double-walker. The word had originally had mildly super- natural connotations—"a wraith of one alive," said Kenzo's German-Japanese dictionary—but it had come to mean simply a double, or an uncanny look-alike.

There was a saying that everyone on earth had a double, a duplicate so identical in every way that they might have developed from the same zygote. Perhaps because Kenzo had no obtrusive or extraordinary features, people frequently told him that they knew someone who looked exactly like him. "Spitting image," they would say. "He might be your miss- ing twin, separated at birth!" So far Kenzo had managed to avoid being introduced to any of these walking wraiths, but he had a feeling that if he ever did meet his own *doppel*, he would *gäng* away in the opposite direction as fast as possible. More likely, from what he had heard about such meetings, neither man would be able to see the faintest resemblance to himself.

These thoughts led him, inevitably, back to the labyrinthine murder case. The one thing he was sure of was that the body in the bathroom at Kinue's house had belonged to Kinue. According to the photographic evidence, Kinue's calves and forearms were not tattooed, whereas her sister Tamae's were densely patterned.

Tamae could not have been killed in Kinue's stead for what- ever reason, because there would have been tattoos on the lower arms and legs of the dismembered body. No such tattoos were found. Therefore one thing, at least, appeared certain: the victim was Kinue Nomura. That didn't mean that Tamae might not be involved in the case in some other capacity. Kenzo had a hunch that Kinue's sister was alive, and he was determined to find the proof, perhaps (with luck) this very night.

Thinking about the riddles of the Tattoo Murder Case made Kenzo's head spin, and he was relieved when the conductor called out, in his mournful voice, "Yurakucho! Please watch your step, and make sure you haven't forgotten anything."

Yurakucho means Pleasure Town, and the pursuit of earthly delights was in full swing when Kenzo arrived. Rows of tiny restaurants and red-lantern drinking spots spilled their light and noise onto the crowded sidewalks, and the air was thick with aromatic smoke from skewered chicken roasting over open fires. Kenzo forged ahead, oblivious to the delicious smells and inviting interiors. For once, food was the furthest thing from his mind.

The place he sought was just around the corner from the teeming station. Nicknamed the Field of Poisonous Flowers, it was a stretch of tree-lined pavement just before the Sugiya Bridge, where streetwalkers plied their trade. Kenzo was a bit nervous, for aside from a couple of forgettable trysts in the Philippines, he had never even spoken to a prostitute.

The women stood in clusters, talking and giggling among themselves. The pinkish streetlight cast a dim theatrical glow, and Kenzo was reminded of the performance of *Swan Lake* he had once seen on a school excursion. From a distance, the women looked like graceful ballerinas striking poses against a backdrop of painted trees. As he drew closer, though, Kenzo got a sense of the sadness and desperation that the women's flashy dresses, bright makeup, and brittle patter couldn't disguise.

How tragic, he thought. Japan had always had a thriving sex trade, but this was different. Before the war there had been a few streetwalkers in the seamier parts of town, but most of the prostitution was carried on in designated brothels, behind closed doors, with a certain decadent *élan*.

Now, though, there were hordes of women standing around all the major train stations hoping to rent their bodies to some stranger for an hour or two, simply because they could find no other way to support themselves. These women were somebody's daughters, mothers, wives, sisters… Suddenly remembering why he had come, Kenzo took a deep breath and approached the nearest group of prostitutes.

"Hey, good-looking," said the tallest of the group. She wore a short, curly blonde wig, but under the heavy Western-style cosmetics her features were classically Japanese.

"Hello, handsome boy," said a short, plump woman. Her gauzy cocktail dress—orange with black and yellow spots— gave her the look of an overweight butterfly, and her cheeks were rouged in perfect circles, like those of a doll.

"Um, hello, good evening," Kenzo said shyly. "I should say right away that I'm not a potential customer, but I am willing to pay for certain information."

"Oo-ooh!" the women chorused in mock excitement. Kenzo was sure they were making fun of him, and he had a strong urge to run away.

"Hey, big spender," purred a woman with a henna-tinted ponytail.

"Handsome *and* rich," quipped the butterfly.

"Wait a minute—are you a cop?" demanded the tall *faux*-blonde.

"No, no, nothing like that," Kenzo assured her, more or less truthfully.

"A private detective, then?" The speaker was a woman in her late thirties, incongruously dressed in a schoolgirl's uniform of middy blouse, pleated skirt, and knee socks, with her hair in two fat red-ribboned pigtails. Kenzo had heard that some men liked that sort of thing. The thought of it made him feel slightly nauseated.

"Yeah, what are you, a private detective?" echoed the other women. Their collective perfume mingled the heady scents of jasmine, gardenia, rose, lavender, sandalwood, and citrus with the ambient urban odors of car exhaust and burned-out buildings. Kenzo's head began to swim.

"A detective?" he stammered. "Sort of. Not exactly. You see—" The women were staring at him with suspicious expressions on their garishly painted faces, and once again, Kenzo felt the desire to flee. *You have to do this for Kinue,* he reminded himself sternly. *She can't rest until her killer is caught and punished.*

Instead of running away, he decided to tell a tiny lie. "The truth is, I'm looking for my sister," he said without batting an eye. "She used to work here, and she went by the name of Sumiyo Hayashi. She looked like this." He took a photo out of his briefcase and held it up.

"Never saw her, never heard of her," said the aging schoolgirl, raising her drawn-on eyebrows. "But if you'll come with me I'll make you forget your sister, and your wife, and all your other troubles, too."

"Thank you very much for the offer. Perhaps another time," Kenzo replied, with far more politeness than the situation warranted. He knew he had made a mess of his first interview, and he wasn't surprised when the women burst into raucous, derisive laughter the minute he walked away.

He tried the next group of women, with similar results: a lungful of cloying perfume, a faceful of flirtatious jokes, an outright invitation or two, and finally, after each woman had confirmed that she had never heard of anyone named Sumiyo

Hayashi, with or without tattoos, an awkward good-bye. Some of the women were quite beautiful and intelligent-looking, and Kenzo couldn't help wondering how they had sunk so low.

It's the damned war, he thought. *It turned everyone's lives upside down, and drained all the innocence out of the world.*

One particularly lovely woman, standing alone beside a tree, caught Kenzo's eye. She was dressed in a simple black satin sheath, with her hair twirled up in a sleek chignon, and for a moment Kenzo tried to picture the two of them together. Not entwined in some tacky hotel room with a blinking neon sign casting lurid stripes across the swaybacked bed; no, Kenzo's heart, soul, and libido still belonged to Kinue Nomura. He just thought it might be nice to walk through the park with a pleasant, pretty female companion and talk about normal things, things that had nothing whatsoever to do with war, or murder, or tattoos, or dismembered corpses.

Then the woman spoke, and Kenzo's modest fantasy evaporated. It wasn't just that she had a rough, uneducated country accent or that her front teeth were chipped and broken; those things didn't help, true, but it was what she said that completely shattered the spell.

"I'll be your best friend till morning, sweetheart," she crooned in a grotesquely seductive voice. "All for the price of a bowl of noodles. I'll do anything you like, even—"

Kenzo was stunned, and appalled. Before the woman could finish her pathetic proposition he thrust a handful of money at her—enough for ten bowls of the finest hand-rolled noodles—and turned on to the next group.

It was nearly midnight. Kenzo was exhausted, but he was determined to talk to all the streetwalkers before he headed for home. It had not been a productive evening so far. One or two of the women had thought they remembered the name Sumiyo Hayashi, but they were unable or unwilling to supply any details.

The photo didn't seem to jog any memories, either. When he brought out the picture of the three siblings the prostitutes cracked jokes about getting tattooed themselves, or asked whether the handsome Tsunetaro was single, or exclaimed over the artistry of the designs. No one recognized the faces of the Nomura sisters. Part of the problem was the rate of turnover. Most of the women had only been working the area for a month or two.

Kenzo's hope was ebbing away as he approached the final group—two thirtyish women in tight-fitting red tango dresses, and a very young girl in a blue Alice-in-Wonderland pinafore who appeared to be half the age of her colleagues, at most. He thought at first that the young girl was just keeping her mother company on the job, so to speak, but then he noticed that the girl was wearing rouge and thickly mascaraed false eyelashes, and he felt the shock in the pit of his stomach. The girl gave him an exaggerated come-hither look, batting her spidery lashes, and he had to avert his eyes in pity and shame. *She must be an orphan,* he thought. *Poor thing.*

After fending off the older women's shrill offers of expert companionship, Kenzo trotted out his searching-for-my-sister lie. Then, in a weary listless voice, he said, "I don't suppose you ever met a woman who went by the name of Sumiyo Hayashi?"

"Oh, you mean Sumi?" said one of the older women, and Kenzo was suddenly wide awake. With her flat-featured, kindly face, the woman looked like some of Kenzo's country aunts, back in Nagano Prefecture. He thought she must be a war widow, doing this to support her children.

"Yeah," the woman went on in a nostalgic tone, "me and Sumi, we were good friends. She was a strange one, though. She never wanted to talk about the past, but I got the impression she was estranged from her family. She seemed to have a lot of anger just below the surface, if you know what I mean, like a volcano. Another funny thing—she always wore the same sort of outfit, no matter what the weather was. Even on the hottest summer nights—and you know how muggy it gets in August. She would show up wearing a long-sleeved dress, with dark tights and high heels. Some of the other girls called her the Librarian behind her back, but the clients didn't seem to mind. She was always very popular. Maybe it's true what they say about modesty being sexier than showing it all."

Glumly, the woman gazed down at her own plunging, ruffled neckline, but Kenzo's thoughts were elsewhere. *Long sleeves to hide the tattoos*, he was thinking, in high excitement. *And dark tights, for the same purpose.*

He held up the photo of the three tattooed siblings, and the woman stared in surprise.

"Oh my," she gasped. "That's her on the right, or maybe on the left. I never knew she had siblings, much less a tattoo. That explains a lot." Warming to her topic, the woman rambled on. "Yeah, old Sumi was an odd one, all right. I was never sure that she was telling me the truth, about anything. She was a real looker, though, like one of those long-faced beauties in the old woodblock prints. We used to have some laughs, I can tell you that, mostly at the customers' expense. You meet a lot of unusual personalities in this line of work, if you know what I mean. Oops, no offense to you, sir."

"None taken," Kenzo said absently. "But wait a minute. You said something about August. Does that mean Sumiyo Hayashi was still working here in August?"

"Yeah, she was here all that month, as I recall, but I don't remember seeing her around in September. She dropped a few hints about some wonderful man she had met who had promised to take care of her, so I figured maybe they ran off together. I wish someone like that would come along and rescue us, but no such luck."

"Us?"

The woman gestured at her two companions, who had been listening quietly, with their shoulders touching like a couple of seabirds huddled against a storm. "Yeah, us," she said. "Me, my sister, and my daughter."

Oh my God, Kenzo thought, *that's her own daughter? Has the whole world gone insane?*

Suddenly he wanted to get out of the unsettling Field of Poisonous Flowers as fast as possible. He gave several bills to each of the women, hoping it would be enough to get the girl in the pinafore off the streets, for one night at least. She couldn't have been more than fourteen, an age when girls should be at home doing schoolwork or reading novels about dogs and horses, or practicing the piano.

When Kenzo reached the corner by the station, he turned to look back. The three women—the daughter, the mother, and the aunt—were deep in conversation with a trio of men whose distinctive costumes identified them as laborers: jersey shirts, woolen bellybands, balloon-legged pants, knee-high split-toed boots. One of the men was swaying drunkenly, and he had his arm draped familiarly around the young girl's fragile shoulders.

"War," Kenzo muttered angrily. "What a lousy, rotten invention *that* was."

It was long past midnight, and a light rain was falling on the ravaged city. Safely ensconced in his tiny lair, Kenzo lit a

244

hand-rolled cigarette and blew the smoke toward the ceiling. He was far too excited to sleep, for he was now convinced that Tamae Nomura was alive, and that she and Sumiyo Hayashi were the same person.

If that was true, though, then how had Tamae survived Hiroshima? Where had she gone with her "wonderful man"? And might it be possible that Tamae's well-documented estrangement from her sister had somehow culminated in Kinue's murder?

Kenzo's head was teeming with questions, but there was a noticeable absence of answers. *What this case needs is a fresh point of view,* he thought. *Or a miracle.*

43

Two months passed. It was well into autumn. The air was crisp and cool, and the leaves of the Japanese maples had turned the brilliant crimson of a geisha's painted lips. On the grounds of Tokyo University Medical School, in the neighborhood of the pond made famous by Natsume Soseki's novel *Sanshiro,* a tall, remarkably good-looking youth was loitering about gazing at the scenery.

The young man's eyes were a distinctive amber color. The large, liquid pupils had the gleam of obsidian, while jet-black eyebrows traced a fine, feathery arc above long, thick eyelashes. His shoulder-length, pageboy hairstyle gave him a slightly androgynous look, as did his flawless ivory skin and the almost feminine beauty of his chiseled features. He was saved from mere prettiness by the dignity and intelligence that suffused his face. In those days when so many people were wearing charred rags or recycled military uniforms, he was dressed like a country squire in a forest-green tweed jacket with matching knickerbockers, long gray herringbone-patterned stockings, sturdy brogues, and a gray tweed doughboy cap.

The young man's name was Kyosuke Kamizu. He had gone from Ikko Academy to the Tokyo University Medical School just after Kenzo Matsushita, and everyone who knew him raved about his brilliant intellect. As a youth of nineteen Kyosuke had already mastered six foreign languages: English, French, German, Russian, Greek, and Latin. During his student days he wrote a long thesis on the topic of integers, which was published in the German magazine *Mathematische Zeitschrift.* These extraordinary gifts and accomplishments gave rise to the sobriquet "Boy Genius," a nickname that Kyosuke himself had always despised.

Naturally, everyone assumed that after graduation Kyosuke would go on to Tokyo University, study advanced mathematics or physics, and then become a great scholar and a distinguished professor, like so many of the boy geniuses before him. Instead, Kyosuke chose to enter Tokyo University Medical School, where he did special research in forensic medicine. In better times he might have stayed on at the university and followed the traditional course of the brilliant academic, from assistant professor through full professor and on to professor emeritus down the road. But the turbulent tide of history swept Kyosuke off course, along with millions of his contemporaries. He was drafted and became a military surgeon, and his wartime assignments took him from China to Java, on the southern front.

Kyosuke was the only son of a well-to-do, aristocratic family of landowners and intellectuals from Kamakura. Before he left Tokyo on a troop tram, Kyosuke said good-bye as if forever to his devoted servants, an elderly couple who had raised him after his parents' untimely deaths in a dreadful act of violence during a visit to New York City back in the 1930s. Although not a practicing Buddhist, Kyosuke was imbued with that religion's sense of the impermanence of things. He had resigned himself to the possibility that he might not survive the war, so he was filled with particularly deep emotion upon returning to the calm, unchanged campus of his beloved alma mater. After gazing around at the tranquil scenery for a few moments, Kyosuke climbed a nearby hill and headed toward the medical school library, which had always been his favorite haven.

Kenzo Matsushita had grown tired of working on his dissertation research and he, too, was taking a stroll around the campus. He was standing under an immense gingko tree, staring moodily up at the overcast sky through a canopy of fan-shaped golden leaves, and he looked around just as Kyosuke approached. Kenzo's face stiffened and turned pale, as if he had seen a ghost, but when he realized that he was looking at the real thing he shouted, "Kyosuke!" in a joyful voice and ran toward his old schoolmate.

"Kenzo! Kenzo Matsushita!!" A smile was playing about Kyosuke's sculptured lips, and faint dimples appeared in his smooth, hairless cheeks.

"Kyosuke, I'm so glad to see you!" Japanese men do not often embrace in public, but Kenzo couldn't help giving his long-lost friend a robust slap on the shoulder. "How wonderful that you made it back safely!"

"Thanks, but I'm not sure 'safely' is the right word. I was beaten rather badly in a detention camp in Java, and I ended up more dead than alive. Somehow I managed to get to Kyoto, and I stayed there considerably longer than I had expected, resting in a hospital. The only good thing was, I got to do a lot of reading."

"That's terrible. But you survived. I mean, we're two of the lucky ones. How long has it been, anyway?"

"I think it's at least four years since we saw each other in Peking."

That hadn't been much of a meeting. There was little free time, and before they had a chance to sit down for a meal or explore that ancient city, they were hustled off with their respective regiments. Kyosuke's train departed first, and Kenzo had a vivid image of Kyosuke at the train window, saluting and mouthing his favorite farewell, *Gardez la foi*.

The war was over at last and here they were, together again in peacetime, both alive and relatively well. Kenzo's glum mood had vanished, and he felt he might burst with joy. The sky, too, had been gray and gloomy, but now the thick clouds parted and a shaft of brilliant golden light illuminated the two men. For a moment they looked like Renaissance seraphs in contemporary dress.

At that same instant, Kenzo had a flash of inspiration almost as brilliant as the sunlight. "Mr. Kamizu," he said with exaggerated politeness, "I know it is terribly rude of me to ask such a thing when you've only just returned, but the truth is I really need your help with something."

"And what might that be?" Kyosuke asked playfully. "Are you having trouble with calculus again?"

Kenzo ignored the schoolboy joke. "It's a long, strange story," he said in a serious tone. "The short version is, I've been dragged into a very complicated murder case. Somewhere along the way I made a huge mistake and caused the investigation to lose a major clue that might have broken the whole thing wide open. My brother is having a terrible time with this case too, and that's why I'm humbly begging for your assistance. Please, Kyosuke, won't you kindly lend us your magnificent brains for a little while?"

Kyosuke laughed. "I didn't realize you knew how to speak such exquisitely polite Japanese. You sounded as if you were talking to a stranger! Seriously, I don't know whether I can be of any use or not, but I'd be more than happy to help to the best of my ability. I wouldn't call it an ulterior motive, exactly, but I do have reasons of my own for wanting to make the world a safer place to live."

44

Kenzo and Kyosuke sat down under a graceful umbrella-shaped willow tree on the banks of the pond. While Kenzo gave a detailed account of the case, from his first meeting with Kinue Nomura to the horrific, heartbreaking murder of Tsunetaro, Kyosuke sat in silence, eyes closed. His face was so perfectly calm and expressionless that it appeared as if he had fallen asleep. Even after Kenzo had finished his recitation, Kyosuke continued to sit like a meditating Bodhisattva.

Finally he opened his eyes and spoke. "You're right, it is devilishly difficult," Kyosuke said. "Yet it's by no means impossible to solve." He bent down, picked up a flat pebble that was lying at his feet and tossed it into the dull green pond. As the ripples spread in shimmering circles around the point of entry, he watched quietly, a reflective smile on his comely face.

Geniuses really are different from you and me, Kenzo thought, as he tried to imagine what might be going on in Kyosuke's superior head.

"Actually," Kyosuke said after the last ripple had faded away, "I've believed for many years that you have an exceptional gift for observation, and for accumulating and analyzing data. But putting all that data together through synthesis and cooperation, that's another matter entirely."

Kenzo nodded his assent, remembering the notes-from-the-teacher that he used to carry home from elementary school, pinned to his sky-blue jacket: "Quick to learn, but does not work well with others."

"Fortunately," Kyosuke continued, "it just so happens that synthesis and cooperation are among my strong points." To a stranger, that statement might have sounded like the bluster of an egomaniacal braggart, but Kenzo knew that his friend had the substance to back up every word.

Kyosuke seemed to be waiting for a response, but when Kenzo just nodded in silent admiration, he began to speak again. "I see what you mean when you call this murderer an evil genius. There does seem to be a sort of genius in the way he made his plan, and carried it out. I'll give you that, without argument. The trick is to match your own thinking with the thought patterns of the killer's disturbed mind. If you're unable to make that leap of imagination, then you'll be wandering around endlessly in a maze of contradictions and absurdities, utterly stupefied by the complexity of it all. At that rate, the case might well go unsolved forever. However, I have no intention of letting that happen."

"Kyosuke, I can't believe what I'm hearing. Are you saying that you think you can solve this case?"

"That's exactly what I'm saying."

"How long do you think it would take?"

"Oh, I'd say… by the end of the week I should be able to give your brother the wherewithal to arrest the murderer." Kyosuke tossed another stone into the tranquil pond.

Coming from an unknown, inexperienced young man, that was an awfully ambitious declaration, and Kenzo was astounded by Kyosuke's brash self-confidence. *He opened his mouth and out came a rainbow,* he thought, recalling the proverb about a person who talks a bigger game than he can deliver.

After a long silence, Kenzo recovered himself sufficiently to say, almost pleadingly, "Don't tell me you've already figured out the secrets of this case."

Kyosuke gave him one of his trademark sphinxlike smiles. "No, no, not even close. All I'm doing right now is considering various hypotheses, trying them out in my mind one at a time. From among those possible explanations, I'll choose the one that seems to be the most logical. Then I'll see whether it matches up with the available data without any major discrepancies. Once I'm sure of the facts and have determined the identity of the murderer, my final step will be to place some psychological pressure on the killer. After that, it's just a matter of standing back and waiting for him to self-destruct. That's really all there is to it."

"That may be all there is to it for you, but for us mere mortals, it hasn't been quite that simple. Tell me, have you found the magic hypothesis yet?"

"As a matter of fact, I have. But it's such an utterly bizarre theory that if I tried telling it to anyone at this early stage, I'd probably be laughed out of the room."

"But how—" Kenzo stammered.

"The thing is," Kyosuke interrupted, "I wouldn't blame anyone for laughing. This hypothesis of mine surprises even me. By comparison, Professor Hayakawa's remarks about non-Euclidean geometry seem quite plausible. First of all, we have to discard the idea that parallel lines never meet, even at the point of infinity. I mean, you can't solve a problem of non-Euclidean geometry by using Euclidean geometry, am I right?"

Kenzo was dumbstruck. "I guess so," he said.

"You have to learn to think in paradoxes, because we're talking about a world where black becomes white," Kyosuke declared. "I'm very impressed with Professor Hayakawa for having been the only one to figure that out so far. He can be quite sharp at times. In this particular murder case, the theory of positive versus negative—in a photographic rather than a conceptual sense—has been put into practice most ingeniously. Black becomes white, and white becomes black. All the investigators were confused by the criminal's elaborate trick, which I admit was diabolically clever. Everyone mistook the positive for the negative, and vice versa."

"Wait a minute. Are you talking about those photographic plates that Professor Hayakawa found in the garden?"

"Yes, that, too, but there's more to it. Those discarded bits of film that the killer scattered around the garden are just a small part of the puzzle. Right now I'm trying to take a more sweeping view of the character of the case, rather than getting preoccupied with minuscule details."

"Oh, I get it. But in scientific terms, in order to prove a hypothesis, you have to verify every single one of its elements. How are you planning to do that with these tangled-up murders?"

"Well, based on the fact that Tsunetaro apparently saw through the entire case based on one glance at the photographs you showed him, I'm assuming that those tattoo pictures are the first key. The second is to do a psychological analysis of each suspect. In the first case, the police investigation came up with five possible suspects, am I right? Of those five, Takezo Mogami is dead, and Usui had already been arrested on the day before the third murder. So let's eliminate those two from suspicion for the time being. That leaves Professor Hayakawa, Gifu Inazawa, and your old school friend Hisashi Mogami. He's the same one they used to call the Black Sheep, I assume?"

"One and the same," Kenzo said, amazed anew at Kyosuke's memory for detail.

"At any rate," Kyosuke went on, "if the culprit is lurking among this group, then we should be able to determine who committed all the murders by doing a psychological analysis of these three men. However, in this case there is a hidden element, which I'll call the X factor. The killer probably couldn't have committed the murders without the help of this X. Person X hasn't yet appeared before us, of course, but as we proceed with our investigation this mystery character will inevitably be smoked out of its hiding place."

"You say 'it,' but X is a woman, right?"

"That's exactly right, because three minus two equals one."

"I see," Kenzo said excitedly. "So the three tattooed siblings minus Orochimaru-plus-Jiraiya equals Tsunedahime, right? That's my theory exactly, that Tamae Nomura is alive and was somehow involved in the murders."

With a faint, cryptic smile, Kyosuke gazed up at the great mass of gray-lined cumulus clouds overhead, as if they might be loaded with clues and not with rain. After a moment he said, "What I'm wondering is why you didn't notice a fundamental difference between the nature of the first two murders and that of the third. Not only you, of course. It strikes me as odd that even the experienced detectives in the police department seem to have overlooked this difference."

"What difference is that?"

"Let's call it a difference in style. Remember, you said that Hisashi Mogami had compared this crime to a checkmate? That's one way of looking at it, but I think it would be more accurate to liken it to the beginning of a chess game. This crime isn't just an artistic creation. It's an outright challenge to an opponent. 'Go on,' these murders seem to say, 'try to solve us.' I don't mean a match between the killer and the police investigators. Rather, it's a match between the murderer and Fate. The person who committed the first two murders calculated the risks and took every circumstance into account, and then just as he was taking a breath of relief, thinking he had literally gotten away with murder, Fate tossed another chess piece onto the board and laughed in the killer's face. That was Jiraiya, of course; the one piece the murderer had overlooked. As the killer was pondering his next move, he suddenly became aware that this new piece had the power to destroy him. The killer knew he had to find a way to dispose of the threat. And that was the end of Jiraiya, also known as Tsunetaro Nomura, the quintessential man who knew too much."

"Ah," said Kenzo, rendered speechless by Kyosuke's clever metaphor.

"Because of the impromptu nature of the most recent murder, there is a flaw in it. Naturally, he tried to conceal the crime, but he didn't have the luxury of time to plan as he did with the first two killings. I'm certain that the murderer must have grown arrogant after those early successes, and conceited people tend to make mistakes."

"And what was that mistake?" Kenzo's head was spinning.

"As I see it, it's the fact that the mystery woman, whom the killer has kept hidden until now, has finally come out into the open. And this is a woman who for some reason needs to cover her arms with bandages, down to the wrist."

"Of course!" Kenzo exclaimed. "Tamae, covering up her tattoos. But why was she wearing a kimono, instead of her usual long-sleeved dress? Oh, I know. I'll bet her savior, her wonderful man, was one of those traditional types who won't permit his woman to wear Western clothes."

Kyosuke gave Kenzo a tolerant smile before continuing with his own train of thought. "The next thing that struck me as odd is that even while he was carrying out his bizarre handiwork, the killer made no attempt to conceal his crimes. In the first murder, he chose Kinue's own house as the staging ground.

Maybe that was unavoidable, but it doesn't make sense that he would cut up the body and hide the torso somewhere, while leaving the head without a mark on it. And while the killer went to all the trouble of locking the bathroom in order to hinder the discovery of the body, he seems to have deliberately left the lights on in that same room. There's no way that the people in the neighborhood wouldn't have eventually noticed that the light had been left on, particularly since they already took a lively interest in Kinue's every move. Even if you and Professor Hayakawa hadn't come along the next morning, the body would have been discovered before too long. That's all fine. However, there was no common-sense reason to believe that the body would be found during the night. So the killer must have had some inside information that led him to predict that someone would see the body in the locked room before morning. I think the light was left on in order to attract the attention of that someone, like a beacon in the night."

"But why?"

"Perhaps it was to tempt a person with peeping-Tom inclinations to look through the crack in the door in the hopes of glimpsing Beauty in her bath." Kyosuke gave a fleeting smile, then continued. "This way of thinking can be seen in the other two murders as well. In the death of Takezo Mogami, a building slated for imminent demolition was deliberately chosen as the stage for the drama. In the third murder, after going to so much trouble to remove the tattoos from the body, why didn't the killer smash the face into unrecognizability while he was at it? If the face had been obliterated, it would have been quite difficult to identify the victim." Kyosuke paused for a moment, but before Kenzo could reply he began to answer his own question.

"Do you understand, Kenzo? Do you see the reason why the killer purposely set it up so that his crimes would be discovered?"

"No, I don't see at all. Is it some sort of psychological disorder, like an exhibitionistic-crime fetish or something?"

"No, it has nothing to do with mental illness. This criminal is like an audacious film director. Nothing is left to chance; he calculates everything down to the millisecond, and he only acts after weighing all the possible ramifications. If you look at it from a utilitarian point of view, that method is infinitely preferable to the usual reckless impulsiveness found in murderers. Am I right?"

Kenzo's mouth opened and closed as if he were a carp gulping air. When no sound came out, Kyosuke continued. "Do you know how to be an ingenious liar? The trick to deceiving people is not to lie your head off from start to finish. On the contrary, out of a hundred things you say, ninety-nine should be completely true. Then at the very end you tell one single, magnificent lie. That's the basic premise of the Machiavellian philosophy of foreign relations: if you overwhelm them with ninety-nine bits of truth, they'll never notice if you sneak in one little lie. This is a basic formula in psychology, too. Thus, our killer seems to have gone to extremes to disclose various aspects of the case—almost gratuitously, it would appear—while being careful to protect certain crucial secrets that were essential to his survival, in the most literal sense."

Kenzo should have known what to expect from the superbrain of Kyosuke Kamizu, whose other schoolboy nickname, besides Boy Genius, had been the Reasoning Machine. Nevertheless, after listening to Kyosuke's impromptu analysis, he couldn't find the words to express his wonderment and awe.

Instead he stood up, dusted off his rumpled khaki trousers, and beckoned to his friend, who was skipping yet another stone across the gray-green water.

"Come on," Kenzo said. "There's something I want to show you."

45

A short train ride later, the two men sat in Kenzo's small second-floor room in his brother's house. On the chipped burgundy lacquer table between them were two untouched cups of green tea and two small round dishes. Each dish held a shimmering dark brown square of bean-paste jelly, which Kenzo's sister-in-law had served with her usual quiet grace before closing the door discreetly behind her. A few minutes later, the discordant sound of one of Mariko's less diligent pupils attempting to plow through the easiest of "Five Easy Pieces" floated up from downstairs.

Spread out on the table were the photographs Kinue had sent to Kenzo for safekeeping. Kyosuke perused each print carefully, while Kenzo stared at his old friend's face, watching for changes in expression. A faint smile played about the corners of Kyosuke's mouth. He didn't say a word.

Next he picked up the assorted notes that Kenzo had prepared on the case over the past few months. Kyosuke was an unusually rapid reader, and he ran his eyes over every line, up to the final page. There he began to make some notes of his own in the margins, with characters so tidy and symmetrical that they might have been mistaken for movable type. Kenzo leaned across the table and swiveled his neck until the cartilage made an ominous cracking sound, trying to see what Kyosuke was writing.

Addendum to Note #3, he read. *In the third murder, only the tattooed skin was taken. In the first murder, the entire torso disappeared. What is the reason for this difference?*

"You overlooked one important point," Kyosuke said, laying down his pen. "I took the liberty of writing it in."

Fortunately, on that day Detective Chief Inspector Daiyu Matsushita came home early for once. Kenzo left Kyosuke in his room studying the case notes while he went downstairs to tell his brother everything that had happened that afternoon. Daiyu had already taken a bath and changed into a loose brown lounging kimono. Now he listened in high good humor, sipping a glass of Sapporo beer.

"I see," he said, when Kenzo paused for breath. "So this is the friend you've spoken of so often, the genius who published a world-class theorem in high school? And you think his powers of reasoning could be applied to solving these murders? Perhaps he'll become a famous amateur detective, just like in your mystery novels, and put us all to shame."

Daiyu's tone was teasing and jocular, but the expression in his eyes told another story. "Kenzo," he went on, "I'd like very much to meet this friend of yours. If he somehow manages to solve this case, I promise that I'll take off my hat and pay homage to him for accomplishing what I've been unable to do. Hell, if he gets me out of this predicament, I'll do better than that. I'll *eat* my blasted hat."

Kenzo could hardly keep his mouth from falling open in disbelief. Coming from the fearsome Matsu the Demon, who never asked anyone for anything, this request for Kyosuke's help was an extraordinary concession.

A few moments later Kenzo led Kyosuke downstairs and introduced him to Daiyu. Kyosuke was deferential yet self-confident, and his behavior toward the chief of detectives evidently made a very good impression. When Kyosuke attempted to take his leave, Daiyu all but barred the door, insisting that Kyosuke stay for dinner.

The three men shared a light meal of rice, miso soup with tofu and straw mushrooms, grilled butterfish, and various savory side dishes. (Daiyu's wife Mariko, as was customary, served them in silence, then ate later by herself in the kitchen.) Between bites, Daiyu and Kyosuke poked good-natured fun at Kenzo's theory that Sumiyo Hayashi, the elusive prostitute, was really Tamae Nomura. They took particular delight in skewering Kenzo's argument that the woman's habit of dressing year-round in dark tights and long-sleeved dresses proved that she was Tamae, covering up her full-body tattoos.

"Lots of women in this country never go out with bare legs or arms," Daiyu pointed out. "I mean, who ever heard of a short-sleeved kimono?"

"That's true," Kyosuke said. "As for the dark tights, I once read in a women's magazine that they are recommended to make legs look slimmer. And you know how self-conscious Japanese women are about having legs that look like a daikon radish!"

After the laughter had died down, the talk turned serious. They discussed the war, the Occupation, and the future of an economically-shattered Japan ruled by an emperor who had announced that he was not, after all, a god. In the course of the conversation Kyosuke effortlessly quoted Chekhov, Chaucer, and Heine, though not in a pretentious way, and always with perfect relevance. His extensive knowledge and breadth of interests were evident at every turn, and before long Daiyu Matsushita's gruff heart had been captivated by the penetrating intellect of this exceptional young man.

After several cups of after-dinner tea, Kyosuke finally stood up. As he put on his handmade brogues in the entry hall, he gave a clear guarantee that within a week's time he would point his finger at the culprit in the Tattoo Murder Case. The investigation was to begin the following morning, and he and Kenzo made a date to meet at ten o'clock.

"*Gardez la foi*," Kyosuke said as he bowed his way out the door. When Daiyu looked quizzical, Kyosuke explained, "That just means 'Keep the faith.' It's the only thing I remember from French class besides *soup du jour* and *cherchez la femme*." That was a gigantic fib, of course; Kyosuke was a gifted linguist and had even won a major prize from the Tokyo branch of the Alliance Française.

After Kyosuke had gone, Daiyu blew out a huge corona of cigarette smoke and said, "That's quite a friend you have there, Kenzo. To have such self-confidence at such a young age… I have to admit, I'm very impressed. I don't understand all the heavy-duty academic stuff he talks about, but I get the feeling he has the kind of remarkable mind that only comes along once every ten or twenty years. If all goes well, I'm not at all certain that he won't be able to solve this case, just as he promised."

46

The following day, precisely at ten o'clock, Kyosuke showed up at Ogikubo Station. In his dove-colored cashmere suit and matching overcoat, with a pale gray fedora worn raffishly down over one eye, he looked like a stylish young English gentleman. Kenzo had also dressed in a suit, though nothing as elegant as Kyosuke's symphony in gray. He had arrived early and had been pacing up and down in front of the station since nine forty-five. As soon as Kenzo raised his hand in greeting, Kyosuke fell into step with him and they began walking briskly toward their first destination.

The Mogami Group headquarters proved easy to find. The company was housed in a two-story building right on the main street, and the glass door bore the words, in rich gold lettering: THE MOGAMI GROUP—ENGINEERING, CONSTRUCTION, GENERAL CONTRACTING. The two men went into the wood-paneled lobby, where several disreputable-looking characters were sitting around a hibachi brazier, talking in low voices. One of the men, whom Kenzo recognized immediately as Gifu Inazawa, leapt up like a jack-in-the-box as Kenzo and Kyosuke approached.

Kenzo spoke first. "Mr. Inazawa, it's been a while. The truth is, we have one or two questions we'd like to ask you, if that's convenient."

Gifu Inazawa was clearly disturbed by this request. His face changed color several times, going from pale to red and back again, until he resembled a large, flustered turkey. Finally he spoke, or rather squawked, in a voice that sounded as if he had something caught in his throat. "Ah, Officer, it's good to see you. It's difficult to talk out here, so please follow me." Inazawa led his visitors to a spacious, well-furnished inner office with a brass door-plate that read TAKEZO MOGAMI, PRESIDENT.

Kenzo suppressed a smile. He had been introduced to Gifu Inazawa at the tattoo contest a few months earlier and had seen him again at the scene of the murder Since Inazawa's stern interrogation by Daiyu Matsushita, the man had evidently gotten it into his head that Kenzo was a policeman, too. The misunderstanding was very convenient.

"No one will be able to hear us in here," Inazawa said, gesturing for the two amateur detectives to sit down in a couple of foreign-looking chairs covered in black leather, while he took a seat behind a large mahogany desk. "Has something else happened?" Inazawa asked in a worried tone. "Who is it this time?"

"No, we aren't here about the murder case today. That's a relief, to tell the truth, because even policemen get sick of talking about nothing but murder all the time. Actually, this gentleman is an old friend of the late Mr. Mogami." Kenzo waved a hand in the direction of Kyosuke, who was somehow managing to keep a straight face. "Mr. Kamizu recently returned from Java, and when he heard about Mr. Mogami's death he was naturally very shocked. He expressed a desire to learn more about what had happened to his friend, and so I decided to bring him along with me today."

Kyosuke stood up and made a formal bow. "My name is Kyosuke Kamizu," he said. "I was treated very kindly by Mr. Mogami on many occasions, and I would like to offer my sincere condolences on the truly terrible thing that has happened."

Following the plan that he and Kenzo had rehearsed on the walk from the station, Kyosuke introduced himself in exceedingly polite terms.

Inazawa breathed a visible sigh of relief. "Oh, so that's how it is," he said. "Yes, it's really been a shock to us all. Even in this dog-eat-dog business, we could never have imagined that such a terrible thing could happen to our boss, who would never have hurt a flea, and who didn't have an enemy in the world as far as I know."

Kenzo stifled another smile at this disingenuous description of Takezo Mogami, who by all accounts had been a rapacious and unprincipled wheeler-dealer with enemies in every ward of Tokyo. "How about it?" he said. "If you can spare the time, won't you tell Mr. Kamizu what happened?"

Obligingly, Gifu Inazawa proceeded to relate the entire story of Takezo Mogami's disappearance and subsequent murder, scratching his head perplexedly as he talked. Kenzo could find no discrepancies whatsoever between this narrative and the statement Inazawa had earlier given to the police.

Kyosuke listened intently to the story, and when Inazawa had finished he said in a sympathetic tone of voice, "This has been really rough on you, too, hasn't it? But from what you've told me I get the feeling that Miss Nomura had quite a crush on you. It must have been very hard for you to lose her just when you were becoming so close."

"It's very kind of you to say that. There's no telling what might have happened if she had gone on living, if you know what I mean." Licking his narrow lips like a hungry wolf, Inazawa gave a lecherous chuckle.

Watching that coarse, sensual face, Kenzo couldn't help thinking that the man was the sort of incorrigible beast who gave all men a bad name. Kyosuke, too, appeared to be stifling a grimace as he said, "From what I've heard, Miss Nomura seems to have been, shall we say, a woman of healthy appetites. Do you know whether she had any trouble with men in the past?"

"No, not as far as I know. I think she had more trouble with women, to tell you the truth. They were all terribly jealous of her, my own wife included. Miss Kinue was the kind of woman who made other women very angry, whether by stealing their men, or living a luxurious life, or just by being beautiful. As for men, though, I do remember that there was a big uproar at one point when someone said Miss Kinue's relationship with the boss's younger brother Hisashi was more than friendly, but that turned out to be just a rumor. Knowing how strongly the boss felt about Miss Kinue, I don't think Hisashi would have had the courage to take that kind of risk, no matter how attracted to her he might have been. And in any case, I don't think she was his type. He's always talking about how much he dislikes tattoos, on men or women."

"Speaking of taking risks, you were about to cross a rather dangerous bridge yourself," Kyosuke said.

Inazawa smiled sheepishly. "I know," he said. "I'm really ashamed of my behavior, acting like a lovesick fool at my age."

"On another subject," Kyosuke said, "how are things with the business?"

Inazawa sighed. "Hisashi has absolutely no ambition, so it's a major problem. He's the boss's only brother, and we had hoped that he would take over the company and run it with our support, but he just keeps saying that he isn't cut out for this sort of business. Not only that, but he's undermining the strength of the company by selling off some important land rights much too cheaply. On top of that, it's been a very difficult time for me, having my behavior regarding Miss Kinue made public by the police. Sometimes I just feel like crawling into a hole, but I can't desert the company."

"Everyone makes mistakes, and what's past is past," Kyosuke said breezily. "What's that old saying, 'There's no shame in being a fool for love.' Oh, by the way, I gather you've taken up dancing."

"You heard about that?" Looking embarrassed, Inazawa ran his hand over his sparse, oily hair. "Yes, well, when you're in this sort of business there are certain things you have to do as a matter of social courtesy."

"Are you sure you aren't doing it for another reason? I hear those dance-hall girls are very charming." Evidently that random remark hit the bull's eye. Inazawa laughed self-consciously, and Kyosuke seized that opportunity to change the subject. "By the way, do you have any other interests or hobbies?" he asked.

Kenzo was amazed that Gifu Inazawa would tolerate such a prolonged intrusion into his private affairs, but he concluded that the presence of a "policeman" had made him more docile than he would have been had he known his guests' true identities.

"No," Inazawa replied, "I'm ashamed to say it, but I've somehow managed to live my life until now without any special hobbies or passionate interests, outside of work."

"But surely you enjoy horse racing?" Kyosuke probed.

"Oh, yes, now that you mention it, I do."

"There's nothing quite like the feeling you get when you bet on a long shot and end up getting a big payoff, is there?"

"You can say that again. I remember back in 1939, in the good old days, I put a bundle on a long shot, and won big. In prewar money, I made over five hundred yen, but it didn't last very long. My buddies and I drank it up in no time, celebrating. Unfortunately that sort of a win is really rare."

"Is that so?" Kyosuke said languidly. He appeared to have suddenly lost interest in the conversation, and after a brief exchange of pleasantries with the ever-obsequious Inazawa, he and Kenzo left the building.

"How's this for a hypothesis?" Kenzo ventured as the two friends walked toward the station. "Inazawa ran up some huge gambling debts, so he embezzled money from the company. When Mogami found out, Inazawa panicked and killed him. As for Kinue, she laughed in his face when he tried to seduce her, and he killed her in a fit of pique."

"Not a chance," Kyosuke said flatly. "I mean, think about it. How could an unimaginative, cowardly pig like that carry out such an ingenious crime?"

"But he certainly seemed to like gambling."

"Sure, he may like to place an occasional bet, but that doesn't make him a big-time gambler, I'm absolutely certain of that. He doesn't have the character, or the capabilities."

"But he doesn't have a perfect alibi, either," Kenzo argued.

Kyosuke pursed his lips for a moment, and then said very slowly, as if addressing a child, "All right. If you're going to be stubborn about this, then tell me. What's his motive? I can't deny that there could be something to your theory about embezzling money from the company, but I don't really see him bumping off his boss over such a small thing. If you propose to make him the culprit, there are just too many things that don't make sense, and too many discrepancies in his behavior. First, he left his fingerprints on the outside of the doorknob of the bathroom at Kinue's house, right? A criminal that careless would surely leave his fingerprints on the inside of the knob as well. He didn't. If he were the kind of sloppy criminal who would not only strew his prints all over the place, but would leave behind a piece of incriminating evidence at the murder scene and go back in broad daylight to retrieve it, I think the police would have solved this case long ago. They wouldn't have needed my help."

There was nothing Kenzo could say in self-defense. He walked along in silence, feeling like the village idiot, and before he knew it they were nearly at the station. "Now what?" he asked.

"Well, I called Professor Hayakawa earlier and was told that he wouldn't be home until early evening. I wonder whether Hisashi Mogami has a telephone at his house?"

"Yes, he does. Shall I give him a ring?"

"No," said Kyosuke after a moment's consideration. "Let's stage a surprise attack, without phoning first. But first, what do you say we grab some soba for lunch? It's my treat, in return for dinner last night."

"You know what I just remembered?" Kenzo said as they wandered through the narrow alleys behind the station, looking for a restaurant that specialized in buckwheat noodles. "The dining room at Ikko Academy."

"Oh, that's a lovely thought," Kyosuke said sardonically, for the dining hall had not been famous for its comfort, or its cuisine. "That reminds me, though, are you still the Ultra?" In their days at Ikko, Kenzo had been nicknamed the Ultra-Extraordinary Eater because of his boundless appetite and his ability to consume prodigious amounts of food.

"You'll find out soon enough," Kenzo said with a mischievous grin He slid open the frosted-glass door of a promising-looking soba shop and bowed low like an Elizabethan courtier, sweeping the ground with an imaginary feathered hat.

47

It's the quintessential sound of lunchtime in Japan: the sibilant din of noodles being aspirated into hungry mouths at great velocity. Kenzo and Kyosuke were contributing their share of noise as they slurped up their extra-large bowls of buckwheat soba noodles garnished with deep-fried tofu strips and sliced green onions in a dark, rich broth. Between bites, Kyosuke went on talking.

"Why do you suppose Professor Hayakawa didn't try to produce any confirmation of his own alibi? It's true that if someone suddenly asked either of us what we were doing on such-and-such a day in the past, we'd be hard pressed to remember where we were or what we were doing. If it were a question of a day or two ago, though, that would be entirely different. You can't very well say you've completely forgotten such recent events, and even if you didn't have any witnesses, the natural human instinct would be to tell the investigators what you were doing. For someone in danger of being charged with a capital crime, to refuse to give an alibi is very strange indeed."

"Maybe the professor was just peeved about having been roughed up by the police," Kenzo said, sprinkling a pinch of five-spice powder on his broth.

"I don't think mere peevishness begins to explain it, in a serious case like this. No, I think there's some secret that the professor doesn't want to reveal, some deep, dark secret that he's willing to risk his reputation and even his future to protect."

Kyosuke picked up his cup and took a sip of hot green tea. "The next thing that strikes me as strange," he went on, "is why, in the first murder, the killer took the entire torso away with him if all he wanted was the tattoos. It would have been much easier to have removed the skin at the scene. As you know, if you take the subcutaneous tissues as well, the skin will keep without spoiling for quite some time even without chemical processing, so there was no need to take the entire torso, bones and all. On top of that, a human torso is very heavy, and it would have been difficult to deal with all the blood pouring from the neck and from the stumps of the limbs. I mean, picture someone staggering along with a huge burden on their back, leaving a trail of blood. Whether it was in broad daylight or in the middle of the night, you'd think such a sight would attract some attention, wouldn't you?"

"Yes, that struck me as strange, too."

"I think it's because no one understands the axiom of criminal economics."

"What on earth is that?" Kenzo said.

"Well, suppose a murderer carries a torso away from the scene of the crime. What does he do with the leftover bones and internal organs once he's stripped off the skin? Actually I must confess that it only just occurred to me now that this sort of problem—the efficient management of crime-related waste products—might be called 'criminal economics.' I'm not talking about something like making dyestuffs from the by-products of coal, what the Germans call *koks*, or 'coke' in English. This is a much more sinister business. But anyway, what happened to all the blood that resulted from chopping up the body? Were there any bloodstains in the garden?"

"Not as far as I know. The bathroom where the body was found had ceramic tiles on the floor and walls, and the water had been left running overnight, so all the blood was probably washed down the drain. The forensics people examined the drain and found evidence that quite a large amount of blood had passed through it."

"A large amount of blood, eh?" Kyosuke drank the last of his tea, replaced his disposable wooden chopsticks in their paper wrapper, and stood up. In the course of the conversation Kyosuke had tossed out a number of hints, but, try as he might, Kenzo had found himself unable to follow his friend's line of thought. He didn't want to seem dense, though, so he didn't ask any of the questions that were in his mind.

The two men left the restaurant and cut across the train tracks. After walking for fifteen minutes through a maze of bombed-out buildings, flimsy barracks, and older houses that had miraculously survived the war, they arrived at the midpoint between Ogikubo and East Ogikubo. The neighborhood was entirely residential, and the house they were looking for turned out to be quite large, though not terribly luxurious. In the spacious garden there was a ferro-concrete outbuilding that appeared to be a studio of some sort.

"Does Hisashi Mogami paint pictures?" Kyosuke asked.

"I really wouldn't know about that," Kenzo replied.

"Never mind, I'll ask him myself. If he's a painter, we'll get him to show us some of his works of art. Often you can understand a person's psychological makeup just by looking at one or two of his paintings."

Kenzo rang the doorbell in the entryway. A plump, middle-aged housemaid told them that Hisashi Mogami was away on a trip and wasn't expected back until the following morning. The two men said that they would call again the next afternoon.

"That was a real waste of time," Kenzo grumbled as they trudged back to the station.

"It couldn't be helped," Kyosuke said cheerily. "You have to be prepared to put up with a little frustration, if you're going to be an amateur detective." Just then a sudden gust of wintry wind threaded its way between them, kicking up a great golden cloud of dried gingko leaves.

"It's really cold in Japan, isn't it?" Kyosuke said, pulling his overcoat closer around him. "I'd forgotten how cold it gets in this country." Whether because he had recently returned from the steamy southern front, or because he was still recovering from illness, the cold seemed to penetrate his woolen clothing and go right through to his rangy bones.

Kenzo shivered sympathetically, although the cold didn't really bother him. "So what shall we do with the rest of the day, until evening?"

"That's a good question. I'd like to go take a look at the crime scene at Kitazawa. Do you suppose we could persuade your brother to come along?"

"It's hard to say. I'm sure he'll try to accommodate us as much as possible, but he has a very busy schedule."

"In that case, call him up and say, 'Kyosuke Kamizu would like to show you the solution to the mystery of the locked room, so please do us the honor of accompanying us to Kitazawa this afternoon.'"

Kenzo stopped in his tracks and stared at Kyosuke. No one believed more deeply in the genius of his friend than Kenzo, but he couldn't help being startled by that bold declaration. After all, this was a riddle that had stumped the entire investigative branch of the Tokyo police force for three long months and now Kyosuke was saying that he was prepared to solve it without ever having seen the murder site. "Are you serious?" Kenzo asked.

"I'm always serious," Kyosuke said impishly. He gave Kenzo a look of bravado bordering on arrogance, and finished it off with one of his catlike smiles. Kenzo's mind was a whirl of emotions as he stopped at a red public telephone and placed the call to his brother. When Daiyu Matsushita heard the reason for the call his voice was suddenly filled with excitement. This made Kenzo even more uneasy, for he knew how his brother hated wasting time on wild-goose chases.

"He's leaving right away, and we're to meet him at Kitazawa," Kenzo said, as he stepped out of the booth.

"In that case, we'd better get going." There wasn't a trace of anxiety in Kyosuke's voice.

Kenzo put his arm on his friend's sleeve. "Are you absolutely sure about this? If by some chance this demonstration should be a flop, it could make the rest of our investigation really difficult. I realize I probably sound like a fretful grandmother, it's just that I'm so afraid of disappointing my brother again. He can be kind of scary, you know."

"You're still a worrywart, just like when we were in school," Kyosuke said. "Listen, this so-called locked-room mystery isn't as big a deal as you think. Anything a human devises can be figured out by another human being."

Right, Kenzo thought. *Especially if that other human being is a bona fide genius.*

48

An hour later, Kenzo and Kyosuke arrived at the former residence of Kinue Nomura in Kitazawa. That dwelling, along with the rest of Takezo Mogami's property, had passed immediately into the hands of his younger brother Hisashi, who had expressed his intentions of renovating the house and putting it on the market. However, the Metropolitan Police had asked that the house be left alone until the case was solved. Even so, the household furnishings had been carted away.

"This place is about as it was at the time of the crime, right?" Kyosuke asked as he stood outside the gate, peering at the property with interest.

"It looks the same to me," Kenzo said.

"This must be my lucky day," Kyosuke said. "If the house had already been remodeled, I wouldn't have been able to prove my theory." Walking ahead of Kenzo, Kyosuke went through the gate.

During the months since the murder, the garden had run amok. People were afraid of entering the scene of a murder and after the initial police investigation was moved down to headquarters, no one had passed through the gate. The dilapidated wreckage of dried-up tomato plants looked like the greenish-gray skeletons of extraterrestrial visitors, and the atmosphere of the entire garden was eerie and untamed. Kenzo's stomach lurched as he remembered the high hopes with which he had walked through this same garden, believing he was on the way to an intimate romantic rendezvous.

"Where exactly were the fragments of that photographic plate?" Kyosuke asked.

"In the back garden," Kenzo said, recovering his composure. He led Kyosuke around the corner of the building. "I'm sure it was right here," Kenzo said, pointing at a spot on the dusty ground.

"I see," Kyosuke said. "And that window with the horizontal metal bars across it, that's the bathroom?"

"That's right. But it isn't possible to get in or out through the window."

"What about this drainage ditch? Does the water come from the bathroom?"

"Yes, that's right."

Kyosuke bent over and lifted up the cover of the drainage system. "Look, this opens!" he said. "So it's just as I thought."

"Surely you aren't suggesting that a human being could fit through that opening?"

"We aren't talking about *Homo sapiens* here," Kyosuke said. "We're talking about *Limax maximus*. I was just trying to find the slug's footprints. You know, the trail of the slug?" Kenzo couldn't help wondering whether Kyosuke had lost his marbles, but his friend's amber eyes were perfectly clear, and sparkling with excitement.

"Ah, gentlemen, sorry to keep you waiting. I had a little trouble giving some pesky reporters the slip, so I came the long way round." Wearing a black overcoat and booming out his unaffected laugh, the bulky, vigorous form of Detective Chief Inspector Daiyu Matsushita appeared.

After exchanging greetings, the three men entered the house. A thick layer of dust covered every surface, and Kenzo was immediately seized by a fit of coughing. He put his handkerchief over his nose, but even through the thin cotton he thought he could detect a lingering odor of blood circulating in the dusty air, and it made him feel sick to his stomach.

Meanwhile, Daiyu was giving Kyosuke a guided tour of the crime scene, illustrating his statements with the forensic photographs he held in his hand.

"This is where we found some bloodstains. This is where the *tansu* chest was. As you can see from the picture, the contents had been ransacked. In this room, we found a glass with some whiskey residue."

"And where's the problematical bathroom?" Kyosuke asked.

"At the end of this hall, on the right." The three men walked down the hall single file and stopped in front of the bathroom. Through the opening in the brown door where a wide board had been cut out, they could see the white tile floor. Kyosuke stepped through the hole into the bathroom.

"Now, where was the slug?" he asked when Kenzo and Daiyu had joined him.

"On that windowsill," the brothers replied, nearly in unison.

"And where's the original crack in the door, the one Kenzo and Professor Hayakawa peeked through?"

"It's here," said Daiyu, pointing to the lower part of the door, "but as you can see it isn't long enough or wide enough for a thread to pass through, much less a slug."

"Ah, I see what you mean." Kyosuke didn't appear in the least perturbed. He stood quietly for a moment, as if lost in meditation. Then he said, "Okay, that'll do it. I've unraveled the riddle now." He looked at the two Matsushita brothers and smiled.

"You've figured it out already?" Daiyu Matsushita's voice held a mixture of incredulity and hope. "Then tell us, quickly. How on earth did the killer get in and out?"

Kyosuke shook his head as if to say, Not so fast. "I'd like to conduct a little experiment right now, and show you exactly how it was done," he said. "But first we have to be sure that all the conditions are the same as they were on the night of the crime."

Kyosuke removed the stopper from the bathtub and turned on the faucet. Because it hadn't been used for quite some time, the water that came bursting out at first was a deep reddish brown from the accumulation of rust. *The color of dried blood*, Kenzo thought.

"This will take a while," Kyosuke said. "While we're waiting, let's go into the other room." He led the way out of the bathroom. The sound of the running water followed the men down the hall, reminding Kenzo of that horrible morning when he and Professor Hayakawa had discovered the dismembered body.

With all its furnishings removed, the eight-mat room formerly used as a parlor looked dreary and uninviting, but the three men went in and sat down on the bare tatami-matted floor. Kyosuke began to speak, using a didactic tone of voice usually associated with the lecture podium. "In a typical Japanese house, it would be very difficult to create a locked room. While each room may appear to be independent, they share a common floor and a common ceiling. So an intruder could crawl along above the ceiling and enter the house through a clothes closet, or slink along under the floor and make their entry by pushing up the tatami matting. Either way, a Japanese-style house presents no challenge to a resourceful burglar. However, this bathroom is different. The floors and the lower part of the walls are covered with tile, and there isn't so much as a ventilation duct in the ceiling. The untiled areas of the bathroom are finished in wood, but it isn't possible to

278

separate or dislodge the boards. The same is true of the door. Unless, of course, you break it down the way the police did."

Kyosuke smiled mischievously at Detective Chief Inspector Matsushita, who motioned impatiently for him to continue. "As for the windows, they were locked securely from inside, and the outside was protected with sturdy iron bars so narrowly spaced that not even a cat, much less a human, could have squeezed through. The door, too, was firmly bolted from inside, and there was no space above or below the door. There's no secret passage of any sort, and we know that the criminal didn't kill himself in here. It is a fact that the torso was dismembered and has never been found. We also know that the killer found some way of entering and leaving this room. The key to solving that mystery is the existence of the slug."

"The slug? But how…" Daiyu and Kenzo exchanged baffled looks.

"Think about it," Kyosuke said. "According to Kenzo, when Hisashi Mogami heard about the slug in the bathroom, his face turned pale and he seemed very surprised. Since the three curses—the snake, the frog, and the slug—seem to be intertwined throughout this case, casting a weird shadow on everything that happens, it's no wonder Hisashi was shocked to hear that an actual slug had turned up at the murder scene. But what about the killer? We can easily imagine his reaction. It's a fact of psychology that criminals tend to be especially nervous and superstitious immediately after committing a crime. There's no way such a painstaking criminal would have overlooked the presence of a slug in the bathroom, so we can assume that the slug entered the room after the murderer departed. If we could trace the path taken by the slug, I think the escape route of the criminal would become clear as well."

Raising his voice a bit, Kyosuke continued, "As a rule, in a bathroom, no matter what type of construction is used, there has to be an intake and an outtake for the water. In this case the intake is directly from the water supply, so it would be impossible for a slug to have gotten in through the faucet. The outtake is the route used by the slug, and it was also used indirectly by the criminal to make his escape."

Daiyu and Kenzo looked at each other in disbelief. They had both completely overlooked that possibility, as if it were a blind spot.

"Once you understand that, the rest is simple. It's just a matter of needles and thread," Kyosuke said casually.

From the bathroom, they could hear the sound of the water overflowing the bathtub. "Well, it sounds as if we're ready to proceed with the experiment," Kyosuke said as he stood up and stretched his long legs. "Shall we go?" With Kenzo and Daiyu close behind, he re-entered the bathroom. The water had flowed over the sides of the bathtub and washed down the tile floor before spiraling into the drain.

"Let's see, we'll need three pieces of thread. We might be able to get along with fewer, but let's try three just to be safe." Kyosuke reached into the pocket of his overcoat and pulled out a sheaf of linen thread and two large straight pins, along with three small chips of wood. He unrolled the thread and cut it into three sections, then attached a wood chip to the end of each piece of thread. He tied two of the remaining ends of thread to the two pins, stuck one pin into the door above the board, under the bolt, then lightly stuck another pin into the wall at the same height as the bolt. He made a small loop in the end of the last piece of thread, this he attached to the handle of the bolt, pulling it horizontal and making it go around the pin. From there he pulled it diagonal and wound it around the pin atop the door, finally wrapping it around the top of the padlock on the window.

"These three chips of wood will eventually be washed away, down the drain, by the force of the water from the tap. Of course, the water stream alone isn't enough to put this apparatus into motion, but afterward the killer would have picked up the wood chip and manipulated the attached string, and that would do it. Watch from inside and I'll show you." Kyosuke ducked under the thread and closed the bathroom door behind him.

As if hypnotized, Kenzo and Daiyu kept their eyes fixed on the bolt of the door. After a moment, the thread began to move smoothly, manipulated from outside. The bolt was moved to the side and fell into the aperture. This loosened the pin which had been attached to the wall, and it fell to the floor and was washed down the drain. It all happened in the blink of the eye, and the next thing the watchers knew the door was perfectly locked and all traces of the mechanism—the strings, the pins, the wood chips—had vanished down the drain.

"I guess that concludes the demonstration," Kenzo said with a faraway sigh, as if he were coming out of a trance.

"Mmm." Daiyu Matsushita nodded his head without comment, his eyes shining with admiration.

"How about it? Did the lock catch?" Kyosuke asked rhetorically as he stuck his head through the hole in the door.

"Thank you very much for showing us that wonderful trick. I have to say, I was really surprised." There was a quaver of emotion in Daiyu Matsushita's voice, but Kyosuke's face remained completely expressionless.

"A mechanical trick like this is nothing special," he said, almost disdainfully. "There's a much more important aspect, and that is the psychological trick that was used by the killer."

"And what might that be?" Daiyu asked politely.

"You people have allowed yourselves to be chased into a psychological locked room. You're stuck in that metaphorical room, making no progress at all, and you haven't been able to set foot outside it since the case began. This trick with the door isn't the sort of thing someone could think up in ten or twenty minutes, so I think it's safe to say that the killer was someone who was familiar with the inside of this house."

"Is that so?" Daiyu Matsushita was silent for a moment, as if he were looking at a lineup of suspects behind his eyelids. Finally, he spoke. "I used to be confused about why the killer left the water running in the bathtub. Thanks to your demonstration, I understand that now. Having the water running was an indispensable part of the trick."

"That's true, but I think there was another reason for leaving the water running, besides needing it to wash the chips of wood into the drain. No, the running water definitely had another function."

"Meaning what?"

"Meaning that from the standpoint of criminal economics, the more use you can get out of a single prop, the more profitable your enterprise will be."

The chief of detectives appeared to be fed up with Kyosuke's cryptic remarks, and when he spoke it was in a low, annoyed voice. "Mr. Kamizu, let's get to the point. Do you know who committed these crimes, or not?"

Kyosuke smiled. "Almost," he said.

49

Professor Hayakawa had married money as well as beauty. He and his tattooed wife lived in Yotsuya in a splendid European-style brick house with leaded windows, wrought-iron balconies, and a classical English garden hidden away behind high brick walls. The house had been spared by some wartime fluke, while both of the formerly elegant dwellings on either side were now bombed-out ruins, overgrown with weeds. A deferential maid, wearing a white apron over a subdued kimono, ushered Kenzo and Kyosuke into a vast reception room. Kenzo couldn't help crying out in surprise when he saw the extraordinary decor.

There wasn't a single painting on the walls, as might have been expected in a Western-style house. Every inch of wall space was covered with framed human skins patterned with complex, brilliantly-colored tattoos. In the corners of the room, instead of marble statues, were tattooed torso-skins draped over wooden armatures. As Kenzo stared at this strange collection, which was every bit as impressive as the renowned display at Tokyo University, a vision of Kinue's decorated body flashed before his eyes.

"Kyosuke," he said, trying to keep his voice casual, "what do you suppose has become of the Orochimaru tattoo? Assuming the murderer cut off the trunk and took it with him, if the skin wasn't removed and treated right away it would soon go bad. For all we know that magnificent tattoo is already ruined."

Kyosuke shook his head. "Personally, I don't think that's the case," he said.

Just then a door opened and Professor Hayakawa appeared. He was dressed in an expensive brown wool kimono, and when he saw his visitors his face broke into a welcoming smile. "Why, if it isn't Kyosuke Kamizu, back from the dead!"

"Sensei, please forgive me for not staying in touch during the war. Now that I've finally made it home in one piece, I just wanted to stop by and say hello."

"I'm delighted to see that you managed to keep yourself alive. If that stupid war had killed a promising young man like you, it would have been a great loss for the entire country." Professor Hayakawa glanced in Kenzo's direction and his tone and demeanor changed radically. "Ah, Matsushita, how very lovely to see you again," he said, his voice dripping with insincerity. "Your brother really gave me a hard time the other day, you know, just because you happened to remember something that was none of your business in the first place."

Kenzo knew right away that the professor was talking about the photographic plate. "I'm really sorry about that," he said. "It's just that everyone was so excited that day, and I was about half in shock myself, and I thought it might be important evidence. I didn't realize you had walked off with it."

"Well, don't worry about it. I made a fairly big gaffe myself, taking the plate in the first place. Please, please, have a seat." The room was furnished entirely in rather stiff Western style, and the three men sat down on large wing-backed chairs upholstered in green and gold tapestry in a fleur-de-lis pattern.

"Sensei," Kyosuke said, looking around, "this is the second time I've been in this room, but I'm struck anew by what a superb collection you've assembled. It's amazing that all these skins survived the war intact. You must have suffered a great deal, worrying about them while you were away."

"I certainly did. I figured it couldn't be helped if the house got hit by a firebomb, but I was so worried about my collection,

I could hardly bear it. When we were evacuated from this house, my skins were scattered all over the country for safe-keeping. I had the devil's own time putting the collection back together. It was a complete nightmare."

"It sounds dreadful," said Kyosuke sympathetically. "Even with my untutored eye I can see that these specimens should be designated as national treasures. I'm sure that future generations will be grateful to you for going to so much trouble to preserve this unique art form."

The professor nodded. "I'd be happy if everyone understood as well as you do," he said, "but unfortunately society chooses to label me 'eccentric' and treat me like some sort of pervert."

"That can't be helped, I suppose. Maybe they'll come to appreciate you in a hundred years or so. That seems to be the way these things work, historically."

Professor Hayakawa laughed appreciatively. Just then the maid brought in three cups of fragrant Earl Grey tea on a silver tray, and Kyosuke took advantage of this interruption to change the subject. "Sensei," he said casually, "I couldn't help noticing that you don't seem to have any examples of Horiyasu's work here." As if to defuse the somewhat personal question, he picked up his flowered porcelain teacup and took a deep breath of bergamot-scented steam.

"Yes, alas…" Professor Hayakawa's face stiffened, as if the question had caught him off guard. "I regret that I've never been able to add a Horiyasu to my collection. Horiuno, Horikane, Horikin, Horigoro, I've managed to obtain a sample of the work of all the famous tattoo artists. Only Horiyasu has eluded me. To tell you the truth, I wanted that tattoo of Kinue's badly, but that murdering bastard beat me to it. Whoever he is, he must really have a fearsome obsession with tattoos. I mean, I know I'm extreme. Yet, no matter how much I wanted a particular tattoo, I would never have the courage to kill someone and steal the skin."

"He really is a scary killer, isn't he?" Kyosuke said mildly. "But then there's the matter of your refusal to give an alibi for the night of the murder, Sensei. I probably shouldn't say this in front of Kenzo, but the thing I've noticed about policemen in general is that once they decide you're a prime suspect, they'll harass you mercilessly. You took a big risk by refusing to divulge your whereabouts."

"That's all very well for you to say, Kamizu, but there's a point after which it becomes ridiculous. I mean, what evidence is there to tie me to that crime? All right, so I was the one who found the body. Matsushita, here, was with me the entire time. And what possible motive would I have had for doing such a dreadful thing to poor Kinue, whom I had known since she was a child? Admittedly, when Takezo died I did come into some money, close to a million yen to be exact. It can't be said that I would have had absolutely no motive for killing Takezo, but killing Kinue wouldn't have increased my inheritance from Takezo by a single yen. The money that would have gone to Kinue, had she survived Takezo, went directly to Hisashi. I had no vested interests of any sort in Kinue's death. Would I kill her just to get my hands on her tattoo? I'm simply not that stupid."

"I don't know, Sensei," Kyosuke said boldly. "I get the feeling that's an evasive answer."

Professor Hayakawa replied in a calm, dignified tone. "If my activities on that night had no connection whatsoever with the murder, then those activities should be my business and no one else's. Look, it's very rare for an ordinary person, however innocent, to be able to produce a flawless alibi for every waking moment of his life."

"Yes, you're absolutely right. A criminal who allowed himself to be captured just because his alibi didn't check out wouldn't be much of a crook, would he?"

"Precisely. That's the problem with the Japanese police force; they need to take a slightly more scientific approach. Their methods are downright barbaric. From what I've heard, if the police get it into their heads that you are guilty of some crime, they toss you into a squalid cell for two or three months. Every day they subject you to hours of grilling, liberally seasoned with kicks and punches, until you finally end up confessing just to make them stop. I mean, after several months of solitary confinement and brutal torture, they could probably get *you* to confess to murder."

"I don't doubt that at all," Kyosuke said. He lifted his teacup and held it in midair for a few moments, evidently lost in thought. "Still, Sensei, you have to admit that there was something a bit unsavory about the way you made off with those photographic-plate fragments, when they were so obviously evidence from a crime scene."

"Ah, yes. Well, that simply couldn't be helped. I mean, when I saw what was on the slide, my old collector's mania came to the fore. Before I knew it, I had slipped the fragments into my pocket. But if I really were the murderer, once I had drawn attention to the fragments, I would hardly have been so foolish as to make off with them, now would I?"

"No, I don't suppose you would." Kyosuke took a sip of his tea and flashed Kenzo a significant glance.

Deftly, Professor Hayakawa steered the topic of conversation away from the murder case. "The world really does seem to have gone mad. Tell me, Kamizu, what do you make of the state of things today?"

"I've only just returned home, so…"

The professor's voice rose with emotion. "I've been back from the war for quite a while now. This country's in the grips of total pandemonium. All over Japan, it's as if eighty million people had simultaneously gone out of their minds. Staple foods are either rationed or else completely unavailable, and the distribution always seems to be running behind schedule. On top of that, the authorities have cracked down on hoarding, and anyone caught laying in supplies is ruthlessly punished. They ignore the theoretical policy of low prices, while indiscriminately raising the prices of cigarettes and railway tickets. In these crazy times stones float and leaves sink, and the larger the fish is, the more easily it slips through the net. I swear, the government today is beyond the powers of comprehension of an honest person like me. If I were a bit younger, I'd be sorely tempted to turn to swindling, or robbery."

Kyosuke smiled. "I remember before the war you were very cynical about the military authorities, and you haven't changed a bit."

"Oh, come on, Kamizu, it's not just me. Anyone who would buy into that load of moronic propaganda they call the Pronouncement from Imperial Headquarters would have to be soft in the head, don't you think? Let's just say that participating in the war wasn't exactly my idea of a delightful experience. Day after day we would sink innumerable enemy aircraft carriers and battleships. I remember counting sixty ships destroyed, each one full of men who probably didn't want to be fighting any more than we did. We didn't have nearly as much success in downing the crucial B-29s, though. Next time we go to war, we should practice with the catapult and the crossbow. Then we might have a better chance of bringing down a few B-29s." Professor Hayakawa paused to take a sip of tea.

Before the professor could launch into another polemic, Kyosuke seized the opening. "Oh, by the way, are you still playing *go*? Just before I left for the front you gave me a couple of lessons, and I remember that you were an awesome opponent."

"Checkers, eh? Yes, that's still one of my passions. But since you're young, you must have improved by leaps and bounds since we last played."

"No, unfortunately I haven't had a chance to sit down and play a relaxed game of Japanese checkers since I put on my soldier's uniform."

"In that case, what do you say to a quick game? You don't mind, do you, Kenzo?"

"Please, please, go ahead," Kenzo said. "Chess is my game, so I've always been more of an interested onlooker when it comes to *go.*"

Professor Hayakawa rang the brass bell on a sideboard behind his chair. When the maid appeared, he asked her to bring the checkerboard and the black and white stones for playing *go*. Kyosuke chose the black stones, and made a courtly little bow to his opponent. Kenzo, meanwhile, was trying to figure out why on earth Kyosuke would suggest playing checkers. The idea of wasting precious investigative time on something so frivolous made Kenzo's stomach churn.

50

After an hour of spirited play, the professor threw in his chips with the score at two games to one. "Kamizu, you win again," he said. "You've turned into quite a player."

Kyosuke bowed his head deferentially. "I had a good teacher."

Professor Hayakawa paused and lit a cigarette, and Kyosuke casually asked, "Sensei, would you like to see something interesting?" He reached into his briefcase, took out the envelope containing the photographs Kenzo had lent him, and passed it across the table to Professor Hayakawa. The professor looked at the photographs, and a strange expression flickered across his face.

"I see," he murmured, as if to himself. "This is Jiraiya, and this is Kinue's Orochimaru, and this is the Tsunedahime that I picked up in the garden." He stared for a long time at the photograph of the Tsunedahime tattoo, and Kenzo noticed that the hand that held the photo was trembling slightly.

"How on earth did you get your hands on these photographs, Kamizu?" the professor demanded. "Do you know who took them and when?"

"Actually, Kinue Nomura gave these photographs to Kenzo at the meeting of the Tattoo Society in August. She told him there was some secret behind the three tattoos, hers and her brother's and sister's, and she said she was afraid that she was going to be killed and have her skin stripped off. She didn't think there was any way for her to escape this horrible death. She promised to explain in detail the following morning, and she said she also wanted to ask for Kenzo's advice. He was on his way to keep that appointment when he ran into you at the front entrance of Kinue's house. I don't have to tell you what happened next."

Kenzo's face flushed with guilt at hearing the lies he had told to Kyosuke repeated out loud. His story really did sound rather unlikely, but the truth was even stranger, and much less socially acceptable.

Kyosuke went on. "The secret, whatever it was, ended up being buried in obscurity. According to Hisashi Mogami, these photos were originally pasted onto the first page of Kinue's album. That page has been ripped out. There's no way of knowing whether there was some explanation on the back. However, the intriguing thing is that Kinue's brother, Tsunetaro, was apparently able to see through the secrets of this baffling case after one glance at these photographs. After that, he telephoned Kenzo and said he would explain all the mysteries in three days' time. Before he could do so, he ended up being murdered himself." Kyosuke took a deep breath.

"I see," said the professor slowly. He fell into a sullen silence.

Kyosuke had played his last trump card but continued to badger Professor Hayakawa with a tenacity that bordered on impertinence. "Sensei," he asked, "why did you say that this case had something to do with the non-Euclidean theory of geometry?"

"Don't you see?" the professor said in an annoyed tone. "The locked room was too perfectly constructed. It would have taken a first-rate genius to have planned and executed such a complex crime so quickly and with such consummate skill. And the thing about crimes committed by geniuses is that ordinary people often find them impossible to solve. Your specialty is mathematics. You should understand. It's sometimes more difficult to solve a particular problem than to create it in the first place."

"I hate to say this, Sensei, but that's a lie. The real reason this case reminded you of the theory of non-Euclidean geometry is something entirely different."

"Why, you cheeky little… !" Professor Hayakawa was seething with rage. The room was suddenly filled with hostility.

"Sensei, let's stop playing games. Why did you pick up that photographic plate?"

Professor Hayakawa had calmed down a bit and seemed to be enjoying matching wits with Kyosuke. "No matter how I explain about my mania, my obsession with tattoos, an ordinary person simply isn't capable of understanding how I feel," he said. "Right now there's one person inhabiting my mind and body—that is, me. But there's another person—another me, so to speak—who sometimes takes over and does unexpected things, and I have absolutely no control over the behavior of that other me."

"Ah," said Kyosuke. "In that case, let's say that the 'other you' is in love with another woman, a woman who isn't your wife. And while you hate and despise that other woman, you still can't forget her no matter how hard you try. Would that be a reasonable explanation for your behavior?"

"That's ridiculous. That's totally absurd!" the professor sputtered angrily.

"I'm certain that you know the secret behind this case. There's a woman lurking in the shadows behind the murderer, and I think you know exactly who she is."

Professor Hayakawa made no reply. A deathly silence descended upon the room, and after a while Kyosuke stood up and murmured some conventional phrases about the lateness of the hour. The professor saw the two men off in the entryway.

As they were slipping into their shoes, Kyosuke fired one last volley. "Sensei," he said, "I think I understand why you didn't offer any substantiation for your alibi for the night of Kinue's murder. If I had a little time, I don't think it would be too hard to find out where you were. What I do know, at least, is that you were somewhere that you didn't want the police to know about. That's why you were willing to take any risk to cover up that fact. Am I right, Sensei?"

All color drained from the professor's face. He leaned against the wall and whispered in a voice that was almost a moan, "Kyosuke Kamizu, you're a very frightening person."

After the two men left, Kyosuke lapsed into small talk about the starry sky and the invigorating chill in the air, paying no attention to Kenzo's repeated attempts to discuss what had just transpired. Finally, as they were preparing to go their separate ways at the train station, Kyosuke said nonchalantly, "Please tell your brother not to worry. I'll solve this case for him within the next three days." He vanished through the brass wicket and ran down the stairs to the platform.

When Kenzo got home, he poked his head into his brother's study and found him reading the funny papers, a half-full bottle of beer at his elbow. From the other side of the house came the sound of Mariko playing *Für Elise*, practicing for her next recital.

Daiyu greeted his younger brother with an air of urgent anticipation. "Quick, tell me! How did the battle go tonight?"

"According to the official report, one enemy aircraft was shot down in the vicinity of Yotsuya and was last seen plunging to earth in a mass of flames. Our air force is in hot pursuit of the vanquished enemy and a daring showdown is in the works, but you'll have to wait two or three days for the results of the sea battle."

293

"Shall we call the big sea battle Operation Kamizu?" Daiyu joked, and he and Kenzo burst out laughing. Kenzo noted as he looked at his brother's happy face and sparkling eyes that this was the first time he had seen him so relaxed since the beginning of the case.

"What about the professor?" Daiyu said. "Is he black or white? Guilty or innocent?"

"The professor is white, and Kyosuke is black. It was really thrilling, just watching it. Kyosuke executed his trademark endgame, and ultimately he beat the professor."

"What on earth are you talking about?"

"A checkers match. *Go.*"

Daiyu was clearly confused. "Stop joking around!" he thundered. "I'm trying to have a serious conversation here!"

"There's no need to get angry," Kenzo said. "As I said, they were playing *go*, and Kyosuke had the black stones. In the end, it looked very much as if he had figured out Professor Hayakawa's secret. He came right out and accused the professor of being in love with another woman besides his wife. He also said that if he had a little time he could ascertain the professor's whereabouts on the night of the first murder, when he claimed to have been wandering around on the Ginza for three hours."

"If your friend Kamizu's theories turn out to be for real, I'll resign my post and recommend that he be appointed as my successor." Daiyu Matsushita wore a wan smile, but Kenzo could sense the deep frustration behind the joke.

51

Everything I loved is lost/My house gone up in smoke… Hisashi
Mogami was singing a plaintive postwar ballad as he polished
the blue-enameled surface of a large pressurized kettle that
stood in the middle of his laboratory. Hisashi's own house
had been spared by the Allied bombing, but he had other
problems on his mind.

He had gone into debt to buy the vat, which he had hoped
to use to manufacture amino acids and dextrose from such
materials as wheat bran, soybeans, and salted fish guts. The
process involved heating up undiluted sulfuric acid under
pressure, so that the protein in the raw materials would
become amino acids, and the starch would be converted to
sugar. The debt had been fortuitously paid off by Hisashi's
inheritance. While the kettle might someday turn out to have
been a good investment, at the moment he saw it as a gigantic
white (or blue) elephant. The desperate food shortages in the
center of Tokyo made raw materials difficult to obtain, and
because he had no reliable sources for his supplies, Hisashi's
laboratory was depressingly idle most of the time.

Hisashi left his empty, gleaming kettle and went to the window. He stared down at the garden and there, under the fallen
leaves, he saw a ripple of movement as a small snake slithered
through the grass. Hisashi gave a histrionic shudder, for like
many of his countrymen he had an almost pathological fear
of snakes. That aversion had not been lessened by a recent,
bizarre experience.

One morning when he had awakened with a particularly
oppressive hangover, Hisashi had wandered into one of those

dark, musty-smelling apothecary shops in the old-fashioned Asakusa district of Tokyo. Before leaving home he had tried Japan's most popular hangover remedy, green tea with an *umeboshi* plum in it, but that potion had done nothing to relieve the infernal pounding in his head. Hisashi was due to speak at a meeting of the Chemists' Society that day, and he was ready to try anything.

"Give me the cure," he said grimly, slapping down a banknote. The wizened Chinese woman behind the counter took a live snake from a cage, deftly slit its throat with a narrow, curved knife, and held the headless but still wriggling reptile over a smudged-looking water glass until it was half-filled with dark burgundy-colored liquid. Hisashi felt a strong urge to cancel his order at that point, but he didn't want to lose face in front of a woman, much less a foreign woman. He snatched the revolting-looking glass and hastily quaffed the fresh-squeezed blood.

It tasted worse than he had imagined, warm and viscous and obscenely sweet, but he somehow managed to keep from throwing up on the spot. He did, however, vomit prodigiously two minutes later, in the alley behind the shop. When his dry heaves had subsided, the narrow street was sprayed with vermilion, as if it had been the scene of a convention of betel-nut chewers. Hisashi leaned against a soiled brick wall, panting and clutching his abdomen.

After a moment he realized that his excruciating hangover headache had vanished completely, leaving him with two new symptoms: severe stomach cramps, and an unspeakable taste in his mouth. *Never again,* he vowed. He had no intention of giving up his long-running love affair with alcohol, but in the future he would stick with more conventional hangover remedies, or else grin and bear the discomfort like a man.

The garden snake had apparently moved on. The dry leaves lay silent and still. Hisashi shuddered again, involuntarily this time, and turned away from the window. His visitors were due soon.

52

Kyosuke and Kenzo returned to Hisashi Mogami's house in East Ogikubo. This time the maid showed them into the drawing room, and Hisashi was there to greet them. "I'm terribly sorry for my rudeness in not being here yesterday," he said effusively. "I didn't get back until early this morning."

The sunlight lent Hisashi's strikingly handsome face a golden cast, and Kenzo was startled by the change in his old schoolmate's appearance and demeanor. Perhaps it was because of the fortune he had inherited from his brother, but Hisashi looked plumper and more prosperous. He even seemed to have an easy new dignity, a relaxed *gravitas* that had been absent the last time they met. He was considerably better dressed, too, in an elegantly cut suit of fawn-colored wool, with a white silk ascot around his neck. In a sartorial sense, he outshone even Kyosuke, who was wearing a conservative double-breasted suit of midnight blue with a white pinstripe. Kenzo, in his worn, baggy brown rayon suit, wasn't even in the running.

Hisashi Mogami's tone was warmly cordial as he bowed to Kyosuke and said politely, "Welcome to my humble abode. I'm Hisashi Mogami."

"I am Kyosuke Kamizu." Kyosuke returned the bow.

"Your stellar reputation precedes you," Hisashi said, bowing still deeper. "It's truly a pleasure to meet the famous Boy Genius at last."

Ignoring the obvious sarcasm, Kyosuke bowed again, then upped the verbal-politeness level a notch. "I've heard a great deal about you, too. Please allow me to offer my sincerest condolences on the unforeseen misfortune that befell your brother. I'm truly sorry for this tragic turn of events."

"Thank you," Hisashi said, his face suddenly solemn. "Considering that the victims were my brother and his mistress, there's probably no one whose life was more closely affected by the crimes than mine. It's only natural that I would try to figure out this case by myself, especially since the police have proved so inept. I even went once to consult with Kenzo, just after the first murder, before my brother's body was found. This is a splendid chance to try out all my current theories, so by all means let's discuss the case. Of course, unlike Kenzo, I didn't happen to be present when the bodies were discovered, so my deductions are based entirely on hearsay, and I can't guarantee that there won't be some factual errors."

The maid re-entered the room and silently set a covered cup of hot green tea and a plate of miniature, steamed, bean-paste-filled *manju* dumplings in front of each of the three men.

Hisashi moistened his throat with a sip of tea and began to speak. "The first thing that strikes me as odd is that there seems to be a strong intellectual element, as well as a bizarreness verging on the grotesque. These are inextricably intertwined. If you assume that the crimes were all committed by one person acting alone, that apparent dichotomy is incomprehensible. However, if the crimes were committed by two different people, the schizophrenic nature of the murders would begin to make sense. I'm sure Mr. Kamizu is aware of this fact from his research, but there are many instances in criminology where complicated crimes have gone unsolved because two separate acts were mistakenly viewed as a single crime."

"I see," Kyosuke said in a voice that seemed to be filled with admiration. "I hadn't thought of that possibility."

Hisashi looked pleased. "If you separate the case into its two different elements," he said, "then you begin to get some inkling of the truth. The first thing that struck me as weird was that Kinue fired her maid at a time like that, when someone was threatening to kill her and strip off her skin. She was so concerned that she told not only me but also Kenzo, whom she had just met. It doesn't make sense that she would have fired her only servant at a time when most people would want to surround themselves with protection."

"I've had trouble making sense of that as well," Kyosuke said hesitantly. He speared a dumpling with a bamboo skewer and brought it slowly to his mouth.

"When I first met Kinue Nomura," Hisashi continued, "I felt very sympathetic toward her for all she'd been through. As I got to know her better, though, I began to feel that she had gotten exactly what she deserved. I really can't imagine what she was thinking of, inviting that creep Inazawa to visit her at home that night. It's not as if she were lacking for male company; my brother was absolutely mad about her. There was no reason for her to pursue a worm like Inazawa. It's possible that he might have known the identity of Kinue's secret lover and used the information to blackmail her into setting up their rendezvous that night. That would explain the mystery of what she could have seen in a nonentity like Inazawa. I don't want to speak ill of the dead, but she really was a terrible woman. Not an hour goes by that I don't curse the day my poor brother fell into the clutches of that dreadful siren. Perhaps it was heredity; I'm sure you've heard about her criminal mother. Someone who would gladly defile her entire body with hideous tattoos could be capable of anything. It wouldn't surprise me at all if she had had a secret lover. That might explain why she fired the maid, too: to be alone."

"So you think tattooing is barbaric? I must say, it's refreshing to meet someone who has a normal point of view about that!" Kyosuke was looking at Hisashi Mogami as he spoke, and he didn't see Kenzo glaring at him.

Hisashi nodded. "To a person with a shred of common sense, the tattoo manias of my uncle, Professor Hayakawa, or my brother, or Inazawa, wouldn't make any sense at all. Personally, rather than that sort of grotesque decoration, I find a woman with large breasts infinitely more appealing." Seeming to realize the tastelessness of his remark, Hisashi quickly returned to the subject at hand. "However, such recklessly immoral behavior couldn't have gone on for long without my brother getting wind of it. Most of the time he was extremely kind and mild-tempered, but his personality had a dark side, too, and he could be suspicious to the point of paranoia. From the beginning he was wildly jealous and possessive of that woman. He suspected anyone who came along of trying to steal her away, even the rag collector and the delivery boys from the neighborhood noodle shop. I should mention that there was a time when he rashly suspected me of having an affair with her, although I soon convinced him that nothing was farther from my mind. Anyway, while that woman was carrying on her dissolute life, my brother was watching her.

"When he finally secured irrefutable proof that she was cheating on him with another man, he set out in a jealous rage to punish the adulterers. Kinue would probably have been dimly aware of my brother's suspicions. She might also have realized that her secret lover had a monomaniacal passion for her tattoos. She might have gotten scared. Those two elements intermingled, and that's why she ended up making that melodramatic plea to Kenzo for protection."

"Yes, I see what you're getting at," Kyosuke said, nodding his approval. "That seems like a definite possibility."

"So now it's that night, the night of that horrible crime. The secret lover came to Kinue's house while she was away at the bathhouse, and let himself in. A moment later my brother came barging in. The visitor panicked and looked for somewhere to hide. Of course, in that house the only door that could be locked was the bathroom, so Lover Boy ended up hiding in there. Meanwhile, my brother hadn't noticed that there was anyone else in the house. Still in a jealous fury, he fixed himself a drink, then put some prussic acid in the other glass. When Kinue came back she drank from that glass and died almost instantly, poisoned. My brother had also brought a gun, but he probably didn't use it for fear the noise would be heard by the neighbors. When he saw Kinue lying dead he was suddenly overcome with regret because he was still deeply, irrationally in love with that terrible woman. My brother lost his desire to take the other man's life as well and left the house as fast as he could. There's about a thirty-minute gap at this point, which may be explained by discrepancies among people's watches and clocks, and the tricks that memory plays. In any case, my brother fled from the murder scene and went out to Mitaka, where he hid in the abandoned storehouse. Sitting there alone in the dark, he became increasingly horrified at what he had done and finally, half-mad with grief and remorse, he killed himself with his own gun."

Hisashi finally paused. "I see," Kyosuke said. "So that explains one of the killers, but what about the second one? Who was that?"

"I'm not in a position to say who it was. But I can tell you what must have happened. The secret lover was cowering in the bathroom, fearing for his life. When he realized that

302

Takezo had left, he was relieved. He came creeping out of his hidey-hole, only to discover the dead body of Kinue Nomura. He must have been shocked and appalled, and his first instinct was to run away as fast as possible. Given his position, he couldn't very well notify the police. But when he tried to make his escape he noticed that there were people next door, looking directly down on him from the second floor, so he went back into the house. He sat there in the living room for a while, staring at the corpse. The cold fact was that he wasn't in love with Kinue the person; he was obsessively attached to the tattoos on her flesh. As he weighed his options, back and forth, he came up with that fiendish idea.

"Like a man possessed, he dragged the body into the bathroom, leaving a trail of blood. Using a saw he happened to find, he dismembered the body, cutting off all the tattooed portions. Then he wrapped the trunk in the kimono that Kinue had been wearing, and concealed the limbs and head in the bathroom. He locked it from the inside, and somehow managed to get out. I don't know exactly how he did that, but when you read detective novels, there seem to be all sorts of methods for doing such things, so I'm sure it wouldn't be impossible. At any rate, as he was about to carry off the torso, Inazawa came through the gate. The secret lover hid in the trees beside the entryway, or someplace like that, and waited for Inazawa to enter the house. The man wasn't worried that Inazawa would discover the body, or what was left of it, since he had left the bathroom door locked. But when he made a careful survey of the area, he noticed that a man—whom we now know was the vengeful yakuza, Ryokichi Usui—was watching the house. The torso-stealer couldn't very well leave under those circumstances, so he continued to bide his time, no doubt sweating bullets. Inazawa came flying out of the house, obviously upset, and didn't notice our friend hiding in the garden. Then Usui entered the house, which meant that the house was no longer under surveillance, and the tattoo maniac seized that chance to make his escape. He smuggled the body to a safe place, removed the skin, and disposed of the remains."

Kyosuke was listening intently, watching the expression on Hisashi Mogami's face. His eyes shone with intelligence. Hisashi took a sip from his teacup before continuing his monologue. "That brings us to the third murder, or rather the third death, since my brother committed suicide. This is how I think that one came about. When Kenzo told the brother, Tsunetaro Nomura, about the murder of his sister Kinue, and the disappearance of her torso, Tsunetaro must have had some inkling of who had been involved. He searched all over Tokyo until he found the man he suspected, then launched a vicious plan of blackmail. He told the man that if he didn't come up with a certain amount of money, he—Tsunetaro—would go to the police and tell them everything. The lover was terrified. He knew that he hadn't killed Kinue, but he wasn't at all certain that he would be able to persuade the police. And of course cutting up the body and making off with the tattoo was clearly a crime in itself. He ran all over town trying to scrape up the enormous sum of money Tsunetaro had demanded, but to no avail. In a panic, he made his fateful decision. He invited Tsunetaro to meet him at that lonely warehouse, ostensibly to hand over the blackmail money. Then he poisoned him, stripped off his tattoos, and left the body where it lay. That's the way I think it happened."

Hisashi clapped his hands. The maid appeared in the doorway and he pantomimed a sipping motion. "Yes, sir," she said. "Right away."

53

"That truly is a splendid feat of reasoning, Mr. Mogami," Kyosuke said, as the maid refilled the lidded cups with freshly brewed green tea. "It never even occurred to me that the two crimes might have been intertwined in such a strange, labyrinthine way." Knowing how competitive Kyosuke was, Kenzo was astonished to hear his friend lavishing so much praise on the equally competitive Hisashi Mogami.

"Nah," said Hisashi modestly, "this theory is just a product of my imagination. You're very kind, but it really doesn't warrant that sort of extravagant praise."

"The odd thing is," Kyosuke said in a light, teasing tone, "your reasoning is so brilliant that it's almost as if you had planned the crimes. It's a good thing you have such a strong alibi!"

"Tell me about it! I swear, my guardian angel must have made me get into a fight on the Ginza that night. Getting thrown in jail was an unexpected blessing."

"True. You strike me as unusually lucky, the sort of person who always manages to turn calamity into good fortune." Kyosuke and Hisashi looked at each other and began to laugh.

Kyosuke said, still smiling, "You never mentioned the name of the second man, the one you called the secret lover, the man who cut up Kinue's body and stole the tattoo. Who in the world was he?"

"All I can tell you is that he is a person of superior intelligence who also has an abnormal attachment to tattoos. I'm certain of that much."

"I see. Well, to my knowledge there's only one person who fits that description, but never mind that now. Your reasoning

305

is exceptional. I wish I could say that I can't find a single point to criticize. The truth is, there are two or three small details that don't sit quite right with me. If you don't mind, I'd like to ask you about them."

"Sure, go ahead." Hisashi looked surprised.

"About the bloodstained saw that was found near the crime scene. According to your scenario, the second criminal got the idea of stealing Kinue's torso on the spur of the moment, after discovering her dead body. In a case like that, the customary behavior would be to use whatever tools happened to be at hand. The maid testified that she had never laid eyes on that particular saw before. So where did it come from?"

"Well, the maid had been fired two or three days before. The saw must have come into Kinue's hands during that interval."

"That's a possibility, I suppose." Kyosuke sounded unconvinced. "In most households, though, there's no need for two or three saws. The police report said Kinue already had a perfectly good one in the toolshed. If she were going to buy another one, she would probably have bought a new one. I mean, what would be the point in buying an old saw?"

"Well, maybe a carpenter or some other workman left the saw behind."

"A carpenter? The tools of his trade? Can you really imagine a Japanese carpenter going off and forgetting his precious saw? And it's hardly likely that the secret lover would have taken a saw along for what he expected to be a romantic tête-à-tête. I suppose the saw could have been a gift from a visitor, although I haven't heard of anything like that since the reign of Emperor Jimmu. People might take some fancy sweets or a box of rice crackers when they go calling, but not a rusty old saw."

"You're pretty sharp yourself, Mr. Kamizu." Hisashi appeared disgruntled by Kyosuke's line of questioning, but he had the grace to acknowledge his opponent's skill.

"Moving on to my second question: Why did the mystery man leave the light on in the bathroom? If he went to all the trouble to create a locked room by some detective-novel trick, I can't imagine that he would neglect to turn off the light."

Hisashi thought for a minute before answering. "On that point, there may be a lie—or an inaccuracy, if you want to be charitable—in Inazawa's testimony. Don't you think it's possible that he unconsciously turned on the switch himself when he heard the sound of running water and went to investigate?"

"That seems like a reasonable explanation, but why weren't his fingerprints found on that light switch?"

"That kind of switch is exceptionally easy to turn on and off. You just have to touch it lightly with one fingertip. It could be moved to the opposite position using only the palm of your hand."

"All right, I'll yield that point. Let's say that Inazawa heard the sound of running water and thought it strange. So he turned on the light switch outside the bathroom. But why had the second man left the water running in the first place?"

"No matter how thorough the perpetrator is, he's bound to blunder. That's almost unavoidable. It's why most crimes end up being solved. But I do think the water was probably left running on purpose, to wash away the blood."

Kyosuke looked puzzled. "Why would he care about washing away the blood? It's not as if the second man had any reason to try to conceal the whereabouts of the remains, or to make it appear that the murder took place at another location. So it wouldn't have mattered to him if the bathroom was covered with blood. Why would a criminal who left the head and limbs

307

thrown down any which way on the bathroom floor, have worried about a little blood? We're talking about a man who went to the trouble of locking the door from the inside in order to avoid having the body discovered. I find it hard to believe he would have left the water running and the electric lights on, since noise and light were bound to draw attention to the bathroom eventually. The water might have been left on by mistake, but the light could have been turned on from inside or outside the room."

"I believe we've been over this already." Hisashi's tone was polite but cool. "This is what they call a vicious circle in debating terms."

A chill descended upon the room. Hisashi Mogami went on smoking his cigarette, but he didn't appear to be enjoying it very much.

"I'm sorry," Kyosuke said with an embarrassed laugh. "I'm afraid that's one of my more prominent character flaws. Ever since I was a boy people have made fun of me for being an advocate of Greek-style sophistry. Still, I have to ask one final question. Why did the mystery man go to all the trouble of lugging the torso off to another place to remove the skin? If he wanted the tattoos, why didn't he do as he did in Tsunetaro's case and remove the skin on the spot? It couldn't have been easy to carry the torso. According to your scenario, he waited hidden in the garden, holding the torso wrapped in a cotton kimono. Why were no bloodstains found in the garden? Tell me, Mr. Mogami, how did the man dispose of that blood?"

When Hisashi made no reply, Kyosuke continued in an apologetic tone. "I realize it probably seems as if I've been doing nothing but picking holes in your reasoning. But you know the old saying, 'The more one has the more one wants.' The basic principles of your theory are so brilliant, and I just thought that if it were possible to iron out a couple of small discrepancies here and there, then the truth would immediately become clear."

"Hmm," Hisashi mumbled through closed lips. "No matter how perfect a theory we might cook up, it's still just academic and abstract. I simply don't expect to understand this case any further than I do right now." Hisashi took a long drag on his cigarette and blew the smoke toward the ceiling. "According to Kenzo," he said, "you compared this case to an endgame in Japanese chess. Do you have some special interest in chess?"

"Just enough so I can create an endgame myself," Kyosuke said.

Hisashi opened the drawer of a nearby desk, took out a notebook, opened it to a page containing a complex diagram, and handed it to Kyosuke. Kyosuke stared at the diagram for several minutes. Then he said, "Ah, I get it. This is an incredible plan. You throw away five major chess pieces, and then you attack with two bodyguards. Knight takes knight, and then you promote the rook…" He went on reading the moves all the way to checkmate, with a rapid fluency that left Hisashi gazing at him in amazement.

"Mr. Kamizu, how much chess do you play? There's no way an amateur could unravel this checkmate so easily."

"I played a fair amount when I was in college," Kyosuke replied casually.

"How about a quick game?"

"I'd be delighted."

The two men shifted position so that they were facing each other across the table, and set up the pieces on Hisashi's antique Japanese chessboard. From the first move there was a sense of wildly competitive excitement, and as the pace increased, Kenzo watched in amazement. Kyosuke's fingertips were trembling as he moved his chess pieces, while Hisashi plunked each piece down on the board with a resounding thump.

The pace of the battle was fast, and improvisational. Toward the end, it appeared to have come down to one move, but Hisashi forcibly promoted his rook to a bishop, and staged a wicked attack. Kyosuke had fortified his camp with three gold and silver bodyguards, but they were suddenly stripped away, and his king was left exposed. Even so, Kyosuke made a typically gutsy move, marshaling his forces for one last desperate advance on Hisashi's well-protected king. It was in vain. Kyosuke's king fell to Hisashi's next move.

Throwing all the pieces he had captured earlier onto the chessboard, Kyosuke chuckled quietly to himself. Hisashi seemed to be relieved that the game was over. As he wiped the sweat from his face, he began to laugh. "I'm impressed, Mr. Kamizu," he said. "You really are strong! I've been playing professionally for years, but this is the first time I've ever met such a formidable opponent who was an amateur. If you had moved your bishop eight-to-two instead of seven-to-three, who knows how the match might have turned out?"

Kyosuke laughed and gave a mock-courtly bow. "What's that old saying: 'The defeated general shouldn't talk about tactics'?" he said ruefully. "I'm happy to have met such a challenging opponent. There's another saying, too: 'One game of chess is worth a hundred years of friendship.'"

After that, the conversation lapsed into meaningless chit-chat, and then Kyosuke casually inserted a question into the light-hearted banter. "Mr. Mogami, are you by any chance a painter?"

"Why do you ask, Mr. Kamizu?" There was something sardonic in the way Hisashi emphasized the respectful "Mister."

"It's just that as we came in, I noticed what appeared to be an artist's studio."

"Oh, that. The previous occupant of this house was a painter, but I've remodeled it and turned it into an experimental chemistry lab."

"That's right, I remember hearing that you had a degree in applied chemistry. What are you researching now? I'd be very interested in seeing your experiments sometime."

"Before the war I was making amino acids and grape sugar—dextrose—and so on, but the times being what they are, there really isn't much to show you now."

"I see," Kyosuke said. He took a monogrammed, steampressed handkerchief from his pocket and wiped some invisible crumbs from his mouth, then stood up. "Thank you very much for your hospitality," he said as Hisashi escorted them to the door. "I hope to see you again sometime soon."

"Please come again, any time," Hisashi replied cordially.

"Gardez la foi," Kyosuke said with a mock salute, to which Hisashi replied without missing a beat, *"Et vous aussi, mon général."*

The air seemed to be chilled by the promise of winter as Kenzo and Kyosuke walked along in thoughtful silence. Kyosuke's hands were stuffed deep in the pockets of his overcoat, his head was sunk in the collar. His eyes, peering out from the folds of his muffler, seemed to be looking into another dimension. As they approached Ogikubo Station, Kenzo couldn't restrain himself any longer. "Kyosuke, have you figured out who the murderer is yet?"

Kyosuke raised his head. "Yes, I have. Meet me at the police station tomorrow at one P.M. We'll go to your brother's office and I'll tell you who committed the murders. Right now I'm late for a rather crucial appointment with a certain lady, so

311

I'm going to say good-bye. Keep the faith, and I'll see you tomorrow."

With that, Kyosuke flagged down an old black taxicab and climbed in, leaving Kenzo on the curb, staring after his enigmatic friend in wonder.

54

"Maybe the serial killer has struck again," Daiyu Matsushita said in an ominous tone of voice, tapping the glass cover of his wristwatch in an exaggerated manner. "I certainly hope nothing dire has happened to your friend, Mr. Kamizu."

They were sitting in the detective chief inspector's large but sparsely-furnished office at police headquarters, waiting for Kyosuke Kamizu. Daiyu Matsushita sat behind a battered-looking metal desk, while Kenzo perched nervously on the edge of a creaky folding chair. The seat of honor, a well-worn brown armchair adorned with incongruous white lace doilies, was reserved for the young genius. Outside the narrow rectangular window lay another gray, chilly day, but the otherwise austere office was brightened by a huge bunch of hothouse lilies in a green glass vase, brought in earlier that morning by a grateful family whose stolen bicycles had been recovered by the police.

Kenzo made a childish face at his brother. "Well, fortunately my friend Mr. Kamizu doesn't have any tattoos, so there's no reason for anyone to kill him and strip off his skin. And besides, it's only five of one and he said one o'clock." Nevertheless, he couldn't help stealing a surreptitious glance at his own watch to make sure it was synchronized with the black clock on the wall.

"There you go again, mouthing off to your elders!" Daiyu joked. "I can't help thinking that Mr. Kamizu may be stumped by this case. Maybe that's why he's late."

"I told you, he isn't late. He's never late!" Kenzo snapped, falling into his brother's trap. Daiyu made a "gotcha" gesture, and Kenzo smiled sheepishly. "All right, why do you think he'd be stumped?"

"Because Mogami's theory is such a splendid one. I'll be the first to admit, it's much better than any hypothesis the department has come up with. Maybe we should hire civilians and soothsayers. I really doubt whether Mr. Kamizu will be able to produce anything half as good. He probably feels he'll lose face because of that, and that's why he isn't going to show up today."

"Not a chance!"

"Look, I don't care who gets the glory for solving this case, but we do need some sort of concrete proof. The reasoning is all in place. I just wonder if your Mr. Kamizu can conjure up some conclusive evidence to make it all come together." Daiyu spoke in a bluff, joking tone, but he couldn't conceal the fact that he was feeling very anxious. He took a deep drag on his cigarette. Then, carefully contorting his lips, he exhaled in the approximate shape of a hangman's noose.

Kyosuke appeared at precisely one o'clock, looking markedly different from his usual dapper, well-groomed self. His eyes were bloodshot, his long hair unkempt. His clothes were rumpled, too, and his face, which wore a somber expression, was abnormally pale. Kenzo was startled to realize that Kyosuke was wearing the same double-breasted blue-and-white pinstriped suit he had worn the day before, and he wondered whether his enigmatic friend had been out all night with the "certain lady" he had mentioned.

"Thanks for coming," said Daiyu Matsushita. "Please, have a seat." Kyosuke settled back into the thickly upholstered chair, closed his eyes, and took a deep breath, like someone getting ready to meditate.

"I gather that you've figured out who committed the murders?" Daiyu said.

"I have," Kyosuke answered, without opening his eyes.

"Well, don't keep us in suspense. Who on earth did it?"

Kyosuke opened his remarkable eyes. Looking from Kenzo to Daiyu and back again, he said softly, "The murderer is Hisashi Mogami."

55

Detective Chief Inspector Daiyu Matsushita sat in silence for a moment, looking as if he had just received a high-voltage electric shock. Slowly, his expression of surprise was overtaken by contempt mixed with anger. "Mr. Kamizu," he said, in a tone that was crisply businesslike. "I have great respect for your brains. But in this instance, I am afraid that you have arrived at an erroneous conclusion. We know for certain that Kinue was alive until around nine o'clock that night, and Hisashi Mogami was confined to a jail cell from that time until nine the next morning. Have you forgotten this simple, irrefutable fact? Or are you just determined to insult the Japanese police force any way you can?"

"No," Kyosuke said calmly. "My conclusion is not erroneous in any way." His voice was cold as a glacier.

"In that case, give us a way to break his alibi. If you can do that, I'll gladly arrest Hisashi Mogami and send him to the gallows." Daiyu stubbed out his cigarette.

"That suits me fine," Kyosuke said. "Let's get started. First, I'll need you to bring in the proprietor of the Ginza boutique, Kyoko Kawabata, for questioning."

"I'm afraid I'll have to refuse that request. Mogami was only with Kyoko from three P.M. until eight, you know. Even if there were a flaw in his alibi for that period, that wouldn't bring us any closer to proving that he killed Kinue Nomura." Daiyu's voice had an undertone of barely controlled impatience, as if he were being called upon to explain something for the tenth time to an inattentive subordinate.

"Yes, yes, I know all that." Kyosuke's patience, too, was

evidently wearing thin. "None of it makes any difference. Please just get her in here as quickly as possible."

Daiyu pushed a buzzer on his desk and Officer Ishikawa appeared, filling the door frame with his imposing martial artist's body. He was carrying a bulky workout bag. Saluting with his free hand, he said, "What is it, Chief?"

"Ah, Ishikawa. Sorry to bother you when you're on your way to the *dojo*, but this is rather urgent. Would you please get over to the Ginza as quickly as possible and bring Kyoko Kawabata back here with you?" Officer Ishikawa saluted and left.

Daiyu swiveled his black leather chair to face Kyosuke again. "In the meantime, why don't you tell me exactly why you think that Hisashi Mogami is the guilty party." He leaned back in his chair and laced his big-boned hands behind his crewcut head.

"Fine," said Kyosuke. He pushed his disheveled hair away from his face. "Let me tell you briefly how I eliminated the other suspects." Speaking with his trademark self-confidence, he proceeded to present his conjectures as if they were corroborated facts.

He began by stating flatly that Ryokichi Usui—who had a foolproof alibi for the third murder—couldn't have committed the first and second murders, either. Usui did corroborate Inazawa's story, and he also provided a valuable clue when he mentioned having spotted a woman who looked like Kinue in Yurakucho. It was highly unlikely that the woman could have been Kinue, so the obvious conclusion was that it was either a doppelgänger or her sister Tamae, who had survived the atom bomb and returned to Tokyo.

As for Inazawa, he appeared to be a man of ordinary intelligence at best, with no imagination to speak of. His lack of common sense was borne out by his behavior around the time of the first murder. During that brief period he (1) took Kinue's unlikely invitation at face value and brazenly went to pay a late-night call on the mistress of his jealous, pistol-packing boss; (2) left a furoshiki-wrapped bundle with his name emblazoned on it at the scene of an apparent murder; and (3) went back to fetch the bundle the next morning, leaving his fingerprints all over the place. Such a bumbler, Kyosuke argued, would be unlikely to have a clever idea like that of the locked room, much less be able to carry it out. Inazawa had no compelling motive and was in Kinue's house for less than an hour. There was no problem with his alibi up until nine o'clock.

"So," Kyosuke wound up, "I ruled out Usui and Ishikawa as possible suspects."

"Whatever your methods, I'm in complete agreement with your conclusions so far," said Daiyu Matsushita. "What about Professor Hayakawa?"

"On the face of things, he appears very suspect indeed. Hisashi Mogami made clever use of all the professor's weak points in order to throw suspicion onto him—his own uncle!" Wearing a look of righteous indignation, Kyosuke turned his attention to the idea of Professor Hayakawa as serial killer.

"In the first murder the tattooed torso was removed from the rest of the body, while in the third murder, the tattooed skin had been completely stripped away. Thus it appeared that the crimes were motivated by a desire to possess those tattoos. More than anyone else, Professor Hayakawa had what might be called an obsession with tattoos. Indeed, it was generally acknowledged that there was no one in the entire country with a more consuming interest in decorated human skin. But would a successful middle-aged scholar, blessed with status, worldly possessions, and a beautiful tattooed wife, be driven to commit murder simply because of his desire to own more tattooed skins?

"It's true that a fanatical obsession with anything, including tattoos, can become so irrational that it overrides common sense. From that point of view it wasn't unthinkable that if the professor happened to stumble upon a gorgeously tattooed corpse, he might be tempted to make off with the tattooed portion. Nor would it be entirely inconceivable that he might have committed a subsequent murder to protect his own interests, if someone had threatened him with exposure. However, Professor Hayakawa had a license to collect tattoos, and he had already built up a world-class collection without resorting to illegal means. The only thing lacking in that collection was one of Horiyasu's works of art, but surely the professor would eventually have been able to obtain a sample of Horiyasu's work without having to risk his own skin by killing for it."

Kyosuke paused for dramatic effect before delivering his final argument. "So the question is, why would the professor risk everything for the sake of one single specimen, which he would have had to keep hidden away in any case?"

Daiyu looked at his younger brother, then back to Kyosuke. "Still, you can't say that sort of thing never happens. I remember a case, before the war, where a well-known archaeologist stole some ancient documents which had been designated national treasures, and he ended up in prison. After the verdict came down, he was quoted in the newspaper as saying that he didn't know what had come over him. He just had an uncontrollable urge to own those documents. 'Possessed by demons,' that was the phrase he used."

"You raise a good point, Chief Inspector, and Hisashi Mogami may have had that very case in mind when he planned to frame Professor Hayakawa. But there's something in the professor's character that would make such an action unlikely."

"What's that?" Kenzo asked, still on the edge of his seat.

"This may sound strange, but it's the professor's famous sarcasm, and his wicked tongue. There's at least a trace of evil lurking in the heart of every man, and the people who express those dark impulses through speech are less likely to have that spiritual poison settle in the internal organs, eventually erupting in some shocking crime. I mean, consider the shy, quiet conformist who goes berserk one day with a rifle or a sword."

Daiyu Matsushita nodded. "Yes, like that soft-spoken bricklayer last week who murdered his next-door neighbors with a sashimi knife because they refused to do anything about their dog's incessant late-night barking."

"At any rate," Kyosuke went on, "in order to test the professor's psychology I challenged him to a game of *go*. As a rule, in matches of chess and checkers, when you find yourself at a disadvantage, there are two ways to try to win. One is to go into a defensive mode and wait patiently for the opponent to make a mistake. The second is the reverse: to launch an all-out attack, turning the board into a site of chaos and confusion. The all-out attack is the method favored by big-time gamblers, but the professor chose the rational, deliberate road. He painstakingly followed the classical rules, taking when it was proper to take, protecting when it was proper to protect, and waging a clean, pretty game. As it turned out, I ended up winning both games. When the last game was over, I was able to eliminate Professor Hayakawa from the list of murder suspects, without a shadow of a doubt. Call it instinct, but I would stake my life on that."

Daiyu Matsushita had been listening intently. The expression on his face was half admiring, half skeptical. "Mr. Kamizu, your methodology is unconventional, to say the least, yet what you say seems plausible enough. But in that case, why did the professor pick up that photographic plate? Was he just possessed by an irresistible urge born of his mania for tattoos?"

"I don't think that was it," Kyosuke said. "That plate hinted at a huge secret, the unraveling of which would have made it possible to solve the case almost immediately. I think the professor must have realized that as soon as he picked up the fragments. He probably wanted to take the pieces home and study them at his leisure; he saw that something was fishy, and that's why the remark about non-Euclidean geometry slipped out. Actually, Kenzo, I hate to say this, but you did a really unfortunate thing."

Oh, great, Kenzo thought, *more guilt,* but the look Kyosuke gave him was pitying rather than accusatory.

"What I mean," Kyosuke said, still looking at Kenzo, "is that if you had just left him alone after he took the plates, this case could have been solved by the professor himself months ago. Of course, that's assuming that he would have been willing to cooperate with the police. At the very least, the third murder would have been prevented."

Kenzo hung his head, and Daiyu said, "Why wouldn't the professor provide an alibi for the time in question?"

"That must have been tearing him apart." Kyosuke rubbed his eyes. "If he could just have offered proof of his whereabouts, he wouldn't have had to put up with being interrogated and held in jail. Yet he didn't dare say the one word that would have saved him from all that inconvenience and discomfort. This is just conjecture, but I think that on that evening the professor was at a place he didn't want the police to know about."

"What sort of place?" Kenzo asked eagerly, his feelings of guilt forgotten as his curiosity reasserted itself.

"Again, this is pure conjecture. It's hard to imagine the professor as a member of a secret society, and I doubt that he was lurking about in some illegal gambling joint. If he had been at another woman's place, he wouldn't have wanted his wife to find out, but there's no reason why he couldn't have told the police in confidence, man to man. So, knowing what we do of the professor's character and interests, that leaves just one possibility: that he was at the studio of some outlaw tattoo artist."

"Yes!" Kenzo said.

Kyosuke's theory was that the professor was at a studio to observe someone being tattooed, possibly paving the way for the eventual purchase of that person's skin. Tattooing was still highly illegal, and the ban was actively enforced. If Professor Hayakawa were to give away the address of the tattoo artist, he would be betraying that person's friendship, and he would risk losing his access to the glamorous, insular world of the art tattoo, forever.

"That was why he refused to speak. He was confident that the truth about the case would eventually come out, but if the worst came to the worst and he was formally charged, he probably felt certain that the tattoo master would forgive him for revealing that artist's address in order to save himself. In essence, the professor decided to risk his own skin to protect someone else's."

Kyosuke smiled slyly. "Of course, this was one reason why you were blundering around in a labyrinth until I came along," he said. "At any rate, the more I learned about the case, the more it appeared as if the only plausible suspect was Hisashi Mogami. Then I met with him and, as you probably heard from

Kenzo, he set forth a most surprising hypothesis. Although his reasoning appeared to be impeccably clear and logical, I immediately sensed that this was just another page from his diabolical plan book. His speech was liberally irrigated with sincerity—the man really is quite an actor. That speech was his trump card, and he had been biding his time waiting for the perfect opportunity to play it. That was his fatal mistake, choosing Kyosuke Kamizu as the sounding board for his fake theory."

Kyosuke paused for a moment, and an odd look flitted across his fine-boned face, as if he were feeling a twinge of sympathy for his prime suspect. After a quick recapitulation of Hisashi's spurious "theory," he continued his own hypothesis:

"The investigation floundered, and Hisashi just sat back on his seemingly impregnable alibi and watched the police chasing their tails. He was close to his aunt, so Hisashi must have known that his uncle, the professor, went out every night to some unknown destination. Knowing his uncle's proclivities, he probably put two and two together and figured out where he was going. So he knew the professor would be in a bind when the police asked him for an alibi. The first and second murders went almost exactly as planned. Of course, Hisashi couldn't have foreseen that Ryokichi Usui would choose that night to break into Kinue's house. He did know that Inazawa was planning to call on Kinue later that night, because that invitation was part of the scheme. Hisashi deliberately left the light on in the bathroom, so that Inazawa would be sure to peek in and see the body. He predicted correctly that Inazawa, who had gone to the house of his boss's mistress with the most scandalous of intentions, wouldn't rush to report his gruesome discovery to the police."

Kyosuke paused and took a long gulp of tepid green tea. "As it turned out, Inazawa couldn't have behaved more perfectly if he had been a Bunraku puppet, and Hisashi the black-hooded puppeteer," he said. "But Fate had another idea, and an unexpected chess piece appeared on the board."

"You're talking about Jiraiya, right? Tsunetaro Nomura?" Daiyu Matsushita said.

"Exactly. When Tsunetaro showed up, holding the key to the secret on which the whole case turned, Hisashi was amazed, and alarmed. He knew he was in danger, so he had to take rapid action, without the luxury of planning that went into the first two murders. He lured Tsunetaro out, killed him, stripped off his skin, and left him in that desolate warehouse. For Hisashi, a tattoo wasn't an object of desire, quite the contrary. But he thought that by removing the tattoos he could draw a parallel with the first murder, and cast even more suspicion on Professor Hayakawa. It was a clever strategy, no doubt about that." Kyosuke paused again and picked up his teacup.

"Shall I order you some hot tea?" Daiyu asked solicitously.

"No, this is fine," Kyosuke said, draining the cup. "One thing about the war, it made things like whether or not a cup of tea is hot seem very trivial. Anyway," he went on in a brisk tone, "let's take a careful look at Hisashi's alibi for the third murder."

"There was a three-hour blank space in Hisashi Mogami's account of his activities. He claimed to have spent that time in a movie theater, but there would have been plenty of time for him to rush back to Tokyo by car, commit the crime, return to Yokohama at high speed, and still have an hour left over. The police assumed he would have been traveling by train, in which case it couldn't have been done. However, because Hisashi's alibi for the first murder was seemingly impregnable, his alibi for Tsunetaro's murder was evidently accepted without being rigorously questioned by the police."

Once again, the chief inspector's face wore a complicated expression: a mix, this time, of embarrassment and annoyance. "Go on," he said shortly.

"Of course, I didn't conclude that Hisashi was the killer on the basis of these things alone," Kyosuke said. "After he had presented his hypothesis, which seemed to suggest Professor Hayakawa as Tsunetaro's killer, I pointed out some inconsistencies. Hisashi appeared agitated by my questions, which he rebutted with varying degrees of success, but he refused to abandon his thesis that the crime had been committed by someone with a tattoo mania. He also made a point of expressing his own deep aversion to tattooed skin."

The Matsushita brothers exchanged a significant glance. "Methinks the gentleman doth protest too much?" Kenzo murmured, paraphrasing some dimly recalled high-school Shakespeare.

Kyosuke smiled appreciatively, then cleared his throat. "At that point," he went on, "I proposed a friendly game of chess. I hold a third-level certificate, and an ordinary person couldn't begin to play against me. However, Hisashi Mogami is a professional player, and I knew that trying to use the chessboard to my advantage was not going to be simple by any means. I launched a mad-dog attack, and by the end of the middle game victory appeared to be within my grasp. But Mogami is what they call a born big-game player. It requires a mysterious combination of brains, courage, and recklessness, and he has them all. He detected a small opening, and he launched a do-or-die offensive. Although I ended up losing the match, I learned enough about Mogami's character to be certain that he was the culprit. It's difficult to put into words, but as I said

325

before I would stake my life on my instincts, the way I did on so many occasions during that horrible war."

Daiyu Matsushita had listened to Kyosuke's monologue in attentive silence. He was clearly filled with admiration, but his face still bore a shadow of doubt. "Mr. Kamizu, your arguments sound very convincing. However, please forgive my rudeness, but I must point out that everything you've said so far is theory or fanciful conjecture that exists only in your own head. I mean, I can't very well charge a man with murder because he beat you at chess."

"That's perfectly reasonable. And that's exactly why I asked you to call Kyoko Kawabata in for questioning. When she arrives, please grill her in detail about Mogami's actions between three and eight P.M. on the day of the murder. And then if you wouldn't mind, please permit me to ask her a few questions. I know it's somewhat irregular—"

"I have no objection to your questioning the witness," Daiyu interrupted, "but why are you so concerned about that particular time period?"

"For the rest of that night there are numerous witnesses to Mogami's whereabouts. During those five hours, the only witness is Kyoko Kawabata, and I have reason to believe that she wouldn't hesitate to lie to protect the man she loves. Also, I think there is plenty of room to doubt the circumstances of Takezo's death as they have been reconstructed." Kyosuke's eyes were alight with determination.

Just then, Officer Ishikawa came into the room and whispered in the ear of the detective chief inspector. "Bring her in," said Daiyu Matsushita.

56

Kyoko Kawabata was a pretty, intelligent-looking woman in her late twenties, with glossy black hair done up in a French roll. Her slender, willowy figure was sheathed in a simple dress of dark blue jersey, and a ruby-studded brooch in the shape of a heart glittered on her lapel. Nervously clutching a lace-trimmed handkerchief, she sat down on a folding chair and smoothed her skirt over her knees.

Detective Chief Inspector Daiyu Matsushita immediately got down to business. "You are acquainted with Hisashi Mogami, is that correct?"

"Yes, we sometimes go out together as friends."

"So your relation is strictly platonic?"

"Yes, that's correct." Kyoko Kawabata looked a bit indignant, but she answered calmly enough.

"You have stated previously that on August twenty-seventh, you attended the Togeki Theater with Mr. Mogami. If you don't mind, we would like to ask you a few more questions about the events of that day."

"I see," Kyoko Kawabata said in a doubtful tone of voice. "As I explained in my previous statement, Mr. Mogami and I had a long-standing date to go to the Togeki Theater on that day. The women who work in my boutique have a tendency to poke their noses into other people's business, so rather than having Mr. Mogami pick me up at work we arranged to meet in front of the theater around three. The curtain went up at about three thirty and we were together the entire time, sitting in adjoining seats. After the show ended at seven thirty, Mr. Mogami escorted me to Yurakucho Station and saw me onto a train for Meguro, which is where I live. That was where we said good-bye, a few minutes before eight."

"Did you stop off anywhere for a cup of tea on the way to the station?"

"Mr. Mogami suggested that we stop for refreshments, but… This is a bit embarrassing, but I was feeling a little under the weather, so I just wanted to get home and lie down as soon as possible."

"What did you do for your evening meal, then?"

"I had brought some rice balls and a thermos of green tea, so we ate in our seats."

"You didn't buy any food at the concessions in the theater lobby?"

"That's right."

"What sort of seats did you have?"

"I believe I gave the officers the ticket stubs when I was questioned the first time."

"Oh, here they are." Daiyu Matsushita reached into a file labeled KAWABATA, KYOKO. "So you had two adjoining seats in Row G, next to the *hanamichi* runway on the right side, is that correct?"

"That's entirely correct, sir," Kyoko said politely.

"While you were inside the theater, did you happen to meet anyone you know?"

"No, not a soul."

"Did anything unusual happen at the theater on that day? For example, were any of the actors taken suddenly ill, or were there any last-minute changes in the cast, or did any of the actors mess up their lines, or fall off the stage?"

"Yes. Now that you mention it, at the end of the second act there was an uproar because someone had apparently committed suicide by jumping from the third-floor balcony, and the beginning of the third act was delayed because of that."

"I see. And may I ask what you were wearing that day?"

"I had on a one-piece dress of iridescent silk, and a pearl necklace."

"What about Mr. Mogami?"

"He was wearing a white suit and a striped necktie. He had on a brand-new Panama hat, and he was wearing white shoes." Daiyu Matsushita lifted his head and looked at Kyosuke with a quizzical expression. He had asked all the common-sense questions, and now he seemed to be saying, What should I ask her now?

"Detective Chief Inspector, could I see you for a moment?" Kyosuke said. The two men walked to the corner of the room, where Kyosuke whispered a few words in Daiyu's ear. Nodding, the chief inspector returned to his seat wearing a severe expression. He then launched a verbal attack on Kyoko Kawabata. "It's obvious to us that your statement is basically a pack of lies," he said. "The person who is here with us today is a famous private detective, and he has located a witness who was at the Togeki Theater on that same day. That person is prepared to testify that you were sitting alone during the entire performance."

Kyoko's face had grown paler by the minute, and she blanched still further when Kyosuke took over the questioning. "Of the two seats, were you sitting in the one nearest to the runway?"

"No, Mr. Mogami was sitting in the seat nearest to the runway, and I was in the one next to that." Kyoko smoothed out her crumpled handkerchief and used it to blot the delicate beads of perspiration that had accumulated on her upper lip.

"We're never going to get anywhere if you insist on lying to us, you know. The seat next to you was empty during the entire performance." Kyosuke spoke coldly, as if he had forsaken all human feeling for Kyoko Kawabata. "The usher working in that section of the theater has given a statement saying that you were by yourself the entire time."

Kyoko's lips began to tremble slightly, but no words came out. She plucked nervously at the pins that held her hair in place while Kyosuke plunged ahead, evidently oblivious to her distress. "You testified earlier regarding Mr. Mogami's costume on that day. Since you work in the fashion business and are presumably more observant of such things than the average person, I'd like to take your word on this point. But if I do that, a strange problem arises. As you know, after parting from you that night, Mr. Mogami got into a brawl on the Ginza and ended up spending the night in jail. When he was booked, a form was filled out by the police which described what he was wearing, and according to that form he had on black shoes. Now, it hardly seems likely that a man would carry a change of shoes with him when he went out, don't you agree?"

"Uh…" Kyoko Kawabata's mouth had fallen slightly open, but no words emerged.

"You're lying, aren't you? Hisashi Mogami asked you to back up his alibi, even though it's a complete fabrication. Well, the charade's over. Did you really think you'd be able to carry it off?"

Kyoko Kawabata's pretty face took on an expression of injured pride. "I'm not lying!" she shouted. "I'm telling the truth. It's all true!"

Coolly, Kyosuke continued his interrogation. "You've been deceived by Mr. Mogami," he said. "Didn't you realize that he's a famous Don Juan? Perhaps he neglected to mention that he has promised to marry at least ten or twelve women, including the daughter of a nobleman, a wealthy widow, and a certain tattooed woman."

Kyoko sat slumped in her seat, shaking her head in disbelief as several hairpins clattered onto the table. An enormous tear rolled down her cheek, a shudder shook her lithe body, and then she lay her head down on the desk and burst into tears. Kyosuke watched dispassionately as Kyoko's luxuriant black hair, finally loosed from its moorings, rose and fell with the force of her weeping like a boat being tossed by a storm.

"That's enough for today," he said. "You may go now, and we'll expect you here tomorrow at one P.M. Please understand that we are sympathetic to your situation and don't want to harm you in any way, nor will you be prosecuted if you decide to change your story and tell us the truth. Give these matters some careful thought, and we'll see you again tomorrow."

Nodding agreement, Kyoko Kawabata wiped away her tears with the now-sodden lace handkerchief. After a halfhearted attempt to tidy her tumbled-down hair, she stood up, bowed silently to the people in the room, and vanished through the door without a word of farewell.

Daiyu Matsushita stared up at Kyosuke's face. "Mr. Kamizu, I don't mean to question your methods, but why did you let that woman go when she was so close to breaking down? One more push and she would have admitted that Mogami's alibi was a tissue of lies."

Kyosuke replied in his usual cool, uninflected manner. "I'm happy to see that you've started to lean in the direction of my theory. But that woman is nothing but a decoy. For the murderer, and for us as well, she's just a convenient tool. Pursuing her any further would just be a waste of time and energy. We've already poked enormous holes in Mogami's

331

story, and that's all we needed to do. More important now is the question of what Mogami will do when he learns his alibi has been demolished. If he wants to do something dramatic, tonight is his only chance because the case is rapidly approaching its finale."

There was a long moment of thoughtful silence. Then Kenzo said, "Since the case is almost solved, can we order some noodles now?"

"The Ultra-Extraordinary Eater has spoken," Kyosuke said, and everyone laughed.

57

The ramen noodles had been ordered, devoured, and cleared away, and Kenzo, after eating twice as much as anyone else, had gone for a short stroll around the block.

Detective Chief Inspector Daiyu Matsushita had ordered constant surveillance on Kyoko Kawabata, who was expected to run straight to Hisashi Mogami. The chief of detectives had also sent a heavily armed team of marksmen and a number of regular police officers to surround Mogami's house. Now Daiyu and Kyosuke were sipping weak green tea and discussing the case while waiting to make their move.

"Mr. Kamizu, you were talking earlier about a mystery woman. That wouldn't be Kyoko Kawabata, would it?"

"No," Kyosuke said. "I don't really think she had a very important role. I'm still not sure how much she knew about the details of all this, but I suspect not very much."

"Actually, when you started to close in on Kyoko Kawabata, I was thinking of trying to get her fingerprints."

"That would probably have been useless," Kyosuke said, shaking his head. "Even if you had taken the trouble to do that, you wouldn't have found her fingerprints at the Kitazawa crime scene. She was never there."

"In that case, the mystery woman is someone else entirely. She's the same woman who lured Tsunetaro out, and she would also have left fingerprints at the Kitazawa crime scene, is that right?"

"That's exactly right, and it's because of that woman that this brilliantly conceived crime could be carried out. If you think about it, she's really a frightening character."

"So who is she, anyway, your mystery woman?"

"I'm surprised you haven't guessed. She's, uh…" Just as Kyosuke was about to make that revelation, a very diminutive, boyish-looking police officer walked into the office and began to give his report in a surprisingly deep, authoritative voice.

"We've just heard from Officer Ishikawa via radio. When Kyoko Kawabata left police headquarters, she went immediately to East Ogikubo and entered Hisashi Mogami's house. We've also received word from the officers who have Mogami's house surrounded, saying that Mogami has been seen there at an upstairs window."

Daiyu Matsushita nodded at the reporting officer, who saluted smartly and left the room. "Mr. Kamizu, what do you think?" he asked.

"Let's get going," Kyosuke said, standing up and stretching his long limbs in a fluid movement. "Let's go to Mogami's house and wait for the fish to swim into our net."

The crosstown rush-hour traffic was horrendous, and it took Kyosuke, Kenzo, and Daiyu nearly an hour to reach the neighborhood police station in East Ogikubo that was serving as temporary headquarters. The early-winter day was already completely dark when they arrived, and the absence of light made the cold seem even more penetrating.

The local policemen were obviously thrilled and nervous at having a big boss in their small domain. After the three interlopers had taken over the shabbily furnished conference room for their command post, they were served a take-out dinner of Chinese-style fried rice and garlicky *gyoza* dumplings, hastily ordered by the precinct sergeant.

"Oh, my," Kyosuke said, looking down at the mound of food. "I'm not sure I can eat again so soon after that noodle feast."

334

"Don't worry," Kenzo said, waggling his eyebrows. "I can eat all three servings, if necessary." As it turned out, it wasn't. The food was unexpectedly delicious, and the three men cleaned their plates. While they were drinking their umpteenth cups of yellowish-green tea, an officer appeared at the door and said, "Kyoko Kawabata has just left Mogami's house."

"Thank heavens," Kyosuke said with a sigh of relief. "I thought it would probably be all right because even a fiendish person like Mogami often has a scrap or two of humanity left. Nevertheless, I had serious reservations about using her as a decoy."

As the Matsushita brothers lit their after-dinner cigarettes—unfiltered Hope brand for Daiyu, hand-rolled for Kenzo—Kyosuke Kamizu said, "It looks as if we have some time to wait, so why don't I go ahead and explain about the second murder. The fact is that this murder was Hisashi Mogami's primary objective. The first murder was designed to draw attention away from that objective, and was really nothing but a diversionary tactic. He had a clear-cut motive for Takezo's murder, and however impeccable an alibi he might devise, he couldn't be certain of throwing the police permanently off the track. The way he achieved his goal was by first committing a murder for which he had a seemingly perfect alibi. He then killed his brother Takezo and made it look like a suicide of remorse, so it would appear that Takezo had committed the first murder. It was a remarkably daring and intricate plan. An elegant solution, indeed."

Kyosuke looked around at his little audience, which was hanging on his every word. "From the questioning of Kyoko Kawabata today, we established that Hisashi's alibi until eight o'clock is full of holes. It's entirely possible that he committed the second murder during that time period. But why did

Takezo go to the haunted house in Mitaka carrying his own fully loaded gun? Clearly, he went there with the intention of shooting someone else. He fell into a trap, and his weapon ended up being used on him instead."

"But what was the purpose of Hisashi's plot? Was it purely for financial gain?" Daiyu Matsushita lifted his gold-trimmed captain's hat—the same one he had rashly promised to eat if Kyosuke solved the case—and scratched his close-cropped head.

"That's exactly right, at least initially," Kyosuke said. "However, I don't believe Takezo would have tried to kill his younger brother just because he realized Hisashi had designs on his fortune. No, I think Takezo's motive was love, which is to say jealousy. Hisashi claimed to have been upset because people unjustly suspected him and Kinue of having an illicit relationship. But was that suspicion really unfounded? I don't think so; in spite of all his pronouncements to the contrary, I think such a connection did exist. Of course, the walls have ears, so Takezo would have learned eventually that his brother was carrying on with his mistress, the woman he intended to make his wife. How would an exceedingly jealous and possessive man like Takezo have reacted? If Kinue had fallen in love with another man, a stranger, that would have been bad enough, but her handsome young lover turned out to be someone he loved and trusted—his own brother. That was a different sort of betrayal altogether. Takezo had no wife or children, and when he saw his hopes for starting a family with Kinue going up in smoke, it's no wonder that he decided to punish Kinue and Hisashi the best way he knew how, by cutting off their financial support. We know that shortly before his death he met with his attorney, Mr. Sayama, and expressed his intentions of changing his will.

336

"Here's another question. Why did Kinue defy Takezo's wishes and enter the tattoo contest? However much of an exhibitionist she may have been, she would hardly have flaunted her naked body in front of a crowd of strangers if the man she supposedly loved asked her not to. Women's minds just don't work like that. No, she was manipulated by Hisashi Mogami for reasons which I'll explain later.

"Of course, Hisashi would have found out that Takezo knew about his relations with Kinue, and he would have heard about the visit to the lawyer. He was probably seized by panic, because—as we know now—he had run up vast gambling debts that his brother had been paying off for years, and if his brother abandoned him, he would face financial ruin. But that wasn't all. Hisashi understood his brother's character very well, and he knew that Takezo's jealousy could lead him to shoot his own brother in the heat of the moment. Hisashi decided that he'd rather be doing the killing, especially since he had been planning to murder his brother eventually in order to get his hands on the inheritance."

With the flair of an expert storyteller, Kyosuke described a selfish soul in torment. Even though Takezo's attempt had failed, it was still chilling to listen to a tale of two brothers intent on killing each other. Kenzo couldn't help thinking that this terrible case was a reflection of the moral bankruptcy and spiritual corruption that followed the Great War.

"Having made his decision," Kyosuke went on, "Hisashi telephoned Takezo at work. He's a good actor, so he probably disguised his voice. When Takezo answered, Hisashi whispered something about Kinue having a secret rendezvous with his younger brother at the haunted house in Mitaka.

"No doubt Takezo was enraged at the betrayal. Without the faintest inkling that a trap had been laid for him, he marched right into its jaws. By the time Takezo arrived at the house in Mitaka, Hisashi was already there, hiding. When Takezo walked through the front door, holding his loaded pistol, Hisashi grabbed him from behind and held a handkerchief soaked in chloroform over his nose until he lost consciousness. Hisashi then dragged his brother's inert body into the storehouse, where he propped it in a sitting position on an empty box. After being shot in the head by Hisashi, Takezo's body collapsed onto the floor. That's the way the second murder took place."

"But why didn't we find any traces of the anaesthetic?" asked Daiyu Matsushita.

"Because any residue would have disappeared after three or four days."

"What if Takezo hadn't showed up with a loaded pistol?"

"In that case, Hisashi probably would have used prussic acid—the preferred beverage of discriminating suicides—as he did in the first murder."

Quite a bit of time had passed, and the cold had become even more biting. Everyone synchronized their watches: seven o'clock. It was necessary to prevent Mogami from escaping while also making sure that anyone entering or leaving his house wouldn't notice it was under surveillance. The appropriate orders had been given, and a discreet but secure police cordon surrounded Mogami's house.

At last it was time to move. As silently and stealthily as ninjas, the five men—DCI Matsushita, Officers Ishikawa and Akita, Kenzo and Kyosuke—crept onto the grounds of the estate. They had already received reports that Hisashi Mogami was in his chemistry laboratory. Sneaking through the garden gate, they tiptoed up to the converted artist's studio and peeked through the window.

A large industrial-type pressure cooker stood in the middle of the room, and Hisashi was walking around and around the blue-enameled vat with long, agitated strides. The room was lit only by a dim lamp in one corner, and in the muted light Hisashi looked like an unkempt, nervous ghost. As he paced in circles, obviously lost in thought, he kept raking his hands through his hair and shaking his head as if in despair. Kenzo felt a pang of sympathy for this doomed man, whom he had known since childhood. There was something distinctly other-worldly about Hisashi's appearance, and Kenzo thought of Daiyu's comment about sending the man to the gallows.

The five intruders crouched in the bushes and waited. Minute by minute, the passing time ticked by, the numbers on their watches glowing in the dark like tiny, luminescent sea creatures. One hour, two hours, three hours, four. The time passed so slowly that to those who were waiting silently in the chilly shadows, it seemed more like four days than four hours.

Eleven P.M. Suddenly a woman wrapped in a long black cloak, her face hidden by a black shawl, walked through the gate. She looked around cautiously. In that instant Kenzo felt as if his heart had stopped beating. *Tamae Nomura!* he thought. *I was right, after all.*

"Kyosuke, that was our mystery woman?" Daiyu whispered.

"That's right. The big fish just swam in."

The five shivering ninjas crept up to the laboratory building.

The former artist's atelier had been divided into two large rooms connected by sliding doors, which now stood open. In the inner room, Hisashi Mogami was still pacing around his cauldron. The other room was a storage room filled with large vials of sulfuric acid, hydrochloric acid, and other chemicals. Concealing themselves in the shadows, the five men peered through the windows and waited.

58

"Darling, is it really true?" The woman appeared to be out of breath. After gasping out those words she collapsed into an antique velveteen armchair. The laboratory was dim, lit only by a single lamp.

"Yeah, it's true all right," Hisashi Mogami replied in a low, weak voice. "And all because I made the mistake of underestimating a weird guy named Kyosuke Kamizu." Hisashi had stopped his pacing and was leaning against his laboratory table with both legs trembling uncontrollably. "It's all his fault, that Kamizu," he said. "Thanks to him the police began to question my alibi from three to eight. He was here yesterday with Matsushita's younger brother. When they started asking questions about the case, I did as we'd planned and spun out an elaborate theory that pointed the blame at my uncle. I had the feeling even then that Kamizu wasn't buying my story, and now it looks as if there's no way out."

"Don't talk like that, darling. Pull yourself together! Maybe they've broken your alibi. That doesn't prove anything by itself. If you just insist that you were off somewhere gambling, it should be all right. As long as your alibi from nine o'clock on holds up, there should be no problem. I mean, I don't think there's any way the police could have figured out about the car, do you? It isn't registered in your name or anything. As long as they don't arrest me, I think you'll be fine." The woman's tone was brave and resolute, and she spoke with absolute confidence.

"You have such a strong spirit, same as always." Hisashi sounded envious.

"Of course I do," the woman said. "I'm really surprised at you, though, falling apart like this. You're supposed to be a man, but you're sniveling like some spineless little coward. You're really useless at a time like this, you know." The words were harsh, but the tone was not devoid of affection.

Hisashi Mogami didn't attempt to defend himself; he just stood in silence. After a moment he tottered over to the sideboard on rubbery legs, and took out a square bottle of whiskey and two glasses. He filled the glasses with the dark amber liquid, then stumbled over to the woman and handed her one glass. Closing his eyes, he downed the contents of his own glass in one desperate gulp.

"Won't you have a drink with me?" he said softly, but the woman just sat staring into the depths of her untouched glass, her back to the eavesdroppers.

"Don't tell me you put poison in it," she said slowly.

"Don't be ridiculous! Didn't I just taste it for poison, right before your eyes?"

The woman raised the glass to her lips as if to drink, then lowered it again. She held it out to Hisashi. "I don't want this," she said. "You drink it. Go ahead, show me it isn't poisoned."

In one quick move, Hisashi brushed the woman's hand away. The glass went flying out of her hand and skidded across the table, breaking several chemical beakers that lay in its path. The whiskey glass finally landed on the floor, where it shattered into a hundred sparkling pieces.

"What do you think you're doing!" the woman shouted, jumping up from her chair. "I knew you were going to try to poison me tonight."

Hisashi Mogami made no reply. His eyes looked as if they were about to burst out of his head, and he was shaking from head to foot like someone in the advanced stages of malaria. All his cockiness had been replaced by fear and despair.

"Two can play at that game, you know," the woman said in an angry voice. "I'm still the only one who knows all the secrets. If I died now you probably think your evil deeds would be forever hidden in darkness, which I'm sure would suit you just fine. Well, I'm sorry to disappoint you, Mr. Criminal Mastermind, but you're not getting rid of me that easily. I'm not some gullible little conquest that you can slip a mickey when she ceases to be useful. Don't you forget that for a minute! I'm just as tough as you are; maybe more so, judging by the pathetic way you've been behaving tonight." The woman stopped and took a deep, racking breath, then continued her tirade.

"Do you really think I could have been your partner in crime, and crossed all these dangerous bridges with you, if I didn't have a very realistic idea of what kind of person you are? I may love you, but I don't trust you as far as the door. That's why I've taken some precautions. If you kill me, a letter that I left with someone—never mind who—will be on its way to the police within a day or two. Along with the photographs, that should be enough to convince them of all your wicked deeds. The truth is, I'd be happy if you'd kill me right now, knowing that before long you'd be swinging by the neck from a high place and following me into the next world. We've often talked about committing suicide together if worst came to worst, so let's do it right now. I think it would be incredibly romantic to make love one last time and then have you kill me and dissolve my body in sulfuric acid. Come on, if you're going to murder me, do it now!"

It was an astonishing speech, and the men lurking in the shadows were shocked.

"Aaah," Hisashi said in a tone of anguish. "Why did you have to fall in love with a rotten scoundrel like me?"

The woman stood up and ran her long fingers through Hisashi's already tousled hair. Gently, she began to shower him with kisses as soft as rain. She kissed his hands, his forehead, his cheeks, and finally his lips.

"Shh," she whispered. "Don't waste time worrying about futile things like that. As long as we have money, life is a party. Don't you remember the vow we made to each other to live fast, die young, and go to hell together?"

"Yeah, well, the time for our honeymoon in hell is fast approaching."

"Don't be silly, darling," the woman said, laying her head on Hisashi's shoulder. "If the police don't arrest me, you'll be fine. I'm sure the police will give up before long, when they see there's no way out of the labyrinth of this case. And when that happens, we'll be home free. So stop worrying and start living. We're in love, remember?" She put one hand inside his shirt and began to trace circles on his chest.

"You're right," Hisashi said. "Everything may work out for us, after all."

"That's the spirit," the woman said. She wrapped her arms around Hisashi's waist and slipped her hands into his back pockets, while he buried his face in her hair. "Everything will turn out fine, if you just stop fretting so much. There might be a spot of trouble with the police. So what. Nothing you can't handle, but for the time being I think I'd better stay away. If you need to see me, just give me a call and we can arrange to meet somewhere."

"Mmm-hmm." Hisashi's assent was muffled by the woman's hair.

"More importantly, darling, I need some money," she said.

Hisashi disentangled himself and moved away. "I just gave you a wad of cash the other day!" he said in an annoyed tone. "Please try to be more careful about how you spend it. I'm going to have a lot of additional expenses. Besides, you know I can't go throwing money around now. That would draw suspicion."

"Oh, come on, don't be such a tightwad. You know you're rolling in dough. And remember, I'm the one who helped you kill three people. I mean, for your sake I even killed my own flesh and blood. It's really unbearable not to have enough money to go out drinking or shopping once in a while. Besides, half of all your money belongs to me. That was the agreement."

Hisashi's shoulders slumped in defeat. "If you want money, it's in the main house in the usual place," he said numbly.

"Well, I'll be running along then. Come on, lover, cheer up!" The woman planted a light, playful kiss on Hisashi's lips, and he pulled her closer into a passionate embrace. As the lovers grew more demonstrative and began to shed their clothes in the dim lab, the watchers turned away in embarrassment.

"Let them have their moment," Chief Matsushita muttered under his breath. "A last taste of pleasure before the roof falls in."

A short while later, Hisashi got up from the couch where the woman still lay like a naked courtesan. As he was putting his clothes back on, the laboratory door burst open. Daiyu Matsushita stood in the doorway, silhouetted against the darkness with his pistol drawn.

"Hisashi Mogami, you're under arrest for murder!" he thundered. "If you're smart, you'll surrender quietly."

Hisashi froze for a split second and then dashed away, dressed only in white boxer shorts. Bullets flew from Daiyu

Matsushita's gun, shattering the chemical beakers on the laboratory table and sending sprays of rose-colored liquid in all directions. From behind the giant pressure-cooking vat, Hisashi Mogami returned fire.

"Darling!" Wrapped in her long cloak, the woman went running toward her lover. Halfway across the room she gave a little scream and collapsed face-down on the floor clutching her breast, the black cloak billowing around her.

Daiyu Matsushita took careful aim and fired. Hisashi Mogami shrieked in pain and fell to the floor, a bullet through the back of his right hand. No sooner had the suspect dropped his gun than Officer Ishikawa pounced on him and put him in handcuffs.

Hearing the gunfire, hordes of police officers came rushing in. "Chief, are you all right?" they asked as they crowded anxiously around their leader.

"I'm fine, I'm fine," said Daiyu gruffly. He wiped the sweat from his brow and looked down at Hisashi, who was lying on the floor, groaning. "See to this man's wounds, then take him down to headquarters and charge him. What about the woman, is she all right?"

"She was shot right through the heart." Officer Ishikawa was crouched beside the body, trying to find a pulse. "One of Mogami's bullets went astray, and she died instantly. I don't see an exit wound. There's nothing we can do for her." Ishikawa stared vacantly at his hands, which were dripping with the woman's bright red blood.

"I see," said the chief. He looked around the topsy-turvy room and his eyes lit on Kyosuke Kamizu, who was standing off to one side. Politely, Daiyu Matsushita bowed his head. "Mr. Kamizu—Kyosuke," he said, "I'm so very grateful for your help.

345

Thanks to you, the case is solved, and I didn't have to disembowel myself in public. I guess the mystery woman was Tamae Nomura, the woman seen in Yurakucho, the prostitute who went by the name Sumiyo Hayashi. Right?"

Kenzo, who was standing nearby, nodded eager assent. "I told you!" he said.

Kyosuke shook his head. "You people still don't get it, do you?" he said wonderingly. "She isn't Tamae Nomura." Every eye was on Kyosuke's impassive face as he repeated, "Don't you see? This isn't Tamae at all. It's her sister, the person you thought was the victim of the first murder. This is Kinue Nomura." As he spoke, he bent down and lifted the cloak that covered the naked corpse.

Everyone in that crowded room gave a collective gasp. The sisters may have had similar features, but the sight of Horiyasu's spectacular masterpiece left no doubt that they were looking at Kinue Nomura. Like a rainbow fading from the sky, the gorgeous Orochimaru tattoo was growing less vivid by the minute as the blood drained out of the body. They stood staring at that fascinating work of art. Something uncanny was happening. Though the body of Kinue Nomura lay still and dead, the great sorcerer's snake on her back still seemed to be wriggling and writhing in agony, as if it were struggling to hold on to its own colorful, one-dimensional life.

59

"Good news," Detective Chief Inspector Daiyu Matsushita said to his brother Kenzo as they sat in Daiyu's office at police headquarters on the following afternoon, waiting for Kyosuke to arrive. "We won't have to listen to your genius-friend's monologue on an empty stomach this time! Some of our detectives recently caught the gang who burglarized a nearby sushi restaurant, and we managed to recover all the valuable lacquerware and ceramics, so the chef decided to show his gratitude by sending over a feast for the entire station this afternoon. Ah, here comes the man of the moment."

Kyosuke was right on time, as usual. He was dressed in winter-white flannel trousers, a black turtleneck sweater, and a gray-and-black herringbone tweed jacket. An oyster-colored silk scarf was slung carelessly around his neck. Kenzo, who had thrown on some wrinkled khaki slacks and an old tan sweater, stared admiringly at his friend's dashing getup.

After greetings and congratulations had been exchanged, Daiyu led the way to a conference room with bare walls of cracked plaster painted institutional green. The three men sat down on threadbare gray zabuton cushions around a low table of cheap varnished wood. "Excuse the prison-camp decor," said the chief, pulling a gargoyle face, "but at least we can offer you something to eat. Ah, here's the first course now."

A very young, shy-looking policeman entered the room carrying a tray laden with several round lacquer boxes filled with artistically arranged sushi. Along with all the familiar varieties of fish, shellfish, and vegetables, there were some expensive delicacies: the adductor muscles of the ark shell clam, jewel-like fish roe, and the dark, flavorful foot of the cockle. The young officer's large ears flushed crimson at being in the presence of both the Big Boss and the now-famous amateur detective. The rookie placed the boxes on the table along with chopsticks, individual plates, translucent pinkish-rose pickled ginger to clear the palate between tastes, soy sauce, tiny pyramids of pungent green wasabi horseradish, doll-size cups, and three small ceramic flasks of warmed sake.

Kenzo reached out eagerly to begin pouring his favorite intoxicant, but his brother barked, "This isn't a party! We're working here, so we need to keep our heads clear. Take away the sake and bring us some cider or something. No, on second thought, just bring some strong green tea in big mugs, like they serve at the sushi shop. Make sure it's good and hot, too."

The three men unwrapped their disposable chopsticks, said, "*Itada-kimasu*," and began to transfer the pieces of sushi to their individual plates. Kyosuke took a bite of raw tuna roll, chewed appreciatively for a moment, and then began to speak.

"Last night the final curtain fell. No one could have predicted that Kinue Nomura would end up losing her life in such a way, but perhaps that was part of the destiny of those three ill-fated siblings. Bad karma, as they say. I suppose the biggest mystery of this case are the tattoos. The brother, Tsunetaro Nomura, managed to figure out the secret after just one look at a photograph. Likewise, Professor Hayakawa caught a brief glimpse of a photographic plate, and later he was able to figure out the connection between the two. It was those photographs that led me to the solution of this case." Kyosuke started to pick out a piece of *kappa-maki* cucumber roll, then changed his mind and settled on an oblong of rice wrapped in seaweed and topped with luminous orange beads of salmon roe.

"It seemed strange that while there were numerous people who had seen Kinue's and Tsunetaro's tattoos, there wasn't a single person who had ever seen Tamae's tattoo in person. But Kinue insisted that Tamae had the Tsunedahime tattoo, and there was even photographic evidence to support that claim, so who would doubt it? It's certainly true that once someone gets a tattoo, it will be with them until they die. If it's just a small one, it can be partially removed by burning moxa or applying certain topical chemicals to the spot, but some traces will always remain. In the case of a full-body tattoo, those techniques simply wouldn't work. If you think along these lines, then when you look at the photograph of the three siblings together, you can only conclude that the two women had very different tattoos. The body that was found in Kitazawa consisted only of four partial limbs and a head, and the most essential part, the torso, was missing. So who was the victim? If it had been Tamae, then judging by the extent of the tattoos in the photographs, there should have been tattooing on her forearms and lower legs. Since no such tattoos were found, then there's no way that the victim could have been Tamae. And therefore, there was no choice but to conclude that the dismembered body belonged to Kinue Nomura. And indeed, that's what everyone concluded."

There was a slight clatter as the Matsushita brothers crossed chopsticks in pursuit of a particularly attractive piece of abalone sushi, but Kyosuke continued unperturbed. "It's an impeccably logical argument, in the abstract. However, the facts as they emerged have proved that this perfectly logical conclusion was, quite simply, wrong. The problem lies in our assumption that Tamae Nomura had the Tsunedahime tattoo, an assumption that is based on the fundamental notion that a tattoo can never be erased.

"To solve this case, we need to assume that a large tattoo can, in fact, be erased. It's difficult to make this leap of imagination, but we must force ourselves to look at a tattoo as something that is not necessarily permanent. I feel the utmost respect and admiration for the intellect and expertise of Professor Hayakawa, who was able to reach this conclusion after one glimpse at the negatives in question.

"There's a basic reason why Professor Hayakawa realized that the photographs were not entirely genuine, that is, the pattern of the tattoos. The world of tattoos is a very superstitious one, and generally speaking, it is taboo to tattoo a snake, a slug, and a frog on one person's body. This is because of the belief that the three creatures will fight among themselves and destroy that person. There are other taboos as well. For example, tattoo artists won't do a Kagekiyo design because it will supposedly cause the bearer to lose his eyesight. There's no way a tattoo artist of Horiyasu's stature wouldn't have observed such taboos. However much he may have despised their wicked, adulterous mother, he certainly would never have put such ill-omened designs on his own children, even if the designs were divided among the three of them. It is a fact that he carved two of the three controversial designs, Orochimaru and Jiraiya, on two of his three children. Therefore, in order to keep the curse from taking effect, he would have had to put a different design—something other than Tsunedahime, which would have completed the three curses—on the third child. That is, on Tamae.

"But then we have the photographs, which plainly show Tamae with the Tsunedahime tattoo. This was one of the primary mistakes made by the police investigators assuming that a photograph is the same as reality. Mogami suspected this would happen, and it was just another facet of

350

his brilliantly thought-out plan. A photograph can create a powerful illusion."

Both Matsushita brothers were hanging on Kyosuke's every word. Daiyu—the chain-smoking Locomotive—had actually forgotten to light another cigarette, even though the one he was smoking had burned down to his fingers and gone out.

Kyosuke popped a piece of flying-fish sushi into his mouth, took a sip of tea, and continued. "I know you've seen actors and actresses in films and on stage who appeared to be tattooed but in actuality were not. For stage plays, a small tattoo can be drawn directly on the skin, while the actors wear patterned tights or body stockings to suggest larger-scale designs. Sometimes the smaller patterns are drawn onto thin silk which is then glued onto the skin, but that doesn't work for a full-body tattoo. Those effects may look all right on stage, where the aim is to create a general impression, but if you photograph them you can tell immediately that the tattoos aren't genuine. Therefore, actors in the movies can't use patterned tights or body stockings to depict tattoos. Since the movies prize realism so highly, film actors have their fake tattoos drawn and painted directly onto their bare skin. I've heard that they use varnish to keep the patterns from being washed away by perspiration, but I can't vouch for the veracity of that. At any rate, when the temporary tattoos are created by that method, they look completely genuine. If you looked at the film without preconceptions, you probably wouldn't be able to tell the drawn-on tattoos from the real thing. For example, what do you think of this photo?"

Kyosuke reached into his briefcase and placed a publicity still from a recent Japanese movie on the table. The picture showed an Edo Period *ukiyo-e* artist in the act of drawing the rough sketch for a tattoo of Yama-Uba, an evil-looking mountain witch, onto the naked back of a beautiful woman. Daiyu and Kenzo stared at the photograph for a moment. Then, almost in unison, they let out a loud *Ahhh* of comprehension.

"Suppose that someone wants to get a tattoo," Kyosuke said. "The first thing the tattoo artist will do is to bring out his portfolio and show the potential client his flash—the tattoo designs in his repertoire. These invariably include an assortment of birds, flowers, humans, mythical beings, and background designs such as clouds, shells, and sea creatures. The client leafs through that big book of possibilities and eventually finds a design that captures his, or her, fancy. Does the tattoo artist immediately whip out his needles and start puncturing the skin? No, the first thing he does is to draw an outline of the chosen design onto the client's skin, with sumi ink and a bamboo brush. The reason for this precaution is obvious. Once the tattoo is under the skin, it can't very well be changed, even if the client decides that it looked better in the sample book. Usually this preliminary sketch is just a simple outline. But sometimes, in special circumstances, the tattoo artist will go to the extra trouble of adding colors and shading.

"Do you see what I'm saying? The photograph of the Tsunedahime tattoo shows one of those elaborate drawn-on-the-body sketches, not an actual permanent tattoo on human skin. Once you become aware of that fact, you'll realize that there is something unnatural about the Tsunedahime tattoo in the photographs. There's a subtle lack of modulation in the shading, and it is all somehow more garish than the muted shades you expect in a tattoo. Tsunetaro and Professor Hayakawa were both tattoo experts, and they noticed the fakery right away. Even Kenzo sensed that something was odd about the photographs, months ago. At the time he dismissed it as a trick of the light, but he wasn't far from the truth." Kenzo had just stuffed a large piece of fermented-soybean roll into his mouth, but he tried to look simultaneously sagacious and modest as Kyosuke continued talking.

"I have no way of knowing why Tamae chose to have that design painted on herself. I can only guess that it was a macabre joke. She eventually got some other design tattooed on her skin, but we have been unable to ascertain what that design was. We can be absolutely certain of one thing, though. It wasn't Tsunedahime. Once you solve this fundamental problem, all the other riddles and mysteries of the case melt away like summer snow." A light film of perspiration had formed on Kyosuke's brow. He took out a monogrammed white hand-kerchief, blotted his forehead, and folded the handkerchief fastidiously before returning it to his pocket.

"Last night we obtained the most graphic proof that Hisashi Mogami and Kinue Nomura were lovers and murder-ous co-conspirators," he said. The three men lowered their eyes at the recollection of the shockingly intimate scene they had inadvertently glimpsed through the laboratory's windows.

After a moment of reflective silence, Kyosuke continued. "The fiendishly clever idea for the murders popped into Hisashi's head one day when he happened to see a woman who looked like Kinue in Yurakucho and realized it was her sister Tamae, whom everyone had assumed was killed when the Americans dropped the bomb on Hiroshima. Hisashi had already decided to kill his older brother Takezo, but until then all his murder plots had been discarded due to some fatal flaw. It's not that he was ambivalent about wanting to kill his brother, he just hadn't been able to figure out how to make it a foolproof crime. He saw Tamae as the missing piece of the puzzle, his passport to the perfect murder. In order to carry out his plan, Hisashi first seduced Tamae and then hid her away in a room somewhere; this explains her sudden disappearance from Yurakucho. Making Tamae his willing slave was not a difficult task by any means. As we've seen, women find Hisashi remarkably attractive, and he seems to be endowed with an ability to bewitch them.

"Tamae was simply a victim of Hisashi's greed, as was Kyoko Kawabata, to a lesser degree. Considering the way things turned out, you could even say that Kinue Nomura was ultimately sacrificed because of Hisashi's lust for money. But it does appear that he was genuinely in love with Kinue, whereas Tamae was just a convenient tool. When his own gain was involved, a human life had no more significance than a mosquito's. As for Kinue, if she had any reservations about colluding in the murder of her own sister, Hisashi managed to talk her out of them. She was as greedy for material things as he was; she was eager to be rid of her odious patron, Takezo Mogami, and most important, like her poor deluded sister, she was madly in love with Hisashi and would have done anything to keep him. From what we've heard, Kinue had never been close to Tamae and had thought she was dead in any case. Perhaps that was how she rationalized it—that Tamae should have died in the bomb blast. Or perhaps she didn't rationalize it at all. From all accounts, she was a cold-hearted, self-centered, hedonistic woman, just like her mother. It seems likely that she was more upset at the thought of Hisashi in bed with her sister than at being a party to that sister's death. At any rate, she was a full partner in the plot."

Kyosuke took a deep breath, and slowly let it out. "So Kinue entered the tattoo contest, and there she met a splendid foil in the person of Kenzo Matsushita. Hisashi, too, realized immediately that Kenzo could be used to advance his nefarious plan."

Kenzo sat in silence, hanging his head, overwhelmed by feelings of remorse, humiliation, and scorn for his own foolish gullibility. But as always, in the corner of his consciousness, there was a small voice whispering, *There's no shame in being a fool for love, and I'd do it again in a minute.*

"If Kenzo hadn't turned up," Kyosuke went on, "they probably would have sent the photos to some newspaper reporter. But because of Kenzo's connection with the police department, he was the ideal conduit for the information—or rather the misinformation—that Kinue gave him.

"All the things she told him about fearing for her life and so on were specifically designed to make Kenzo, and everyone else, assume that the dead body in the bathroom belonged to her. It was all a big charade. If you think about it in a rational manner, the things she said were very strange indeed. At that time, Kinue hadn't yet received the threatening letter from Ryokichi Usui, and it's hard to believe that a woman from such a tough background would get into a tizzy over some vague feelings of foreboding. But because the circumstances of the murder seemed to coincide with her fears about someone wanting to kill her and steal her skin, no one ever questioned the veracity of her original remarks. From the time she met Kenzo, every action Kinue took was focused on making it appear that she had been murdered. The photographs she gave to Kenzo, the words she spoke, the photographic plates that were dropped in the garden behind the bathroom; everything was carefully designed with that one objective in mind. As for the photo album, one page was ripped out and almost certainly destroyed. There must have been some explanation of the tattoo photos written on that page, and it would have been disastrous if that information had fallen into the hands of the police."

Kyosuke paused and helped himself to a piece of rolled sushi made with the pungent leaves of the *shiso* plant and tart *umeboshi* plum paste. After savoring those distinctive flavors for a moment, he said, "Regarding the second crime—that is, the murder of Takezo Mogami—there's no need to add anything to the explanation I set forth yesterday. By the time Takezo learned about Hisashi and Kinue's affair and began talking about changing his will, some time after the tattoo contest, Hisashi was just about ready to kill him in any case. In fact, it was Hisashi who arranged for word of the affair to reach Takezo's ears. Prior to that, Takezo just had a vague suspicion that Kinue might be fooling around behind his back."

Kenzo flushed, even though he knew his friend couldn't possibly be talking about him. Oblivious to Kenzo's discomfort, Kyosuke forged ahead.

"Once he had killed his brother, Hisashi was able to pour his energies into Tamae's murder, which I'll keep calling the first because it was discovered first. In order to make it appear that the body parts in the locked room belonged to Kinue, he had to use only the portions of Tamae's corpse that corresponded to the placement of Kinue's tattoos. This was an absolute condition, but it wasn't his only concern. He also had to make sure that the body would not be autopsied. With modern forensic medicine, the time of death can be estimated quite precisely by dissecting the internal organs. Not having access to Tamae's internal organs, they estimated her time of death at between six P.M. and midnight, which turned out to be correct. But just as Hisashi imagined it would, that estimate left a lot of latitude. During that time, Kinue made a point of going to the public bath and showing off her tattoo. On the way home she purposely stopped and chatted with a neighbor in order to advertise the fact that she was still alive at that hour. Thus, since the investigators knew that Kinue was alive as late as nine o'clock, they were tricked into shortening their estimate of when the crime was committed to the hours between nine and eleven P.M. That, of course, was a time period for which Hisashi had a perfect alibi. With what we know now, we can confidently estimate that the murder and mutilation of Tamae Nomura actually took place between six and nine.

"Since the corpse belonged to Tamae and not to Kinue, I can state with confidence that the scene of the murder was not Kinue's house in Kitazawa. It would have been ruinous to have the people in that neighborhood catch a glimpse of the living Tamae, or even to guess at her existence. If anyone realized that Tamae had survived the war, then Hisashi's elaborate plan would have fallen apart. In that case, where was the murder committed? I'm absolutely certain it took place in Hisashi Mogami's laboratory. Do you remember last night when Kinue blurted out those horrifying words about killing her and dissolving her body in sulfuric acid?"

The Matsushita brothers nodded somberly.

"Well," Kyosuke went on, "Hisashi was conducting experiments, using a giant pressure cooker to make amino acids and dextrose by means of chemical reduction, right? That kettle was lined with lead. If you filled it with sulfuric acid and turned on the heat and the pressure, disposing of a human body or two would be a relatively simple matter. So, after coolly killing his brother, Takezo, with his own gun, Hisashi rushed back home to wait for Tamae to arrive for what she doubtless thought would be a tender romantic rendezvous. Hisashi would have given his maid the day off, and his house is in a residential neighborhood so there isn't much foot traffic. On top of that, the laboratory is in a separate building that can be reached without going through the main gate, so it was a nearly ideal place to carry out his plan. After Tamae entered the laboratory unseen by anyone, Hisashi probably strangled her from behind. He may have used chloroform or his favorite offering, the poisoned cocktail. Once she was dead, he cut off her head and limbs. He stuffed her torso, including the thighs and upper arms, into the kettle. He then turned on the heat and the pressure, poured in the sulfuric acid, and dissolved her body. The entire operation would have taken an hour or two. He then packed up the remaining head and limbs, and sped over to Kitazawa by car. So you see, it wasn't a matter of the torso's having been taken away." Kyosuke's voice was filled with excitement. "Instead, the head and limbs were carried *in*."

60

The Matsushita brothers were awestruck by Kyosuke's revelation that the severed head and limbs found in Kinue's bathroom had been imported, and the much-talked-about torso had never been present at all.

"That's just diabolically clever," Daiyu said, pounding his forehead with the heel of his hand. "He really played us for a bunch of fools."

"I never would have figured it out in a million years," Kenzo said, shaking his head. "No, make that a billion years."

While his audience was still reeling, Kyosuke proceeded to reintroduce the pet theory he called "criminal economics." From the point of view of a criminal, he suggested, a crime is a sort of entrepreneurial business enterprise.

A cool, cerebral criminal like Hisashi Mogami, who concocted his murder scheme with the primary aim of material gain for himself, couldn't very well afford to overlook the basic rules of economics. Not only would it have been a lot of trouble to cut up the body at Kinue's house and then attempt to smuggle the torso out, but there was no need to do it that way. It was infinitely easier to commit the crime elsewhere and bring in the necessary body parts. It was a sort of optical or psychological illusion, like an Escher print. To figure it out, it was necessary to perceive white as black, and black as white.

Turning the bathroom into a locked room was just a mechanical trick, albeit a rather sophisticated one. But why would a murderer take the trouble to turn the scene of the crime into a locked room in the first place? The most common reason would be to make it appear that the victim had committed suicide, but that obviously didn't apply here. It might be that the criminal wanted to make his escape without leaving any traces. A third possibility is that he just wanted to lend a tinge of the supernatural to the case, since there is something intrinsically eerie about a locked-room murder.

Whatever Hisashi's motivation, the fact was that the locked room helped conceal the larger plot, by diverting the police's attention. The ploy didn't involve magic or the supernatural— it was a purely mechanical trick, a feat of engineering—but the locked room did lend an extra measure of creepiness to the murder scene. Mogami must have known that sooner or later someone would figure it out, but in the meantime he managed to confuse and distract even the most seasoned investigators.

Here Kyosuke evoked one of his favorite concepts. "Even after the actual locked room ceases to be a mystery," he intoned with an oracular air, "the locked room of the mind remains an enigma. From the time that all of you saw the locked room, you were completely convinced that a crime had taken place inside that room, and that preconception colored your investigation. There was no way for you to escape from the psychological locked room constructed in your own minds. This complicated and obfuscated the case, and it also caused the crucial clue of the photographic plates to be overlooked. On that point, Mogami's thinking was so brilliant as to be truly scary."

The Matsushita brothers made sounds of assent as Kyosuke moved on to the next topic. "The fact that there were no traces of blood in the garden is perfectly natural, since the actual murder, which must have been incredibly bloody, had taken place miles away in Hisashi Mogami's laboratory. Mogami couldn't very well cart along buckets of blood when he trans-ported the body to Kinue's house, just to make it look like the scene of a gruesome murder and dismemberment, but if too little blood were found at the spurious 'scene,' then people might suspect that the crime had been committed elsewhere. Leaving the remains in a bathroom was a splendid solution. Because he left the drain open and the water running, Mogami was able to create the impression that all the blood had been washed away. However, being the perfectionist that he was, it's likely that he also put a fair amount of blood in a bottle or jar and brought it along. He would have used this to create the signs of a struggle elsewhere in the house, and then poured the rest down the drain, knowing it would show up eventually in the forensic investigation."

Next, Kyosuke touched on the difference between the way the tattoos were disposed of in the first and third murders. In the first murder, he explained, Mogami needed to make the time of death appear as wide as possible so that his alibi would work, while in the third murder he simply abandoned Tsunetaro's body after removing the tattoos, so he didn't have to worry about carting off the bulky torso.

"Why," Daiyu Matsushita asked, "did Kinue invite Inazawa to visit that night?"

"For the sole purpose of having him discover the corpse. Because he's such a simple man, his behavior was absolutely predictable, and sure enough, according to Mogami's script, Inazawa was distraught after finding the body and ran off without notifying the police. The only deviation was Usui's unexpected appearance, which delayed Inazawa's discovery of the body, but in the end that didn't cause so much as a tremor in Mogami's alibi. His plan worked perfectly. At around seven o'clock he transported Tamae's head and limbs to Kinue's house by car, dumped them in the bathroom, and turned it into a locked room. Then he went to the Ginza and picked a fight with some drunken yokels. He got himself arrested and spent the night safely in jail, thus arming himself with a seemingly unshakable alibi."

"But what about Kinue's strange behavior?" Daiyu said. "She goes around saying she fears for her life, but instead of hiring a bodyguard, she fires her maid, thus leaving herself alone in the house. She then invites Inazawa to her house for a midnight rendezvous, and telephones Kenzo and Professor Hayakawa. She removes her cash and valuables from the house, makes it appear that she has been drinking whiskey with a visitor, and after setting up all the stage props, she disappears."

"That's all true," said Kyosuke, "and it was all part of the setup she planned with Mogami. Oh, by the way, I assume you've realized by now that the 'mystery fingerprints' belonged to Kinue herself. The prints the police ascribed to Kinue, thinking she was the victim, actually belonged to Tamae. The ever-meticulous Mogami had taken the time to plant Tamae's fingerprints at the scene, probably by using one of her severed hands." Kenzo shivered involuntarily at that ghoulish image as Kyosuke began to sketch the next chapter of the story.

"When Mogami was released from jail, he was consumed with worry about what had happened overnight. Disguising his voice, he placed a call to Kinue's house, hoping to kill two birds with one stone. That is, he wanted to check whether things were going as planned, and also to introduce a 'mystery man' into the equation. He did get Kenzo wondering: Who is this guy who knows Kinue so well that he addresses her by her first name?

"Once the police started wandering down that kind of diversionary side street, the already complicated case became increasingly convoluted and confused, and they ended up in a quagmire.

"After Mogami had confirmed that Kenzo was at the crime scene, he was able to relax a bit. Later, he was happy to receive a call from the wife of Professor Hayakawa, his aunt, because that provided an ideal pretext for going over to Kenzo's house to find out what he knew about the murder and its aftermath. During that visit, Hisashi managed to underscore his own alibi and put on a show of concern for his missing brother and his uncle, Professor Hayakawa. He was also able to ferret out details of the investigation from Kenzo. Still, when he heard about the bizarre presence of a slug in the bathroom, Hisashi couldn't help shuddering at the symbolism, since the slug tattoo, Tsunedahime, was associated with his murder victim, Tamae Nomura. In his nervous state, he may have wondered whether that live slug might be her ghost, come back to haunt him. The fact that Tamae didn't actually have the slug tattoo didn't make any difference because at that point nearly everyone believed that she did."

Kyosuke looked from Kenzo to Daiyu, as if to make sure he had their attention. Both brothers were listening raptly, leaning forward slightly with hands gripping the edge of the table. Apparently satisfied, Kyosuke continued his monologue.

"No doubt the startling appearance of that slug was just Fate's way of putting the finishing touch on this most artistic of crimes—what painters call 'adding the eyes to the dragon.' It became an uncanny symbol for the case, as did the riddle, 'The slug dissolves the snake...' That magical formula turned out to be eerily accurate. Another curious thing is that Tamae—the elusive Tamae, also known as Sumiyo Hayashi—led a rather sluglike existence, almost as if she had the power to appear and disappear at will." Kyosuke paused, dipped a piece of mackerel sushi in some soy sauce, chewed reflectively for a moment, ate a couple of slices of pickled ginger, took a gulp of strong green tea, and resumed his account.

"Hisashi Mogami was discreetly calculating the time when Takezo's body would be found. If it was discovered too soon, they would find traces of the anaesthetic, but too long a lapse might have made it harder to verify Hisashi's alibi and could also have interfered with Hisashi's inheritance. So he chose to stage that part of his play at the so-called haunted house in Mitaka, which was slated to be torn down in a few days, and both those problems were brilliantly resolved.

"Hisashi's carefully constructed plan yielded excellent results, from his point of view. The police quickly jumped to the conclusion that Takezo had killed Kinue, then turned his gun on himself. However, since they had no actual proof of that, they were obliged to follow every other lead, as well. In the meantime, Takezo's huge fortune fell into Hisashi's hands, and the double murderer must have been laughing—quite literally—all the way to the bank. Everything seemed to be going smoothly when an unexpected person appeared on the scene. Kinue's brother Tsunetaro, repatriated from the southern front, surfaced in Shibuya, practicing his outlawed trade."

Kyosuke paused. "Tsunetaro might eventually have become involved in the case by some other means," he said, "but we have to face the unpleasant fact that his involvement, if not his death, was hastened by Kenzo's visit to his tattoo studio."

Kenzo, who was already feeling as remorseful as a man can feel, hung his head. Kyosuke shot him a sympathetic glance, then proceeded with his conjecture.

"Tsunetaro learned the details of the case from Kenzo, and when he saw the photographs that Kinue had given to Kenzo, he immediately understood what had happened. Tsunetaro, of all people, would have been well aware that Tamae didn't

364

have the Tsunedahime tattoo. He may even have been the artist who drew that temporary tattoo on his youngest sister as an adolescent prank. Realizing right away that something suspicious was going on, Tsunetaro began spying on Mogami. Perhaps he saw Kinue sneaking in and out of the laboratory, but somehow he managed to track her down. By following Kinue, Tsunetaro was able to confirm his horrible suspicion that his other sister, Tamae, had been the actual victim. He must have been shocked and horrified. Without considering the possible consequences, he made the tragic decision that cost him his life.

"If Kinue had turned herself in to the police at that point, she would probably have been sentenced to life imprisonment rather than hanging, and she might eventually have been released on parole. That was Tsunetaro's last brotherly gesture, trying to talk his sister into doing the right thing. He evidently gave a deadline of three days. After that, he told her, he would have no choice but to go to the police himself.

"When Kinue told Hisashi Mogami about Tsunetaro's ultimatum, he must have shuddered at this unexpected blow from Fate. Tsunetaro had been listed as missing in action, which for a soldier usually meant he had been killed. It was a surprise, and a major inconvenience, to have Jiraiya suddenly appear on the scene. Mogami probably spent some sleepless nights trying to figure out what to do. He didn't have the luxury of time.

"From Mogami's morally bankrupt point of view," Kyosuke concluded, "he had no choice but to commit a third murder in order to cover up the first two."

Kenzo let out a sorrowful sigh and shook his head. "If only I had told my brother what was going on, it never would have turned out this way."

"Well, there's nothing you can do about it now," Kyosuke said. "It's easy to have the wisdom of the gods after the fact. As Goethe says in *Faust*, all we can do as humans is to bumble along as best we can." Giving Kenzo another reassuring glance, Kyosuke resumed his dissertation.

"Because the third murder was unanticipated, Hisashi didn't have time to concoct a meticulous plan as he did with the first two. However, he did see the chance to implicate Professor Hayakawa by removing the tattooed skin and leaving the body to be discovered. By rushing to Yokohama by car, he somehow managed to provide himself with a serviceable alibi. He then rushed back to Shibuya at top speed, and he used Kinue to lure Tsunetaro out. Mogami probably told her to say something like 'I'm going to turn myself in to the police now, so will you please come with me?' However, this plan required Kinue to show herself in public. Mogami decided to have her wrap her forearms in bandages in order to suggest that she was Tamae, covering up her tattooed arms. Kinue probably told her brother that she needed to stop off at the room where she was living, and there she must have given Tsunetaro a drink laced with cyanide. Mogami showed up then and put the dead body in the car. He drove it to the warehouse in Yoyogi, stripped off the tattoos, and left the corpse behind. Then he sped back to Yokohama, making it in time so that his alibi would stand up.

"That alibi was by no means perfect," Kyosuke concluded, "but luckily for Mogami, Professor Hayakawa's alibi wasn't exactly a thing of beauty, either. And thus it was that the curse was fulfilled, and the snake ate the frog. Or in this case, the toad." Orochimaru, the sorcerer with the giant serpent familiar. And Jiraiya, the rival sorcerer with his enormous toad.

The amateur detective paused and surveyed the selection of fish-and-rice tidbits that remained on the platters. While he had been explaining the sinister secrets of the killers, Kenzo and Daiyu had made short work of the sushi spread. Kyosuke finally settled on an oblong piece of vinegared rice topped with sea urchin. He washed this exotic morsel down with a sip of tea, and then he began to speak again.

"Chief Matsushita, I hate to say this, but you had your chances to solve this case along the way. For example, when you figured out that the running water and the electric light showed that the murderer didn't really intend to hide the body, that was a truly splendid deduction. But if you had taken it one step further and realized that in fact the killer's aim was to call attention to the body, this case might have been solved then and there. The same thing is true of those bandages. It was because Kinue had *no* tattoos below her elbows that she had to wrap her lower arms in bandages, not the other way around. The trick of making something appear to be hidden when the real intention is to call attention to it was used two or three times in this case. It's almost painfully obvious, in retrospect." Kyosuke shook his head and gazed reflectively into his mug of tea before taking another small sip.

"That's easy for you to say, Kyosuke, you're a genius. But there's no hope for an ordinary guy like me. If you hadn't come along, I don't know if I would ever have solved this case." So saying, Daiyu Matsushita cracked his first smile of the day. "Seriously, that was really something the way you went after Kyoko Kawabata yesterday." The chief picked up his chopsticks and held them poised above two equally enticing morsels of seaweed-wrapped *non-maki*, trying to decide which to devour first.

"I just hate to see anyone get away with lying like that," Kyosuke said with a wry smile. "But think about it. Of all the people who were questioned about the day of the first murder, the only one who came up with a foolproof, documented alibi for the time of the crime was Hisashi Mogami. Aside from him, I noticed right away that everyone else had the usual vague, sloppy explanations. Natural human alibis, in other words. That much was deduction, but I was bluffing the rest of the way. I just got lucky with a few of my guesses."

Kenzo was only half-listening, for he was thinking about the Tsunedahime photograph. What a terrible role that harmless-looking photo had played! First it was used to create the impression that Tamae's dead body belonged to Kinue, then it became the indirect agent of Tsunetaro's destruction. Just one small rectangle of paper, light and shadow, ink on skin...

The three men fell silent as they finished up the last of the sushi and drained their mugs of tea. "Kyosuke, I really don't know how to express my gratitude," said Daiyu Matsushita in his hearty way. "Thanks to you, all the facts of this strange and baffling case have become clear at last. But the one thing I still don't understand is why Kinue would have wanted to be Mogami's accomplice, to the point where she was willing to kill her own brother and sister and let herself appear to have been murdered."

"That perplexed me, as well." Kyosuke gave a rueful smile, but his tone was serious. "A single person like me really doesn't have the proper qualifications to speculate about the delicate mysteries of love, or the mystical abyss of sexuality. But I think it's obvious that Kinue was deeply in love with Hisashi Mogami. For all her experience with men, for all her *femme fatale* appeal, I think it was probably the first time that she met a man she couldn't bear to live without. Her passionate attachment to that man was really a scary thing, and I believe it was exacerbated by the criminal blood that was flowing in her veins, the outlaw legacy of her adulterous mother. Oh yes, Kinue had motivation galore in allowing Hisashi to stage her own phony death to bind him to her, to get a share of Takezo's huge fortune, and to gain freedom for both of them. If they were accomplices in crime, there was no way he could discard her. Like that giant serpent on her back, she had him entangled in her coils."

"And Mogami? What do you make of him?"

"Whatever you may think of his character, you have to feel a grudging admiration for the sort of mind that could conceive and carry out a sophisticated crime like this. However, somewhere along the way his genius became warped, and he took a wrong turn into the realm of pure evil. At the end, he was left without a shred of humanity." Kyosuke's voice was filled with emotion, and a rosy flush mantled his fair skin.

Daiyu Matsushita's face was fairly brimming with gratitude. "Kyosuke, I can't begin to thank you enough. With your inspired help, we were finally able to solve this baffling case, and I am deeply grateful. Tell me, how can I ever repay you?"

Kyosuke raised his pale hand in a dismissive gesture. "There's no need for any sort of repayment," he said. "Ever since I was a child I've had a strong abhorrence for the forces of evil, because of the way my... because of something that happened to someone very close to me. Come to think of it, that's probably part of the reason why I went into the field of forensic medicine. If my humble efforts help to rid society of one evildoer, that's reward enough for me."

Kyosuke untangled his long legs from under the table and stood up. He extended his hand to Daiyu Matsushita, who had also gotten to his feet. The detective chief inspector's eyes were filled with deep emotion as he took Kyosuke's small-boned hand in both of his large ones, and gave it a long, tight squeeze.

61

Kyosuke and Kenzo left the police station together, turning up their coat collars against the chilly air. After passing
under the Bridge of the Cherry Blossom Fields, they headed
down the wide pedestrian boulevard that ran alongside the
Imperial Palace, with its high stone walls, medieval moat,
and flocks of long-necked swans. The two men walked for a
while in thoughtful silence, until Kenzo suddenly blurted out,
"Kyosuke, I owe you an apology."

"Why is that?"

"There's something I've been hiding from you. It's about
that woman, Kinue Nomura. The thing is, we, um, she and I—"

"There's no need to tell me that sort of thing now," Kyosuke
interrupted gently, holding up his hand. "The truth is, I had
an inkling about that from the very beginning. Your story
about receiving the photographs at the tattoo competition
just seemed too unnatural. I can only imagine the sort of con-
trivance she must have staged in order to get the photos into
your hands. You mustn't blame yourself, though. That woman
chose the road to ruin of her own free will. Your only fault was
being a bit naive and trusting, but she was a very clever and
desirable woman. You were simply out of your league with
someone like her."

Kenzo shot a quick glance at Kyosuke's face. He wasn't sure
that he liked being described as naive and trusting, as if he
were some gold-toothed country bumpkin. The thing that
bothered him most, though, was the realization that Kinue had
merely been using him, that all her sweet words and sighs of
passion had been part of a diabolical, cold-blooded charade.

Kyosuke was already off on another subject. "Actually, you probably thought that my logic today was in perfect order, but there was one flaw. As a rule, the artist just sketches the portion that he's going to be tattooing that day onto the skin. For example, if he's going to be drawing a human figure, he might just sketch the face on a given day. So a completed design like that of Tsunedahime in the photos wouldn't have been an under-sketch at all."

"Well, if that's the case, where did those photographs come from?" Just when he thought all the mysteries had been solved, Kenzo found himself confounded once again.

"The truth is, I arrived at my conclusions with the help of a certain woman. She's the wife of a man who has some standing in society, so I can't tell you her name. At any rate, the day after we visited Professor Hayakawa at his home in Yotsuya, I went with that woman to the house of the artist who had done her tattoo. I ended up staying there for most of the night, observing the process. I've never been a fan of tattoos, but I have to admit, it was absolutely mesmerizing."

Kenzo stopped in his tracks and put his hand on Kyosuke's sleeve. "Kyosuke, who is she, that tattooed woman?" he asked excitedly. "Is it Mrs. Hayakawa?"

Kyosuke gave an eloquent shrug. "I'm afraid I'll have to leave that to your imagination," he said. "A matter of chivalry, you know. It was quite a remarkable evening, I must say. The tattoo artist lived in an old house with lots of small rooms, and all the walls were plastered with photographs of people with tattoos. There was one entire room devoted to pictures of Westerners with their untidy-looking sushi tattoos. After seeing that unsightly display I realized that the art tattoo is one area in which Japan can still claim to be the best in the world."

"Wait," Kenzo said. "Did you find out why they call them sushi tattoos?"

"I gather it's because they're scattered about on the skin like pieces of sushi with no artistic continuity or coherence. At any rate," Kyosuke said, "there was a big book of tattoo sketches, but they weren't what I expected at all. I was disappointed at first. Then I came across something else in that album, an entirely unexpected harvest. It was a photograph that depicted dozens of tattooed men and woman, naked at a public bathhouse. I think it must have been a meeting of the Tattoo Society. Among those people, there was an eleven- or twelve-year-old child. The child had an adorable face, even with his eyes closed against the flashbulb, and on both his arms and over his chest, there were delicately shaded tattoos in a chrysanthemum pattern. Of course, there's no way an elementary-school student would have such a splendid tattoo. His parents or someone must have had it drawn onto his skin for the occasion, just for fun. But no matter how hard I scrutinized that photograph, I couldn't see any difference between that child's fake tattoo and the real ones on the adults."

"I see," said Kenzo, stopping in his tracks. A passing US Army truck honked its air-horn and a cloud of gray doves that had been roosting in a nearby tree suddenly flew up into the air with a communal squawk and a great flapping of wings.

"Needless to say," Kyosuke went on, "that photograph vindicated my theory. It also raised the question of why Tamae would have had such a large tattoo painted on her body, and then had a photograph taken. That woman I mentioned just now told me her own strange story, and after that I finally understood everything. Apparently there are some men who simply cannot feel sexual desire for a woman with undecorated skin. As Hisashi Mogami put it, for that sort of man a tattoo

372

is an indispensable erotic catalyst. However, a full-body art tattoo isn't something you can acquire in a day or two. So in cases of erotic emergency, I suppose a temporary tattoo might bridge the gap."

The mystical abyss of sex—it was small comfort to Kenzo to realize that even Kyosuke Kamizu's incisive intellect had a hard time fathoming that ancient conundrum.

Knitting his eyebrows, Kyosuke pursued his line of thought. "As you know, all the men and women who passed through the Nomura household were lavishly tattooed. Kinue's first lover was a tattooed photographer, and it seems likely that Tamae, too, might have fallen in love with one of the tattooed men she met. If her original motive for getting tattooed was to please this lover, then it's conceivable that she had the picture of Tsunedahime painted on her skin as a sort of unrealized dream, or a sneak preview, while she was trying to persuade her reluctant father to tattoo her. Or perhaps she just wanted to give her lover the illusion that he was making love to a tattooed virgin, as a way of keeping his interest until she could get a real tattoo. Who could have dreamed that while the fake tattoo would have faded away after one night of pleasure, its recorded image would come down through the years and end up being the basis for a series of truly horrific murders?"

Kenzo nodded. "Then it was natural that Professor Hayakawa would have suspected something just by glancing at the negative of the photograph," he said. "But Kyosuke, I've been meaning to ask what you meant that night when you said that Professor Hayakawa loved a woman who was not his wife, but also despised her. Who were you talking about?"

"Kinue Nomura, of course. Or maybe he was just in love with her Orochimaru tattoo. The way I imagine it, the professor might have had an inkling that Kinue was still alive even before he saw the actual photographs. I think Professor Hayakawa was filled with contradictory emotions. He despised Kinue for being involved in a murder, yet he wanted her (and her remarkable tattoo) to be safe, and to go on living. The love of skin, the love of tattoos there are things in that shadowy, sensual world that are impossible for an uninitiated person to understand." He turned and looked at Kenzo, and for a moment Kenzo thought he could see the reflection of that mysterious realm in Kyosuke's lucent amber eyes.

EPILOGUE

Several months sped by. Winter turned to spring, the cherry trees burst into joyous bloom, and the residents of the slowly recovering city of Tokyo began to feel that there might be hope for the future, after all. Hisashi Mogami was tried in the First Court of the District of Tokyo, convicted of multiple charges of first-degree murder, and sentenced to death by hanging.

That same week, a new exhibit was installed in the Specimen Room of the medical school of Tokyo University. It was Horiyasu's masterpiece, Orochimaru, the great sorcerer-and-serpent tattoo that had once adorned the body of Kinue Nomura. Now it hung from the ceiling of that vast chamber of history, beauty, and horror, like a macabre mobile.

"Good God, they've turned her into a torso!" Detective Chief Inspector Daiyu Matsushita caught the eye of Kyosuke Kamizu and they both laughed, without mirth. "There seems to be a strange sort of symmetry, though, don't you think?" Daiyu added in a serious tone. "The initial murder case featured four limbs and a head without a torso, and now we have a torso minus the limbs and the head."

"'Fearful symmetry,'" Kyosuke said, quoting William Blake.

Kenzo Matsushita was standing on the other side of the sensational new exhibit, lost in bittersweet reverie. *Once upon a time, this tattoo was alive. It danced on the skin of a beautiful woman while I held her in my arms.* Kenzo took a deep breath as he recalled that magical night in the darkened gambling room of the Serpent Bar. In his rational mind he knew it had all been a calculating charade on Kinue Nomura's part, one small strategic move before her headlong descent into hell. For Kinue, their evening of passionate lovemaking had just been a meaningless flirtation, the means to an unspeakably loathsome end. But for Kenzo, the night he had spent with the exquisite snake-woman was an unforgettable memory: the sweetest of dreams, the most delicious of delusions.

"She was a frightening woman," mused Professor Hayakawa, half to himself. "But I still find it difficult to despise her entirely. And even though I didn't get to add it to my collection, at least I'll be able to visit her tattoo like a shrine, whenever I feel the urge."

Kenzo nodded in silent agreement. Some secret part of his heart, too, would always have deeply romantic feelings toward the doomed woman who had once inhabited this brightly patterned skin with so much passion and verve. He walked slowly around the torso, which was swaying in the April breeze like a ghoulish kite. The giant serpent that raised its long neck on the right shoulder still looked as if it were alive, and Orochimaru himself, wrapped in his chain mail and sorcerer's robes, seemed to be gazing down at the people gathered below with a superior smile, as if to say, "Puny mortals, I'll outlast you all."

The four men stood silently in front of the torso, each lost in his own thoughts. The orchid-colored smoke from the cigarettes of Daiyu Matsushita and Professor Hayakawa rose to the ceiling and formed an eerie nimbus around the disembodied tattoo, like a ring of clouds around a troubled moon.

Kenzo stared at the smoke. *It's as if the sorcerer Orochimaru had conjured up an ominous stormcloud,* he thought, but that didn't seem quite right.

And then it hit him. That lavender cloud was like the smoke from funeral incense, a final offering to the souls of the victims in this terrible case: Takezo Mogami, Tamae Nomura, Tsunetaro Nomura, and Kinue Nomura, the love of Kenzo's life so far.

While his companions moved on to another part of the room, Kenzo stepped up to the tattooed torso and furtively placed his lips on the sneering mouth of the sorcerer. "My wonderful, beautiful lover," he whispered to Kinue's disembodied skin. "I'm sorry I couldn't save you." Kenzo's eyes felt suddenly wet, and he bit his lip and turned away.

———

MORE JAPANESE CRIME AVAILABLE FROM
PUSHKIN VERTIGO

Seishi Yokomizo

PUSHKIN VERTIGO

THE HONJIN MURDERS

The award-winning
murder mystery classic

'The master of ingenious plotting'
Guardian

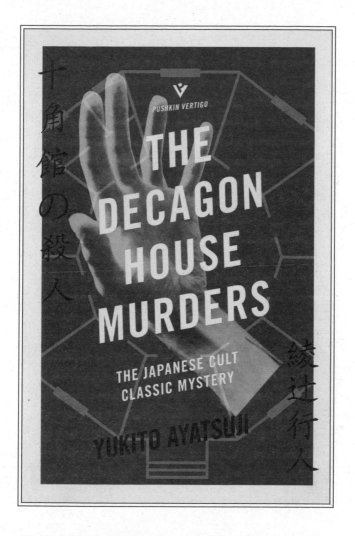

十角館の殺人

綾辻行人

PUSHKIN VERTIGO

THE DECAGON HOUSE MURDERS

THE JAPANESE CULT CLASSIC MYSTERY

YUKITO AYATSUJI

'Every word counts, leading up to a jaw-dropping but logical reveal'
Publishers Weekly **(starred review)**

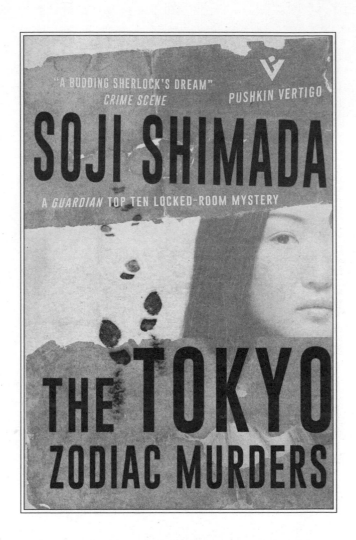

PUSHKIN VERTIGO

SOJI SHIMADA

A *GUARDIAN* TOP TEN LOCKED-ROOM MYSTERY

THE TOKYO
ZODIAC MURDERS

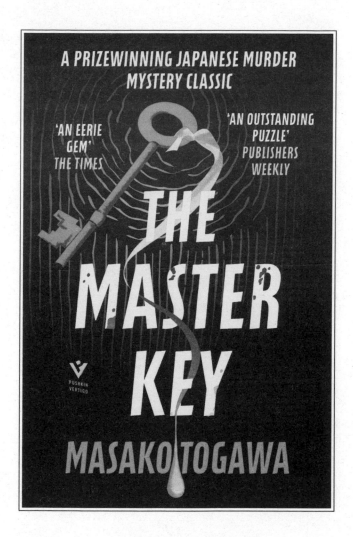

A PRIZEWINNING JAPANESE MURDER
MYSTERY CLASSIC

'AN EERIE
GEM'
THE TIMES

'AN OUTSTANDING
PUZZLE'
PUBLISHERS
WEEKLY

THE MASTER KEY

MASAKO TOGAWA

'An outstanding puzzle mystery'
Publishers Weekly